T·J·PUBLISHERS

CHANGING THE RULES

FRANK BOWE

FOREWORD BY: SENATOR BOB DOLE

T·J·PUBLISHERS

CHANGING THE RULES

FRANK BOWE

FOREWORD BY: SENATOR BOB DOLE

© 1986, Frank Bowe

T.J. PUBLISHERS, INC.
817 Silver Spring Avenue, 206
Silver Spring, Maryland 20910

Printed in the United States of America. All rights reserved.
ISBN #0-932666-30-2 Paper
ISBN #0-932666-31-0 Cloth
Library of Congress Catalog No.: 86-050365

*For my family—my mother, my sister,
and Phyllis, Doran, and Whitney—and to
the memory of my father.*

Foreword

Changing the Rules speaks to me on several levels. In one sense, it is an intensely personal account of a decades-long struggle against disability. In another, it is a romp through the recent past—a fresh, nostalgic perspective on America from the 1940's to the present. This is also a story about parenthood and the lasting effects of a father's values. And it is an insider's account of a long-overdue civil-rights revolution that changed the rules and improved the quality of life for people with disabilities.

Frank Bowe has given us an important, deeply moving book. He has taken his story and related it to the public policy issues on which he has worked as a civil-rights leader. Because he was "mainstreamed" into local public schools long before the term was even coined, his book looks behind the scenes of the current emphasis upon educating handicapped children in the "least restrictive environment" and teaches us what mainstreaming really means. It details how society's "rules" on the role and status of people with disabilities have been changed, particularly by section 504, "the bill of rights for disabled Americans." And *Changing the Rules* draws upon his experience with the United Nations to chart a course for future work on disability throughout the world.

At the center of this book stands a father, a man who insisted upon a set of values that were perhaps contrary to the received wisdom of the times. It is popular today, at a time when many Americans are rediscovering fatherhood, to celebrate the "new" father who is involved in the daily life of the family. Although fathers in past generations might not have spent as much time at home as some do today, their beliefs and values were always with us and their eventual deaths hit us hard. Frank began this book in an effort to explain what his father, who died in 1982, had meant to him.

The author and I both became disabled at about the same time and coped with disability in small-town, rural settings. I was older at the time, of course, but his recollections of how the 1940's and 1950's small-town culture shaped a person's character mirror my own. There is something about the plains of Kansas and the valleys of central Pennsylvania that tells you to keep going, that even though others are there for support, you're going to have to do it on your own.

Perhaps what is most impressive is Frank Bowe's understanding that overcoming a handicap is not an end in itself, but rather is a step that an individual who is disabled needs to take in order to do something else, to make a difference with his or her life. This conviction, which shapes the entire narrative, sets *Changing the Rules* apart from other stories about surmounting disability. At one point in this book, he articulates this philosophy when he says: "I knew that someday I would awaken the dream, and follow its beckonings wherever they might lead." This book traces the awakening of that dream.

I speak for my colleagues in both Houses, and on both sides of the aisle, when I say that rights and opportunities for people with disabilities enjoy truly widespread support. As important as are the historic changes described in this book—particularly the emergence of section 504 as one of the greatest civil rights statutes ever enacted—we must continue our commitment to full participation of disabled persons in all aspects of American life. In this way, the disabled children, minorities, and veterans of tomorrow need not face the same forbidding obstacles that Frank and I confronted.

Washington, DC   Bob Dole
October, 1986   Majority Leader
                                                       U.S. Senate

Chapter One

A moment earlier, I had been ensconced before the television set, engrossed in the drama of the last points of the U.S. Open tennis finals, oblivious to everything but the tension of the moment and the spin of the ball.

Suddenly, that was forgotten, as if it were far in the past and in another place. The drawing room, Poor's mansion, and Tuxedo Park, New York, itself had shifted, I sensed, into a different dimension. For I had seen her.

Her shoulder-length (no, elbow-length!) brown hair sparkled in the lingering light of the setting September sun. She walked with an arresting grace across the parquet floor, yet her bearing implied that she was entirely unaware of her striking femininity and fragile beauty. I saw her smile in greeting as someone approached to welcome her to the mansion. A second passed, and she laughed, a hand reaching up to smooth her hair, the gesture suggesting, somehow, a beguiling innocence untouched by the vicissitudes of life.

How I crossed the room to her side I do not remember.

"Hi," I ventured. "What's your name?"

"Phyllis. What's yours?"

"Frank. I'm going to marry you."

For a flicker of a moment, her smile disappeared. Then, those round brown eyes softened with humor as she replied: "Sure, you are!"

And she was gone to find the room she'd been assigned. I watched her leave, dimly aware of the fluttering lace curtains she touched in passing as she headed for the paneled stairs.

"O.K., lover boy, time for business." Martin Sternberg, who had persuaded me against my wishes to spend the week at the mansion, threw me a knowing wink and gestured back into the drawing room. It took me some time to remember what I'd come here for, since now only one thing mattered.

"Martin!" I urged. "You've got to tell me who she is!"

He smiled indulgently. "One of the new teacher-training students we'll be working with this week. I believe she came down from Boston."

I sighed. "She's the most beautiful woman I've seen in my twenty-six years. Martin, I've met thousands of women, all over the country, but I never met a woman before. Am I making any sense?"

"No," he laughed. "You better forget her for the next few minutes. We have a meeting now."

1

I followed him into the drawing room for our faculty planning session, but scarcely paid attention as he reminded the group of instructors that the week was to be a "total immersion" experience in learning sign language. The trainees, all master's degree candidates in New York University's deafness education program, would spend the next six days learning "how to talk with their hands." He explained that the conference center we were using was once the home of the man behind *Standard & Poor's*. The university had rented it for a week to provide a setting conducive to round-the-clock instruction. Then Martin pointed to me.

"I've asked Frank to leave his research projects and doctoral studies to join us for the week. And, Frank, I think it will be good if you begin the program tonight by talking about deafness—what it is, what it means, why sign language is important."

I nodded vaguely, my thoughts on Boston. Where had she been? Tremont Street? Cambridge? Back Bay?

With effort, I forced myself to concentrate upon the matter at hand. I was present to explain deafness to this group of graduate students. I thought about the small-town Pennsylvania toddler traumatized by a month in a huge New York hospital. I remembered the beatings, taunts, and never-ending loneliness as a child in elementary school. I winced at the memory of the terror I had felt competing against the smartest students in our high school, all of them in full possession of their faculties. I remembered the despair I had felt when as a college graduate one door after another closed in my face, and I could not imagine what I was supposed to do with my life. I shook my head again in amazement that I had made it this far—and in wonder about what the coming years would bring.

Half an hour later, as the students gathered for our first session, I saw *her* enter the large living room in the company of two other women. She sat with them, toward the back of the semi-circle of students before me, giving me a brief glance that revealed nothing more than casual amusement.

"Deafness," I began, my eyes riveted on hers, "is, for me, much like living in a glass box. I can see through, but somehow I can't reach out. People pass by, so close I could touch them, laughing, talking, arguing. Yet it is as though they were in another life. If any of you has watched a movie on a transcontinental flight without using the earphones, you will have a sense of what I mean."

Have you flown out of Logan, my eyes asked her, or into Kennedy or LaGuardia? How could I have missed seeing you?

"Perhaps the most devastating effect of deafness, aside from the social isolation it so often imposes upon children, youth, and adults, is its constriction of linguistic development. A child born deaf, or deafened while a toddler as I was, does not acquire through effortless osmosis, as you did, the English language in all its baffling nuances and endless complexities. Rather, that child must be taught, letter by letter, syllable by syllable, word by word, a language that does not obey its own rules.

"What does this mean, this being alone in the world, apart from others, denied the very coin of the realm? While I was in college—I majored in English at Western Maryland College in Westminster—I read a poem by Theodore Roethke that captured, I think, the human emotions behind the facts you will learn about deafness. It's called 'The Waking,' and I will give you three lines:

I wake to sleep and take my waking slow.
I feel my fate in what I cannot fear.
I learn by going where I have to go.

For me, particularly in the teen years, that was how it was."

I paused.

"For deaf people, sign language serves as a bridge to people and to English. By learning this language, you are reaching out to us, literally extending a helping hand. I think that's why we're here: to reach out a hand, one to another, and grasp the hand of one another."

I don't remember much of what happened after that. Somehow, the session came to an end. Students and instructors departed in twos and threes for other rooms in the mansion.

I turned to find her beside me.

"Frank," she began. "Frank, that was a beautiful speech. Who wrote it for you?"

I smiled. "Oh, someone you don't know but might like to meet. Me."

"You wrote it? But Professor Lloyd said deaf people have fifth-grade reading levels."

I nodded. "Often, that's true. I worked hard, for some fifteen years, before I got the knack of it."

We were alone in the room.

"You know," she said, "I was an English major, too. I'm not sure how much good it did, though. My honors thesis was on the houses in Henry James' novels. Somehow, it doesn't seem quite relevant now."

She was smiling.

"I know what you mean. My honors thesis was on suicide. That doesn't seem relevant any more, either."

"Suicide?"

"Well, actually, it was on Albert Camus and the existentialist issue of suicide as a rational answer to the absurdity of life. My life at the time did seem pretty absurd. I had no idea what I was supposed to do once I left college.

"What I wanted to do more than anything else in life was to be a reporter. Drew Pearson and Jack Anderson were my idols. And, then, one day I discovered that what reporting is, actually, is writing down what has not

3

been written before. And where do reporters get their information? By talking to people, in meetings and on the telephone. Those were things I could not do. And I had no way of knowing how I could do them.

"It was one thing to realize that I have nothing in my ears. It was something else altogether to understand that as far as the world was concerned, I might as well have nothing between them either."

"And do you know now what you'll do with your life?"

"You mean aside from marrying you?" I countered. "Just teasing. Yes, I do."

"And what, pray tell, is that?" She was serious, interested.

"You won't laugh?"

She shook her head, the long straight hair swinging serenely as her eyes sought mine.

"My family raised me to live a life driven by dreams. I want to keep living that way. Since you're an English major, you probably remember Langston Hughes' work. He has some lines about seeing what happens to a raisin in the sun and a dream deferred too long.

"I've learned how to do what it is that I want to do. My life has purpose, meaning, value now. I've sacrificed too much getting this far to give up."

Phyllis said nothing. We walked back to the drawing room. Sitting by her side on the couch, I broke the silence. "Enough about me. Tell me about you. Are you from Boston?"

"Oh, no," she laughed. "I'm a New Yorker. I just went to Boston for college. I spent some time doing kidney transplant research at Harvard Medical School. Then, one day I heard an advertisement designed to recruit teachers of deaf children. The ad used The Who's recording of 'Tommy, Can You Hear Me?' I wrote for information, and they told me about NYU. So, here I am."

"I'm glad you are."

She laughed. "You know, Frank, I've been thinking about it, and now I know what it is about you that puzzles me so much. Your speech is excellent. It really is. There's just the hint of an accent that I can't quite place."

It was my turn to laugh. "My speech. I've been told that I sound like a cross between Henry Kissinger . . ."

"No, it's not that."

". . . and Donald Duck."

Her face softened in laughter as she shook her head, that remarkable long straight brown hair swinging from side to side. "No. That's not it. I studied at the Sorbonne in Paris before going to Boston. And I've traveled throughout Europe, from the Scandinavian countries to southern Italy. I know a European accent when I hear one. So, whoever told you that you have a German accent doesn't know what he's talking about. As far as

4

Donald Duck is concerned, I can assure you that you sound nothing like him."

As I listened to the silence that followed, it occurred to me that Phyllis was about to make a major change in her life. I sensed that she would appreciate some reassurance now, on the eve of her voyage into a world she scarcely knew, that the trip would be worthwhile, that the degree she pursued would help her do something important. So I told her about a brilliant but mistakenly diagnosed deaf five-year-old boy I'd found in a class for retarded children, able only to communicate through gestures. I talked about a forty-seven-year-old man unable to hear, lipread, speak, read, or write, because he had never received the education he needed— and about his aging mother who was terrified of what would happen to him after she died. I shared with Phyllis my sense of awe as a fourteen-year-old girl, handicapped by deafness, emotional disturbance, and visual impairment, emerged one day from her shell to reach out to the world around her.

Phyllis listened quietly, and I sensed her body slowly relaxing. Then we talked for a while about English literature, comparing notes on Keats and Shelley, Wordsworth and Arnold, and about her adventures trying to translate Old English. She spoke of her love of Chaucer, I of my enjoyment of the Romantic poets. Gradually, we moved to a discussion of the more bleak modern poets and to the existentialist view of man as alone in the world.

"You remember how Camus died?" I asked her. "The Frenchman who argued so passionately that life was absurd, that nothing has any meaning? It was in 1960. He was a passenger in an automobile accident.

"So fitting, wasn't it, and so tragic? The irony, for me, is that he was so very wrong. The lives of others give our lives meaning. Camus seems never to have understood that."

She nodded and gave me a smile as if to say: "My thoughts exactly."

For a long while we simply sat together. There was no need to talk merely to fill the space between us, no need for idle chatter about the weather, the university, or any other neutral topic. Words had become unnecessary. What I wanted to do was simply to live the moment, completely content that she was beside me.

At length, Phyllis spoke. "I never thought it would be so easy to be with a deaf person. I feel totally relaxed. It's something I didn't expect."

"What did you expect?"

She shook her head. "I really don't know, Frank. I'm not responding at all to your deafness. We're talking like two old friends, two English majors. And I'm enjoying it."

"You must tell me more about yourself, Phyllis."

"You, too. I hope to get to know you much better."

I touched her shoulder. "Someday, you will."

5

Lewisburg, Pennsylvania, during the halcyon years between World War II and the Korean Conflict, was a quiet township of some 5,000 people dominated—as it is today—by two large institutions: Bucknell University and the Federal Penitentiary.

Bucknell's influence on the town was enormous. An outstanding private university, specializing in engineering and what were then called "the hard sciences" of chemistry and physics, Bucknell by its very presence made Lewisburg much more an intellectually oriented town than any of its neighbors. Many of the important political figures in local and county government were Bucknell alumni, as were numerous bankers and merchants.

Fully half of the faculty at the local secondary school, Lewisburg Joint High School, had Bucknell degrees. Pressure for academic excellence was strong at the high school because the parents of many students were also Bucknell graduates; indeed, they had met and courted on its campus. The university's social and athletic events provided the bulk of the town's entertainment. Aside from autumnal football games, winter basketball games, and spring dramatic arts presentations, there was not much in the way of spectator recreation available in the town.

The Federal Penitentiary, located on the northern outskirts of town, was if anything more famous than Bucknell. It was at Lewisburg that Alger Hiss served his five-year sentence after being convicted early in 1950 of espionage, the case that catapulted Richard Nixon to national fame. Hiss was joined later that year by Frank Costello, an alleged mob figure who had been found in contempt of court during Estes Kefauver's investigation of organized crime in New York City. Much later, Teamster boss Jimmy Hoffa would serve time at Lewisburg, as would prominent members of the Nixon administration responsible for Watergate.

A standing joke in town was that Lewisburgers either went to Bucknell or they went to the Pen.

Lewisburg in the late 1940s was one of several villages its size that had grown up along the Susquehanna. About ten miles north on the other side of the river stood Milton, a manufacturing center. Sunbury, home of the region's major newspaper, *The Daily Item,* was and is some twelve miles south of Lewisburg, at the juncture of the east and west branches of the river. The entire Susquehanna Valley area has been solid Republican country, happily isolated from the turbulence of postwar New York and Washington. The nearest city of any size is 20,000-population Williamsport, then almost an hour's drive to the north. Harrisburg, the state's capital city, stood nearly two hours to the south. As for Pittsburgh and Philadelphia, the state's two large metropolitan areas, both were nearly a day's drive from Lewisburg.

It was shortly after my mother began attending Bucknell University that she met the man who would become my father.

Mom was the oldest of four children born to Milton attorney William T. Windsor. Raised on his farm, Walnut Dell, on the outskirts of the town, even as a sophomore she still felt acutely conscious of just how naive she was compared with her more urbane college classmates. But, having absorbed without question her parents' conservative moral and political values, she also felt the need to assert herself as an individual. She was not living on campus, but commuting daily from the farm in Milton.

Dad was the youngest of the seven children of William J. Bowe, of Manhattan and Spring Lake, New Jersey. Hearing about a manufacturing job from a friend in Milton, Dad gave up a basketball scholarship at Fordham University just a few weeks into his freshman year. He understood that this act of rebellion would cut him off from his family's financial support, as indeed it did. But, like my mother, he wanted to shape his own life; unlike her, he felt no sense of guilt about acting on his convictions.

It was 1937. The nation was still mired in the Depression doldrums. Forty percent of the population had been impoverished in 1930, and the rate would be a staggering fifty percent by 1940. It was no time for a nineteen-year-old to give up a handsome scholarship at a prestigious university to journey to still-depressed central Pennsylvania. But that imprudent decision was very typical of my father: iconoclastic, relishing a challenge, confident in the face of oppressive odds, and scornful of the "easy way" of doing things.

They met in 1941 when Kitty Windsor came to visit one of her classmates at the house where he was renting a room. Smitten by this "dashing, confident New Yorker who knew no fear," my mother was, she later recalled, swept off her feet. "I chose him," she said with pride, "not the other way around."

Both felt adventurous: Mom because she was following the dictates of her heart after a lifetime of submitting to her parents' desires; Dad because he was starting a new life far from Manhattan.

The war interrupted their romance.

Enlisting in the U.S. Army shortly after Pearl Harbor, Dad was assigned to Fort Sill, Oklahoma. It was there, on March 27, 1943, that he married Kitty Windsor. My mother remembers feeling intense pride in herself for making so rebellious a move, so final and irrevocable a statement in the face of her parents' disapproval. She returned to Milton with a salt-and-pepper terrier named Pepsal to set up her own apartment and take a job as a reporter for the *Milton Standard*.

Dad headed for France and Germany.

When my father returned to Milton after VJ Day, his eyesight was permanently damaged. For the rest of his life, he wore thick bifocals and avoided any exposure to war scenes, whether on television, on radio, or in newspapers or conversation.

7

My parents bought a three-story home on Front Street in Milton, renting out the lower two stories to permanent and temporary renters. With the Army discharging a million men a month in late 1945 and early 1946, housing space was desperately short. Rooms at the Hotel Milton, down the street from my parents' home, were overbooked regularly, leading the hotel to refer some of their excess guests to Mom and Dad.

Although his work and her responsibilities around the house kept them busy, the postwar years in Milton were special times.

Sundays were for taking a leisurely drive through town in the family Crosby motor car, affectionately called "Jello" because of a balky suspension system. During the week, they spent their free hours listening to a big Magnavox radio, favoring Edith Piaf and Paul Robeson, or walking through town, laughing at the gingham dresses and cotton stockings of the older women, smiling at the dirndl skirts of the younger girls, and marveling at the crackly wash-and-wear shirts that were just then coming into general use. Saturdays, after washing Jello, they would walk to the local Rialto to catch a movie. Their favorites were Charlie Chaplin films.

One evening, while painting their floor in the Front Street house, my mother became seriously sick. She beamed through the tears the next day, though, when she learned that she was pregnant. In a burst of activity, Mom and Dad turned one room on the floor into a nursery. Mom bought a *Better Homes and Gardens* baby book and began following religiously its detailed instructions about how to be the perfect mother-to-be. She soon added *The Common Sense Book of Baby and Child Care,* by then little-known Benjamin McLane Spock.

Like millions of expectant parents in their generation, my parents had no doubt about their ability to give their children a life much better, much richer, and, above all, much more fun than what they had known as children. My father was sure I'd become, like him, a piano virtuoso and a top athlete. My mother was determined that I'd follow her to Bucknell. Because both had grown up in parent-dominated households, they resolved that their family would revolve around the children. If sacrifices had to be made, they, not the children, would make them. But they were confident the sacrifices would be few and far between. It was characteristic of the times that their optimism knew no bounds.

It was not long, however, before their buoyant mood was seriously challenged.

At Geisinger Medical Center in nearby Danville, Mom learned she had Rh-negative blood. A nurse explained that "Rh-factor incompatibility" had just been discovered to be an important cause of deformities in newborn babies. Were the father Rh-positive, as Dad was, and the mother Rh-negative, the child had better than a fifty-fifty chance of being born "permanently damaged." Those words "permanently damaged" immediately evoked a lifelong confinement to a state institution. The rights of disabled people in 1947, indeed for almost three decades to come, were few and far between. No local public school anywhere had to admit or provide accommodations for a handicapped child. No employer in any state had to hire or accommodate a disabled jobseeker. No public building had to be accessible to people using wheelchairs.

The doctor was pessimistic. "Kitty, I'd advise you not to buy any baby furniture or clothes. In all likelihood, your baby will be dead at birth."

That warning, plus a scary article in *Life* magazine about the condition, which the periodical called *erythroblastosis fetalis,* caused Mom and Dad to monitor my fetal movements with great care, searching for any signal that something might be irregular or unusual about my growth. So the fact that I kicked exuberantly while the crowd cheered at a Bucknell basketball game that winter was taken as a reassuring sign. I must be O.K., they thought, for I was an active fetus indeed.

On March 29, 1947, a Saturday morning, I broke my mother's coccyx bone during delivery, scratching the top of my head from ear to ear. I entered the world as a seven pound, eleven ounce infant looking perfectly normal.

"He looks just like a miniature W.C. Fields with that squashed nose," Dad joked. Both were relieved that the doctors' dire warnings seemed groundless.

Piling me into Jello, they returned to the Front Street house in Milton determined to start a new life after months of agonizing worry.

"We're going to do everything right from this point on," Mom announced. Picking up the by-now dog-eared *Better Homes and Gardens* baby book, Mom set out the routine she and I would follow each day.

"Now, every morning I'll give him orange juice and cod liver oil. Then he has a sun bath. Before his nap, he gets a regular bath. Then, after lunch, I will take him for a walk in the carriage so he gets some fresh air. Then he gets another nap. By that time, you'll be home, and we can take it from there."

Dad wasn't as organized as he liked to think he was, especially when it came to playing with me.

His job each evening was to give me a bath. Watching him one night, Mom burst out laughing.

"What's so funny?" Dad asked, two soapy hands cradling my chest.

"I can't help it. You're handling him like he was made of spun sugar. You look like you're afraid you'll break him."

"Well, what am I supposed to do?"

"Play with him, honey. He's a person, not a china doll."

My father was dubious, but he soon discovered that Mom was right. I was a pretty tough customer, a boisterous infant he could toss into the air and catch with joyful abandon. Soon he was dancing around the living room floor, holding me chest high, and swinging to the tunes of Dizzy

Gillespie and Charlie Parker on the new Columbia Microgroove records.

The schedule Mom left for her mother when she and Dad left me with my grandmother for a weekend illustrates the care two worried parents lavished on me, as well as the influence of Dr. Spock on my upbringing:

"7 A.M. Average waking time. He wants a full bottle of milk, half boiled water and half canned milk, right away. Change him after his milk, not before; otherwise, he'll raise the roof. He will now go back into bed until about 8.

"8 A.M. Ready to get up for good. He now wants a small juice glass full of orange juice (usually one large orange, or two small ones), which he will drink himself. Then his oleum-percomorphum drops.

"8:30 A.M. He'll go in his pen now for at least an hour. Don't go to him every time he cries, unless it is hard and determined.

"11 A.M. He now eats about one-third of a large jar of meat and vegetables, half a jar of vegetables, and half a jar of pudding.

"11:30 A.M. Change his pants and tuck him into bed with a bear. If he throws it out, just let it stay out.

"1:30 P.M. He'll probably get awake about now. Now he has another bottle of milk. He likes this bottle almost cool.

"2:30 P.M. No point in trying to pen him anywhere now. He wants the freedom of the house and preferably a walk or play outside. Don't feel you have to play with him; he's just as happy by himself.

"5:30 P.M. He's usually ready for supper by now. He has the yoke of a soft-boiled egg, half a jar of fruit, and a generous helping of cereal. Then he can have a cookie (or ten) while you eat. If he's bad, cart him out into his pen and leave him there, even if he shrieks bloody murder.

"6:30 P.M. Bath time. He likes the water warm when he gets in. Watch out for him standing in the tub; he does this quite suddenly. Then put him to bed. No point in putting a cover on him or getting up to cover him at night. He's not used to it. Put the bear in the bed with him, pull down the shades, kiss him goodnight, and walk firmly out, closing the door right away. Sometimes, he'll cry for fifteen minutes or more when he doesn't want to go to sleep. Just let him lie there. Unless he sounds hurt, just let him alone, and he'll drop off again."

At fifteen months, in mid-1948, I stood one day, walked toward my father, whose hands were outstretched in front of him in joyous anticipation, and then abruptly turned around and waddled the other way, a wide grin on my face.

"That little devil," Dad grumbled.

"I told you he had a wacky sense of humor," Mom laughed. "Now you've seen it, too."

One evening, Mom sat on the living room couch reading me "Hansel and Gretel." Mid-way through the story, just as the witch ordered Gretel to stoke the fire, I moved from her side to sit on her lap. A few moments later, I was on the floor. Mom laughed, patting her stomach, and motioned me back to her lap. When I fell again, she laughed and patted the couch beside her. We finished the story sitting side by side.

As Mom gave me a book to play with, my father put down his newspaper.

"Kitty, have you noticed how Frankie has his own pronunciations for things? Thank you is 'Danka.' Fire trucks are 'bire tucks.' And he calls himself 'Boyji.' It just seems a funny way to talk."

Mom reached for the newspaper. "So what? Half the children on the block are harder to understand than he is."

"You don't think it's strange?"

"Not at all. Don't worry about it. I'm sure in time he'll outgrow this baby talk."

"Well, all right, Kitty. It's just that I've never seen an eighteen month old say 'Boyji on the biji' when he rides his stroller."

"How many eighteen month olds have you seen?"

"Well, all right."

"Now that that's settled, what are we going to call the baby?"

Two months before my second birthday, Mom suddenly left the house for a week. I was disconsolate, even with Dad home from work to keep me company. I wouldn't play, nap, or take a bath without screaming for my mother.

Dad figured a change of scene might help, so he took me to my maternal grandparents' farm in Milton, hoping I'd think the week was a special vacation trip. It didn't work.

"I want Mommy."

"Soon, honey."

"I want my Mommy."

"Please eat your supper."

"I want Mommy to feed me."

"Mommy's not here now, son. Please eat."

"I won't! I won't!"

By mid-week, Dad was desperate.

One evening, he brought to the farm a small German Shepherd puppy. I was hiding under the kitchen table, determined to stay there until my mother returned.

The dog found me there, licking my face, my hands, and even my feet. It was love at first lick.

"I think she's hungry, Boyji," Dad said, taking out some dog food.

"Can I feed her? Can I? Huh?"

"Well, sure, son. Why don't you two eat together? I'll put your food here on the table, and between bites you can feed the puppy."

11

That's how Dad finally got me to eat.

"What shall we call her, Boyji? We'll need a name for her since she's now part of our family."

"Golly! Is she really ours?"

"She sure is, son."

"Golly! Wow!"

"O.K., son. We'll call her Golly."

On January 25, 1949, Dad brought me back to the Front Street house.

There I found Mom, to whom I refused to say a word, and a bawling baby sister, whom I loved immediately. They named her Robin. I called her "Bebe."

When my sister was one year old, I contracted measles for the first time. Shortly thereafter, I caught it a second time. Both episodes involved very high fevers.

Mom and Dad called Dr. Samuel Dawes, the family doctor, and insisted he come to the house, even though it was late at night.

"Doctor, you've got to do something," Mom begged him.

"Mrs. Bowe, I don't understand why you think this is measles. He had it a while ago. Children usually don't have measles twice, because, after the first time, the body builds up antibodies that prevent recurrence of the disease."

"Well, whatever it is, he's running a frightful temperature."

Fifteen minutes later, Dr. Dawes announced that he was going to stay most of the night until the fever subsided.

"It's measles, all right. But I still can't understand how he could have got them."

"What about the fever?"

"It's still high. Mr. Bowe, Mrs. Bowe, we have a new miracle drug that I'd like to give Frankie. To be honest with you, it's still rather experimental. But I believe this will bring his temperature down faster than anything else I could use. At this time, that seems the important thing."

Mom looked to Dad for a decision.

"Use it," he said. "But first tell me what it is."

"Streptomycin," Dr. Dawes responded.

My fever soon disappeared, but I remained a bit groggy. A few days later, the last vestiges of illness vanished, and I was allowed to play outside again.

It wasn't long, though, before my parents noticed that something was wrong.

"He's pale, isn't he, Kitty?" Dad asked when he came home for lunch one afternoon.

"Well, yes," Mom answered. "I think since the measles, he's been rather nervous."

Dad ran into the house and came back carrying some pictures.

"Look, Kitty. Here's a picture we took last summer. Notice the chubbiness, the red apple cheeks, the ruddy complexion."

"Yes. Our little fat football player."

"Well, that football player isn't here any longer. Unless I miss my guess, we have a pole vaulter here."

"It's no joking matter, honey."

"I'm not joking, Kitty. You can see it as well as I can. And he acts different, too. Quiet. Withdrawn. I don't like it."

The problem was one they felt they had to face alone. Having rebelled by marrying my father, Mom felt she could not go to her parents for help; she feared their rejection. Any difficulties she encountered in this marriage she would have to resolve on her own. My father, for his part, was too proud a man to admit that he could not face and handle his own family's crises.

By mid-April, 1950, Mom and Dad were convinced that the "something wrong" was my hearing. The first signs they noticed were small ones.

I loved playing in our backyard, which overlooked the Susquehanna. With Tim Spotts and Billy Kay, two neighborhood friends, I would rush to the edge of our yard to watch motor boats as they roared past our house. Now, on some mornings I would not hear the boats. On other days, I could hear them in the morning but not in the afternoon.

Another favorite ritual of mine that year had been rushing to the front of the house whenever I heard Jello, the Crosby, bringing Dad home for lunch. In June, my parents noticed that I no longer heard the car's arrival.

One morning, Dad came into my room before leaving for work. I was still asleep. He stood in the doorway and called: "Frankie! Time to wake up!"

I didn't move.

Dad moved to the middle of the room and raised his voice: "Frankie! Wake up, Frankie!"

No response.

He stood at the side of my crib, holding the bars, and shouted: "Frankie! Frankie!"

Nothing.

Finally, he touched me on the cheek.

I awoke instantly.

That evening, my parents debated the meaning of the morning's events.

"I think something's happened to his hearing, Kitty."

"No, it can't be. There's got to be some mistake," Mom insisted.

"Well, he is a deep sleeper," Dad conceded.

"I'm sure that's it," Mom said. "When I went into his room to dress him this morning, he turned around as soon as I walked in. He must have heard me."

"What about the boats on the river? The car at lunchtime?"

Mom shook her head. "I'm sure he was just too busy playing to notice."

Dad would not be mollified. "I think we should get his hearing tested. The sooner, the better."

The next morning, Mom called Dr. Dawes, but he didn't feel qualified to examine my ears. He did recommend an ear-nose-throat specialist in Lewisburg, however. Mom and Dad took me to him one morning.

"Now, Frankie," he said, sitting on a swivel chair not two feet from me. I could see him clearly. "Frankie, I want you to listen carefully and say what I say. Understand?"

I nodded.

"Horse."

I answered immediately: "Horse."

"Cow."

I looked into his eyes and back at his lips.

"Cow."

"Right, sonny. Now: Dog."

"Dog."

"Cat."

"Cat."

He patted me on the head, handed me a lollypop, and turned to face my parents.

"You're crazy," he declared. "That boy hears as well as I do."

The examination was not enough to quiet my father's suspicions. Day after day, he devised ways to test what I could hear.

Coming into the living room one Saturday morning to find me engrossed with some building blocks, Dad banged two books together.

I didn't flinch.

Walking toward me, he repeated the banging.

Finally, when he was only two feet behind me, I turned.

"Kitty," he told Mom when I had gone back to my blocks, "I'm almost certain now."

"But you said he turned."

"Yes, but not until I was almost on top of him. Hmmm. I wonder whether he felt the air. Yes, maybe that's it. When I banged those books together, it created a burst of air that he might have sensed. Maybe he didn't hear it at all."

Mom shook her head. "Then how do you explain his hearing test in Lewisburg?"

14

"I've been thinking about that, too, Kitty. You noticed that the doctor sat right in front of Frankie. He talked to him. Never once did that doctor cover his lips."

"What are you saying?"

"That perhaps, just perhaps, Frankie was reading the doctor's lips."

"You mean that he's taught himself to lipread?"

"Maybe, Kitty. Maybe."

One night in early May, I caught a cold.

By the next afternoon, Mom was worried enough to call my father home from work.

"Honey, I've got this terrible feeling in my stomach that you're right. Maybe it's worse now that he has a cold, but I know, with this dreadful certainty, that Frankie can't hear."

"At all?"

"At all."

My father sat stunned. "Well, we'd better take him to Geisinger, then."

The medical center doctor my parents consulted was skeptical at first. "Mr. and Mrs. Bowe, we don't as a rule, you know, admit children who only have a cold. We'll do it this time, because of your concern about Frankie's hearing. I'm giving him some antibiotics. In forty-eight hours, an audiometrist will test his hearing."

"Why not now, doctor?"

"Because of the cold. We won't learn anything about his hearing until he's recovered from that. You'll just have to be patient."

Two days later, the tests began.

Mom, Dad, and I sat in a small carpeted room with about a dozen toys scattered about. "Play with him here," the audiometrist, a young woman with curly brown hair, told my parents. "Keep him occupied. I'm going to make some noises. Don't let him know you heard them. Okay?"

Mom and Dad nodded.

The woman began with a large rattle. Standing behind me, she shook it, coming closer and closer to my head, without letting me see her.

I didn't respond.

She replaced the rattle and picked up a whistle. Waiting until she was satisfied I was concentrating on the toy cars in front of me, she blew the whistle, took a few steps toward me, and blew it again.

"The rattle makes a low sound, the whistle a high one," she told Mom and Dad. "Now, I'm going to try the drum."

I looked up suddenly from the cars, searching first Dad's face and then Mom's. Receiving no response, I returned to the cars.

A few minutes later, I sat up again. This time, I looked behind me, catching the audiometrist with her drum.

She smiled and gave it to me to play with.

"You'll hear some other sounds now. Keep playing with him. Remember: don't let him know you hear something. O.K.? See if you can get him to play with the cars again or with the toy train. Anything that doesn't make noise."

Over the next ten minutes, Mom and Dad watched as I raced my cars. They noticed me look up startled after one particularly loud tone, searching the room for its source. I responded to the same sound once more but not to any of the other tones.

Mom and Dad anxiously awaited the audiometrist's return.

"Well?" demanded Dad.

"All I can tell you at this point is that he doesn't respond to anything but very low tones and even those only at high decibel levels. I suspect he can hear more than he showed me today. And I think his hearing will probably get better as he gets a little older. He may still be affected a bit by the cold he had the other day."

"What does all this mean?" Dad asked.

"I don't want to be more specific now, Mr. Bowe. There's so much that I don't know yet. I'd prefer to wait until we can test him again before I say anything more definite."

"I want something more," Dad told her, "and I want it now. Does he have a hearing loss?"

"Mr. Bowe, it does look as if he has one. How much of a loss is more than I can say with confidence now. Why don't you talk with the doctor again and bring him back in a few weeks. We'll know more then."

Mom and Dad sought out the doctor. He didn't offer much more information, but he was definite about something else.

"Mr. and Mrs. Bowe, I want to see Frankie again in two weeks. When he comes back, I strongly recommend that we have his tonsils removed and probably his adenoids as well. These can become infected, you know, and the infection could spread to his ears. That's a chance I don't want to take."

"Well, I suppose that's sensible," Mom said. "But couldn't you tell us more about his hearing?"

"The audiometrist told you to wait, Mrs. Bowe. You'll just have to wait."

When we returned to the hospital two weeks later, it was for two days. Mom slept in the room with me, since I refused to stay in my crib alone.

The day after my operation, Mom met with the surgeon who had supervised the tonsil and adenoid removals.

"Well, Mrs. Bowe. The tonsillectomy was a success. I'm pleased the adenoids are safely gone, too."

"Doctor, I hope you won't think me ungrateful. I'm not," Mom said, rubbing her hands together as she always did when she became nervous.

"But he's acting so strange."

"Your son is?"

"Yes. I don't know how to put this. I guess I have the strange feeling that I'm losing him."

"Losing him?"

"I'm afraid the operation traumatized him. He seems almost to be in shock."

"Mrs. Bowe, I'm sure you'll find you're overreacting. After he's been home a few days, you'll find that it was just a normal case of post-operation nervousness."

When Dad came to pick us up and take us back to Milton, he also noticed my trance-like behavior.

"My God, Kitty. What happened in there?"

"I don't know. He's been like this since yesterday. The doctor says he'll bounce out of it in a couple of days."

"I don't like the looks of this, Kitty."

"I'm afraid you're right, honey. I don't like it either, not one bit."

Two weeks later, Mom and Dad held a family conference at the kitchen table.

"He's not out of it yet, that's for sure!" Dad slammed his fist on the table. "If those doctors did this, I'll personally dismember every one of them."

"You've noticed how thin he's getting?"

"Yes, Kitty. How could I miss it? And irritable! It seems every time you steer him away from the stairs or take a toy out of his mouth, he cries."

"What are we going to do?"

"I've been giving it a lot of thought. You realize, Kitty, that this house is now filled with memories for Frankie of everything that's gone wrong in his three years here. In the backyard, he is reminded every day that he can't hear the outboard motors any more. Almost every room in the house must tell him something about the life he used to know—and can't have any more. Besides, you know how concerned we both are about his running out into the heavy Front Street traffic."

"What are you leading up to?"

"Moving. I think we should move."

"Move? Are you serious?"

"As serious as I've ever been in my life. I've been thinking about Lewisburg, where I play tennis every weekend with Donald Ross and the other guys. It's quiet there. And with Bucknell right in the town, Frankie and Robin won't even have to leave home to go to college."

"College? At a time like this, you're thinking of college?"

"You bet I am. I'm more sure than ever that our little boy is going to come out of this all the stronger for the ordeals he's had to go through."

17

The Mensch Agency broker who took them around Lewisburg started with the new homes near the Bucknell golf course. My father displayed his famous subtlety when the broker mentioned the prices.

"Absolutely out of the question! Show us the other end of the price scale. Do it right now. Then we'll work our way back to something we can afford."

My mother was a bit embarrassed. This was one of many instances in which my father's dogged insistence upon being himself, regardless of social conventions, caused my mother to reflect ruefully that it was one thing to delight in being rebellious by marrying a nonconformist, but it was something else altogether to live with him day in and day out.

"Well, there's a nice home at the foot of the campus, not far from the river. It's worth a look."

"Let's go," Dad said, impatient as always with preliminaries.

The house turned out to be an unpainted grey wood structure near the railroad tracks on Brown Street. As the broker had said, it faced the campus. A pleasant surprise were the four tennis courts just opposite the tracks.

"What do you think, Kitty?" Dad asked, as soon as they were out of earshot of the broker.

"I'm afraid of the tracks. The idea of Frankie walking anywhere near those tracks terrifies me."

"We'll have to teach him to stay away from them. What else bothers you about the house?"

"Nothing else, really."

"Good. Here's what we'll do. We'll give Frankie the big bedroom at the front. Robin's crib we'll place in the back bedroom. From our room in the middle, we can reach either one in seconds."

"I like the fact that the bedrooms all open into each other. It seems so friendly and open."

"Right, Kitty. I think this house has a lot to offer. I'll be back as soon as I beat a good price out of that agent."

"Ask him who lives here now."

"Oh, didn't you hear? A retired philosophy professor at Bucknell. He moved away months ago. That's one reason I think I can get a good price."

"O.K., honey. Despite all the work it needs, I think this house will help us make a fresh start."

"Right. We've all been pretty battered lately. We need something good. This, I pray to God, is it."

The day we moved in, a big boxer dog crossed the street and headed for me.

"Frankie, hold my hand," Mom said. "I don't like the looks of this slobbering dog."

I ignored her.

"Hello, Friend Dog," I said, lifting the dog's paw in a handshake.

Dad moved to stand beside Mom.

"You know," he told her. "That's the first reaching out he's done in months."

"Yes. I think you were right about this house."

"Let's hope we're both right."

A few days later, Dad came home for lunch to find Mom singing in the living room.

"Don't tell me. Let me guess!"

"No. I'm not pregnant." She laughed.

"Then what's this?"

"Would you believe that this neighborhood that we thought was just about devoid of kids has suddenly revealed itself to contain no fewer than twenty-two children?"

"I'd have said four at the most."

"Some two dozen! And most of them are Frankie's and Robin's ages. Can you imagine! They'll never lack for friends around here."

"Looks like we made a good decision."

"I can feel it. We're on the way. At long last, thank God, we're on our way."

I was fascinated with Robin's toilet training. She was getting a lot of attention from Mom every time she went into the bathroom. That was attention I wanted.

To make things more interesting, I took Robin aside one afternoon as we were playing in the backyard.

"Now, Bebe. Listen careful."

Her big blue eyes looked into mine.

"Mister Tiger lives in the bathroom at night."

I glanced furtively at the house. Mom was nowhere to be seen.

"Mister Tiger," I repeated. "Big, mean, Mister Tiger. At night. In the bathroom."

She looked like a piece of cotton candy tastes. I almost felt bad about being nasty to someone so innocent. Almost, but not quite.

"Growl," I concluded.

The next morning, Dad wasted no time in setting me straight about how wrong I had been.

"Frankie, I want you to tell Robin right now that Mister Tiger does not live in the bathroom."

I gulped. "Uh, Bebe. Mister Tiger doesn't live in the bathroom."

My father wasn't satisfied. "At night. Or any other time."

I repeated: "At night. Any other time."

"There never has been a tiger, and there never will be one."

"Right."

"Tell her, not me!"

"Right, Bebe. There's no Tiger."

"Thank you. I'm afraid you've set your sister's toilet training back a few weeks."

Mom walked in. "More than a few weeks, Frankie."

"But I'm not going to spank you."

He looked at Mom.

"Your mother and I feel that what you did was wrong. You understand that, don't you?"

I nodded.

"At the same time, though, we're almost glad you did it."

He took my hand.

"Frankly, son," Dad continued, "we were waiting for the old you to come back. We've missed you for quite a while now."

"Welcome back, Frankie," Mom added.

"Welcome back, you little devil," Dad echoed.

Once a month, Mom or Dad took me to Geisinger Medical Center for a checkup. After the gland operations, they didn't want to take any chances.

During our July visit, the Geisinger doctors told my father about an internationally renowned ear specialist, Dr. Edmund P. Fowler, Jr. They recommended that I be taken to Columbia-Presbyterian Medical Center in Manhattan to see Dr. Fowler.

"You see, Mr. Bowe, we've been watching his development carefully. We've tested his hearing several times. I have reason to believe, and my colleagues agree with me, that his hearing is permanently damaged.

"We've not had much experience here with profound hearing impairments. But Dr. Fowler in New York has. If anybody can help your little boy, that somebody is Edmund Fowler."

Chapter
Two

Deafness means being alone.

You don't hear the sounds people make as they move about in the house; there is no connection with others unless you can see them.

Being deaf, too, means that even when others are in the room with you, you don't know what they say to each other.

There is no incidental learning. None.

Your sister learns by overhearing conversations between your parents. She learns by listening to the radio while she plays with her toys. She learns by watching television programs. She learns by talking to her friends.

You do none of this.

You sit quietly, doing whatever you happen to be doing, oblivious to what is going on around you.

It means, as well, that whenever a family member wants to tell or ask you something, that individual must attract your attention by touching you or moving within your field of vision. And then begins the slow, agonizing, emotionally draining process of communicating.

Words are repeated until they are understood. Ideas are expressed three, four, or five times through different words and different sentences. You catch a word here, a word there, and guess about the rest.

Very quickly, despite their love for you and desire to include you in the daily life of the family, your parents and siblings talk to you only when necessary.

There is no idle chitchat, no talking for relaxation.

You do not pick up the bits and pieces of someone's character, personality, interests, and worries that others get in the course of talking "about nothing."

You know your mother, your father, and your sister only from what you see them do and say directly to you.

Slowly, surely, your isolation grows.

Mom was sitting at the breakfast table when I came down one August morning.

I plopped into the chair next to hers. "Ugh! It's raining," I groaned.

My mother laughed.

Setting a plate piled high with hot pancakes before me, she patted my head with one hand while she gave me the syrup with the other.

I drenched the plate in my favorite syrup, expertly catching the overflow with the fingers of both hands. Mom said nothing while I ate. Finally, licking the plate clean, I sat back with a sigh.

"It's too wet to play outside today," Mom said as she set down her coffee cup. She watched me closely, to see if I understood. Dissatisfied, she tried again: "We'll have to wait until the grass dries before you can go out." Still not sure I understood, she tried a third time: "You'll have to play inside this morning."

I nodded. "Is Bebe up yet, Mom?" I asked, referring to Robin.

"Yes, honey. You can play with her while I clean up down here." She nodded and pointed an index finger to the ceiling.

I bounded up the long staircase and burst into Bebe's room. She was lying on her back in the crib, staring at the six light bulbs dangling from the fixture on the wall. Suddenly, I knew how to make the morning more interesting. Dragging a straightbacked chair to the bureau, I climbed on its top and reached for the first of the bulbs. I was astonished to find it hot to the touch. Pulling my hand back quickly, I blew on my fingers while I looked around the room. Bebe was watching me closely. I climbed down, moved the chair to the opposite wall, flicked off the light switch, and pulled the chair back to the bureau.

With a delighted shout: "Out the lights!" I carefully unscrewed the first bulb and smashed it on the floor. Bebe looked startled. I didn't know whether she was about to laugh or cry. Three more bulbs "outened" their lights before the door behind me burst open, and a very angry Mom barged into the room.

"Frankie! Don't you dare!"

"But Mom . . ."

"Oh, my Lord! Just wait 'til your father hears about this!"

Before my father heard about that, I'd become bored again. Picking up a drumstick, I shouted at the top of my lungs: "Listen to Bebe cry!" and bopped her on the head. Pleased that the predicted consequences followed my action, I repeated the performance. I was about to try a third time when I was lifted unceremoniously from the crib and given the beating of my young life. It was the first time Mom had ever hit me. Usually, she left that sort of thing to my father.

After about an hour of screaming in my room that went unrewarded with an appearance by my mother, I wandered into the bathroom to blow my nose on toilet paper. Wanting to see if my face looked sufficiently forlorn to warrant sympathy from my father when he returned home for lunch, I climbed onto the sink and examined myself closely in the mirror. A few moments later, I opened the medicine cabinet and inserted aspirin and vitamin pills into my mouth. I was about to open a nose dropper when Mom pulled me from the sink.

She dragged me screaming into the kitchen and forced me to drink five glasses of milk.

My father found us there.

Before he could say anything, Mom gave him a blow-by-blow account of the morning. "Your son seems determined to send *us* to Geisinger Medical Center," she fumed.

"That bad, huh?" He turned to me. "Frankie, you and I are going to have a little talk. But first I want to discuss something with your mother."

I busied myself with some building blocks, delighted to have escaped punishment.

I did not understand anything my parents said, but whatever it was that they were talking about, they stood by the door for an awfully long time.

Eventually, they turned to me. Dad sat at my side, picked up a block in one hand, and twirled it slowly.

"Frankie. I've got some bad news."

Sure he was going to punish me at last, I began to cry.

To my surprise, he lifted me to his lap. Turning my face to his, he spoke slowly and carefully, repeating himself from time to time to make sure I was following his words.

"You'll have to go away to see a special doctor, Frankie."

It took a while for the words to sink in.

"I know you don't want to see another doctor. But this one might help you hear again."

"I can hear fine."

"No, honey, you can't. You can't even hear the trains go by on the tracks across the street any more."

"I can, too!"

"What about the record player? You turn it way up now and put your right ear up against it."

"Yeah, but I can hear it. I can hear Tubby the tuba, and I can hear the tortoise." To prove it, I added: "He may be slow, but he's sure."

"Frankie, those are songs you learned while your hearing was better. You know them by heart now. When we put on a record you don't know, you tear it right off."

"That's not true!"

"Let's just say that this is the last one. OK, Frankie? I promise. No more doctors after Dr. Fowler."

That did it.

I spent the afternoon playing near the Bucknell University softball field on the other side of the tracks. Golly, my German Shepherd, followed me all the way up the hill that led to the university's main buildings. As I sat and looked down at my home on Brown Street, Golly chased squirrels and birds up and down the hill. Somehow, the squirrels always reached the trees just before Golly caught up with them. None of that seemed to bother Golly. She was happy just being alive.

Dad tucked me into bed that evening. Years later, he still remembered our talk.

"I wish I was Golly," I told him. "She can play. No doctors."

Dad brushed his thick brown hair back across the top of his head. "When she gets sick, she does."

"When she gets a stick? Huh?"

"Sick, Frankie. When she gets sick. Ill."

"Oh, sick."

"Right, sick. When she gets sick, she has to go to a doctor."

"I'm not sick."

"I know. But your ears are. Soon, we'll know why. Then maybe we can make your ears get better."

I nodded. "How soon?"

"It may be a while, Frankie." He paused. "I don't know how long."

"An hour?"

He laughed. "Maybe a week, maybe two."

"That long?" I sat up and stared at him.

"I hope not. I don't know."

He took my hands in his.

"Mom tells me you were busy today." Dad laughed. "I hear you turned Robin into a drum."

"A drum? I didn't have a drum."

"No. I mean, you hit Robin on the head."

"She didn't have a drum. Nobody had a drum."

"Forget it."

"Get it? The drum? What drum, Daddy?"

"No drum, son. Let me buy you a drum after Dr. Fowler sees you. O.K.? Now, get to sleep." He turned out the lights and walked downstairs.

"Kitty, I'm glad he's going to have his hearing tested. It's getting so hard to make him understand me."

"I know, honey. It's like that for me, too. Sometimes, I just can't get through to him."

"But I don't think he understands yet how long this trip will be. Kitty, I want you to talk to him every chance you get about Robin, me, the house, Golly, even the pancakes he had for breakfast today."

"O.K. I will."

"Because no one can take us away from him, you know. His memories of us will keep him company while he's away."

Dad paused. "What I mean is, keep telling him that no matter what happens about his ears, Robin, Golly, and I will be here for him when he comes home."

"Sure, honey. I just hope something good happens. Nothing is the way it used to be around here. He's nervous and irritable; I'm tense; you're tense; even Robin seems to notice it. Whatever is wrong with Frankie's ears, I hope Dr. Fowler takes care of it. Because it's about time we got on with our lives. I don't know how much longer I can take this suspended animation.''

About all I remember of the next day's trip to New York is my fascination with the Pennsylvania Dutch country of eastern Pennsylvania. Almost every red barn we passed had an intricately designed ''hex'' symbol on its side to ward off evil spirits. We saw several horse-drawn buggies filled with black-clad Amish folk. Mom explained that the Amish lived very simply, without electricity, cars, and tractors. I remember, too, that the trip took an incredible length of time. It was almost dinner time when we finally passed over the George Washington Bridge and headed south to the upper East Side apartment of Dad's sister.

From her living room window, I could see more lights than I could count. Dad draped an arm across my shoulder and with his other hand turned my chin so that I faced him.

"New York is the city that never sleeps, Frankie. At just about any hour of the night, you can get anything you want somewhere in this town."

By the time I went to bed, I had forgotten all about Dr. Fowler.

Mom had breakfast ready when I awoke in the morning. She remembered, much later, that she was shaking her head from side to side with nervous jerks as she listened to her sister in law give her directions to the medical center.

"What's the matter, Mom?"

"Oh, Frankie. It's just that I hate this city. I'm deathly afraid you and I will get lost in the huge crowds out there."

"Where's Dad?"

"Um, honey. Dad had to go back. He has to take care of Bebe, you know."

A somber Mom and I took two buses to Columbia-Presbyterian Medical Center. Mom squeezed my hand so hard I had to switch hands every ten minutes or so. I didn't argue with her or ask her to be more gentle; one look at her hard-set, fearful, and determined face told me to be quiet. At last we arrived at the medical center. Its imposing stone structure, with a steep staircase also in stone, seemed cold and impersonal. It was also huge.

Dr. Fowler's gimlet eyes carried no hint of warmth. I took an instant dislike to the man. I didn't like the way he treated us, either. For what seemed like an hour, he grilled my mother with question after question, pausing only occasionally to glare at me, his fish-shaped face hardening into a frown.

Finally, he stepped out of the room.

"What's happening, Mom?" I whispered.

25

"I think Dr. Fowler is convinced I'm a neurotic witch who beat you into this state," she sighed. "That means, he thinks I'm the one who needs a doctor. It's O.K., honey. I'm sure he just wanted to rule out psychological causes before he examines you." She tapped her forehead.

Sure enough, Fowler re-emerged with a scary, long needle. It looked like a silver pen. I screamed. But Dr. Fowler was, I quickly discovered, a strong man, and with my mother's help (my mother!) he soon had me fast asleep. I later learned that he examined my nasal and ear passages, finding nothing unusual that might help explain my hearing loss. There was no outer ear damage in either ear. After I woke up, Dr. Fowler did some audiometric tests of my hearing. Much later, Mom recalled his verdict.

"This little boy has no hearing at all, that I can measure, in his left ear. In fact, Mrs. Bowe, I strongly doubt he ever did. It's highly likely he was born deaf in that ear. Now, tell me again, was there anything in your pregnancy or at childbirth that might have done this?"

"The only thing, like I told you, Dr. Fowler, is the Rh factor. I'm Rh-negative, my husband is Rh-positive. But since Frankie is Rh-negative like I am, I didn't think . . ."

"We'll decide that. Now, there's some hearing left in the right ear. Let's see what we can make of it." He paused, writing on a slip of paper. "This is a prescription for niacin," he told my mother. Niacin is nicotinic acid, part of the vitamin B complex. As a prescription drug, it was designed to get the blood circulating more normally in my head, since Fowler thought circulation irregularities might be affecting my hearing. "After you get back to where you're staying, give this to him twice a day. Then come see me Monday."

We were dismissed.

It was early afternoon when Mom and I returned to my aunt's apartment.

Mom gave me the niacin. Five minutes later, I dived under the sofa cushions, screaming: "Turn off the hots! Turn off the hots!" She leaped to the sofa and buried my head in her lap, both hands rubbing my hair steadily and rhythmically. Then she lifted my head to face hers.

"Frankie, your ears! The right one is white, and the left one is bright red! Dr. Fowler didn't say anything about this. I don't know what to do."

When she gave me niacin again the next morning, I burrowed under the pillows, holding both ears. This time, Mom noticed, the right ear was red, and the left one white. Immediately, she called Dr. Fowler's office to report the irregularities. It was a short conversation.

"Well?" asked my aunt, walking into the bedroom.

"The secretary says Dr. Fowler will look at it on Monday, when we have our appointment."

"Nothing else?"

"She told me to stop being hysterical. Well, I'd like to know why. Here

I am, 300 miles from home, with a three-and-a-half-year-old whose ears don't work right any more. Every doctor I see tells me the same thing: 'We don't know, Mrs. Bowe.' It sounds like a line from Robert Browning.''

"I'm sure it will all work out, Kitty.''

"You see, that's exactly what I keep telling myself. But after so many doctors and so much confusion, with us in the middle of this huge city, I'm really starting to have doubts. You saw how that medicine hurts Frankie. Well, I've seen him given shots, pills, you name it, and none of it has helped. None of it. He's suffering, for what I'm just not sure any more is a worthy cause.''

"You don't have a choice, really, do you, Kitty? You do have to try this.''

"That's what your brother always says. 'We have to try, Kitty. We have to try.' Well, mark my words. I don't like this Fowler any more than Frankie does. I'm afraid, I really am, that this is going to be nothing more than a big disappointment.''

My mother dragged me kicking, screaming, and biting to the Medical Center Monday for our meeting with Dr. Fowler. On both buses, she held me with a vise-like grip. Both of us were exhausted by the time we reached he doctor's office. I sat in Mom's lap, my arms held immobile, as Fowler probed both my ears with small lights, made some notes on a scratchpad, and sat back.

"This little boy will have to stay here for some tests, Mrs. Bowe.''

"What kind of tests, Doctor?''

He tossed his hands into the air. "What not? Since I don't know what might have caused his hearing loss, I need to test for just about anything. We'll look for damage from measles, from the Rh factor, from meningitis, from hereditary factors, anything else that looks promising.''

"For how long?''

"I would say a month, Mrs. Bowe.''

Mom's head slipped back against the chair; her mouth opened slightly.

I watched the color drain from Mom's face. Although I didn't understand what he was saying, I was angry at Fowler for making my mother so upset.

"Mom! Are you O.K.?''

"I guess so, honey.'' She looked at Fowler. "May I have a few moments of privacy with my son?''

"I'll get a nurse,'' he said.

"Frankie,'' Mom began, after we'd gone into a small office across the hall from Fowler's office. "Honey, you'll have to stay here for a while. Maybe for a month, but I hope not that long.''

"How long is a month, Mom?''

"Too long, honey. Oh, about four weeks. Um, thirty days. Let's see."
She paused. "Remember Bebe's birthday is in January? And yours is in March. So from the time we celebrate her birthday to the time we have your party, it's two months. One month is half that long."

"Will you be with me, Mom?"

"Every morning, you bet. And every day until late in the day. They won't let me stay here since it's the children's ward, but I'll be here every single minute that I can."

Her hands on my shoulders, Mom felt my body shaking.

When I spoke, my voice was an uncertain whisper.

"You can't stay?"

"They won't let me. I'm too big." She tried laughing, but I saw her eyes were wet.

"Tell me again, Mom."

"O.K., Frankie. I'm shouting, you know. I want to be sure you understand what I'm saying."

She went through the story three more times until she was satisfied that I understood what would happen.

As we emerged from the office, I saw a nurse crying. She came over to me and put both hands on my shoulders.

"Little boy, I want you to know you've got the most understanding Mommy I ever saw."

The next ten days were a nightmare.

Far from home, the world suddenly hushed, doctors and nurses hovering about, saying I knew not what; needles and pills and medical instruments shoved and stuffed and inserted into me; my mother, my only contact with reality, taken from me each evening; crying myself to sleep every night only to awaken to the dread certainty of more threatening assaults, never understanding why all of this was happening; yes, it was a nightmare, one that wouldn't end.

A nurses' station stood at one end of the children's ward. The upper halves of each of its walls were made of glass; the bottom halves looked like the grey metal on my father's tool boxes. The nurses' station was the center of my life that month. It was from there that Mom emerged each morning and through there that she left each evening. My meals, too, came out of that part of the room. In between meals, nurses brought pills, liquids, and other medications. And it was from the nurses' station that the doctors arrived for their daily visits. I looked to the nurses' station as a way of structuring my day.

Mom arrived at the medical center each morning to find me hiding under my crib.

It didn't take me long to realize that early morning was the doctors' favorite time to operate or examine me. There were days when life was reduced to a simple problem: survive the morning hours.

My first operation was for a spinal tap. Mom remembers her feeling of helpless agony at the sight of my terrified face exploding with joy at seeing her when I emerged from the tests.

"You're a very brave little boy, Frankie. I'm proud of you."

"What happened, Mom?"

"They drew some fluid from your spinal cord. They will look at that now, to see if it tells them anything."

"Oooh. I'm real sore, Mom. My back, my bottom, it really hurts."

"That must be the medication wearing off. I'll tell the nurse."

Later, when I was back in my crib, Mom showed me a dozen books she'd brought for me. These children's books played an unexpected role in my hospital career.

One day not long after the spinal-tap operation, a doctor tried talking to me. I ignored him. He put a finger into the book I was looking at. I ignored that, too.

"You see?" he nodded to his colleagues.

Fowler and his team spent the next two weeks exploring a psychosomatic theory that "explained" my hearing loss by saying that it was caused by psychological rather than physical factors. Psychosomatic illnesses were somewhat novel at the time, but suspected to be very common, particularly in children subjected to anxiety or tension.

Mom told them that I just wanted everything over as fast as possible. Noncooperation with the doctors seemed, to my three-year-old mind, the best strategy, she explained.

Fortunately for the doctors, my mother was able to defeat my little games, to get me to cooperate at least minimally in the endless series of examinations that filled my days. Her, I trusted. Soon the doctors dropped their psychosomatic theory.

Next came the encephalograms. Because viral infection in measles sometimes causes measles encephalitis, which, in turn, produces high body temperatures that destroy nerve fibers, Fowler's team wanted to explore my head for evidence of nerve damage. I wouldn't sit still for these tests, so Mom showed me pictures in some books for the seemingly endless time the tests took. I learned later that the encephalograms confirmed Fowler's hypothesis that my blood circulation was irregular, probably as a result of the fevers I'd run when I'd had the measles, but not so unusual as to be a likely cause for my hearing impairment.

A three-year-old's greatest enemy is time. Once I got through the morning operations, I usually had a great deal of time on my hands. I remember walking around the children's ward, memorizing all the faces I saw. It was my way of measuring the passage of time. As the chubby little boy with the head bandages left to be replaced by another little boy with bandages on his chest, I knew at least several days had passed. When this child was in turn replaced by a small boy with jerky legs and arms, I knew more time was gone.

Two or three days were lost altogether as I caught a bad virus cold from one of the other children. I slept most of those days, but when I awakened, feeling hot, from a nightmare, I found myself frighteningly dizzy.

I'd been dizzy before, but not like this.

I remember the entire room spinning violently. Once I fell out of the bed, my head hitting the steel siding of the hospital crib. Another time, I awoke to find Mom standing beside me. I jumped for her, eager to feel the warmth of her protection, and missed her completely, hitting my head against the sideboards. Sometimes, after fifteen minutes or so, the dizziness would go away; other times, though, I could only escape it by falling asleep again.

After I'd been at the children's ward for ten days, Mom confronted Dr. Fowler one afternoon on his rounds through the ward. She demanded that I be allowed to spend nights with her and be at the hospital only for the tests.

"I come here in the morning to find him beside himself with joy at the sight of me. When I leave, he looks so distraught I'm afraid for him at night. And when he got sick, I really thought I was losing him. Now he's over that, thank God, and as his mother, I know that he needs to get out of here."

"I think you're making a mistake, Mrs. Bowe."

Mom put her right arm around my shoulders.

"I think not, Dr. Fowler. You've had almost two weeks. That's got to be long enough for twenty-four-hour observation to tell you whatever it's going to tell you."

Mom's new strategy of insisting on her rights and mine worked; the next day, I was allowed to leave the ward, although I was under strict orders to be back by eight the following morning.

It felt so good to leave the children's ward! I breathed deeply outside the door leading from the Medical Center. I jumped down the steps two at a time. At the bottom, by the curb, I sang out loud. As Mom came down the steps, I hugged her with both arms.

"Hey, Mom!" I shouted. "Let's go home and never, ever come back."

"Believe me, Frankie, it makes me feel so wonderful to see you looking so relieved, so happy, so free at last. I'd like nothing better than to go home right now."

"Good. Here we go!"

"Honey, let's go to the hotel. I want to talk with your father first."

I watched as she telephoned him. After a few minutes, I left the living room area to sit on the bed I'd slept in only a few times since coming to Manhattan. I didn't notice her walk in behind me.

"When do we go, Mom?"

"Frankie, your father says, and I think he's right, that if we leave now, we've wasted the past two weeks. We need to give it a little longer to learn something, anything really, that will make it worthwhile."

I didn't say anything.

A few hours later, after supper, I asked my mother to come into the bedroom with me.

"Mom, didn't this radio make a lot of noise before?"

"Yes, dear."

"O.K. Listen." I turned up the volume.

"What are you saying, honey?" she asked. "You know that you can't understand sounds you don't know."

"I can barely hear the sound, Mom. It's so quiet in there."

"Did you put your right ear against the speaker, like you do at home?"

"Yes, Mom. It didn't help much."

She stared at me. Suddenly, I saw my mother fall onto the bed, her body wracked with sobs.

I dreaded sleep at night, because I knew the Medical Center was going to get me in the morning. For weeks, I fought as no three-year-old ever did against a mother as Mom dressed me, pulled me to the buses, and dragged me into the dungeons of Columbia-Presbyterian.

Once there, I sat upright in the crib, my entire body tensed, dreading the next examination. By early afternoon, when most of the tests were completed, I was exhausted.

I took a nap one afternoon. I dreamed about fire trucks, flashing lights, and sirens. The medical center was going up in flames. I was secretly glad. Then the smoke reached my bed. I woke up screaming.

"What's the matter, Frankie? Did you have a bad dream?"

"Fire trucks, Mom."

A nurse walked over to my crib. "Anything I can do, Mrs. Bowe?" she asked.

"Don't let her touch me, Mom," I shouted.

"It's all right, honey."

"All night? I don't want to stay here all night. Oh, Mom, please."

"Do you think he's hysterical?" the nurse asked.

Mom's face hardened into a mask. "Absolutely not. Frankie just misunderstood me."

"I hear them again, Mom. Fire trucks. They're coming."

My mother was baffled.

A while later, Dr. Fowler stopped by on his rounds. He examined my ears closely and asked me to open my mouth for him to probe with a small piece of wood.

"Mrs. Bowe, tinnitis is quite common with hearing loss. This little boy's ear nerves have been damaged by whatever caused his deafness. The nerve hairs are jangling in there, making him think he is hearing sirens."

"Isn't there something you can do about it?"

"I don't think so, Mrs. Bowe. He'll probably hear noises like this for the rest of his life."

Mom took me to F.A.O. Schwarz that afternoon. I wandered around the store as if in a trance. Stuffed animals that were larger than I was, one-foot-long model train cars with real working lights, and aisle after aisle of games surrounded me everywhere I went.

"What would you like, darling?" Mom's face looked like Christmas morning.

"You mean I can have anything I want?"

"Yes, darling. Anything at all."

I was torn between the trains and a gigantic erector toy set.

"Uh, Mom." I looked around the store again. "Can I take my toy home?"

"Frankie, you certainly can. Pick out what you want, and I promise you can take it to Lewisburg with you."

I beamed. "Really? The engine."

Mom bent down on her knees. She placed one hand on my shoulder, and with the other caressed my face.

"You know, Frankie, that's the first time I've seen you smile in an awfully long time. I really missed that smile."

The following week was spent in a futile effort to get me to accept a hearing aid. Two very patient audiologists, not knowing why I was terrified, but guessing from my mother's haggard expression that the two of us had been to Hell and back, gamely tried to get me to agree just to put on an aid. I refused. They showed me a half-dozen other boys and girls in the office, all of whom wore body-model hearing aids like the one the audiologists wanted me to try. I shrugged. When one technician decided to put it on me anyway, I tore the aid from his hands and threw it on the floor. Then I tried to send the technician to the same place.

That Sunday, Mom took me to Fort Tryon Park, near the Cloisters in the Bronx. There, she bought a huge wooden stick with a five-pound wad of tan-colored candy on the end.

As soon as she gave it to me, I swung it at her with all my might.

She is the one forcing me to go through all of this, I thought, and at last I had a weapon to hit back.

As patient and understanding as ever, though, she calmed me down.

"Look, Frankie. Those kids over there! Kids your age. On the swings."

"I don't know them, Mom."

"But honey, you will, in just a moment. I'll find out their names and tell them yours."

I shook my head.

"You've always played with kids before," she said, her face looking puzzled and upset.

I shrugged. "I don't know them."

One afternoon, a few days later, after we'd returned by bus to the hotel from the medical center, Mom sat down on my bed.

"Honey, are you sick again?"

"Stick? I don't have a stick, Mom."

"I mean, do you feel well?"

"Just tired, Mom."

"Because you seem so listless, so flat. It's like you've given up. You don't care any more."

"Was I different, Mom?"

"Yes. You fought them every step of the way. You kicked. You bit. You hit. You were so plucky, so full of spirit, that even if you were angry at least I knew you were alive.

"Every day when I'd take you to the Medical Center, you were like a tiger. You wore me out totally even before the day started at the hospital. Now you just walk with me. You don't fight any more."

"I want to go home, Mom."

"You will, honey. Very, very soon now."

"Good."

"This will be our last week."

I looked at her in surprise.

"One more week! Hey, wow!! Super, Mom!"

"That's how I feel, too. By Friday, they'll have had five weeks to find out what they can."

To celebrate, we went to Fort Tryon Park. This time, Mom bought me a huge red balloon. Filled with helium, it stayed up regardless of what I did. I'd never had one before; all mine had been air-filled balloons that fell to earth soon after you let go of them. I had to hang on to this one with a long string, or it would fly away from me.

"To home!" Mom said.

"To hope?" I asked.

"That, too," she laughed. "To home and to hope."

I turned to lipread what she said after that and stumbled over a small rock.

The balloon was gone.

As I watched it disappear in the clouds above me, I leaned into my mother's body and cried uncontrollably. I was still shaking three hours later when Mom gave me some medication to put me to sleep.

It was all getting away from me. I didn't know why—and I didn't know how to stop it.

The next day, Mom laid out her ultimatum. This was it: no more tests. She got a fierce argument from Dr. Fowler.

"But, Mrs. Bowe, Frankie is an interesting case. We've not seen many whose hearing has been lost so recently. Most parents wait much longer than you did to seek help. We'd like to keep him here for some more tests. Who knows what we'll find?"

"Friday he goes home. And that's it."

"Well, Mrs. Bowe. As I say, I think you're making a mistake."

Mom stood her ground. "What can you tell me? What have you learned in all these weeks that will help me and my boy? Please, give me something to make it all worthwhile."

"Well, Mrs. Bowe. This will take a while. Come down to my office."

He sat behind his desk, motioning Mom to sit in the armchair at one end.

"Mrs. Bowe, your little boy is deaf. I would say he's been deaf in his left ear since he was born. As for his right ear, that looks as if it happened just a few months ago. It may have been the fevers he had from measles. It may have been the streptomycin he was given to lower those fevers. It may have been something else. I just don't know. Without further tests, I have no way of knowing."

"When you say he's deaf, Doctor, what do you mean?"

"That he's deaf. That he can't hear people talk. And, I don't like to be this blunt, Mrs. Bowe, but I have to; he never will."

"Never?"

"Never."

"But a hearing aid?"

"Will help him a little, if you can get him to wear one. Frankie is the most violently uncooperative patient I've ever had here. I think he's totally out of control. I would be amazed if he allows you to put an aid on him.

"Even with a hearing aid, Mrs. Bowe, he won't understand a word anyone says. Or a word he says himself."

Mom sat very still in the armchair.

"We will send an aid to you in Lewisburg, Mrs. Bowe. But don't expect it to be a miracle. All it will do is help him be aware of sound. And teach him to read people's lips. He's already surprisingly good at this. Teach him to be better. It's the only way he'll ever understand anybody."

"The telephone, doctor?"

"No. You'll have to forget that, Mrs. Bowe."

Mom took a handkerchief from her pocketbook. "Doctor, isn't there something you can do? Anything at all?"

"Mrs. Bowe, I realize this is a shock to you. All of this. But I have to be honest with you." He paused. "There's nothing we can do to help your boy."

Mom and I left the next morning on a train for Harrisburg. My father and sister met us at the station.

Robin wore a green coat, a hat, and a new plaid dress.

Although I was still sixty miles from home, the sight of her made me feel that I was at last rid of those terrible people at the medical center.

"Oh, Bebe! Oh, Bebe!" I cried, picking her up and swinging her in my arms.

For ten full minutes, I held her tight.

I was coming home.

Chapter Three

I jumped out of the car as soon as we reached the house in Lewisburg. Golly leaped into my arms, smothering my face with licks. She sprang again, knocking me to the ground. I lay, my back on the grass, as she circled me, flicking her tongue first to my hair and then to my hands. As she bent to lick my face again, I pulled her to me, and we somersaulted across the front yard.

With Golly at my heels, I ran up to my room, I touched my bureau dresser first, running my hand over its smooth surface. I sprawled across the chair by my window, rubbing its padded arms. When I lay on my bed for the first time in five weeks, Golly jumped up with me. We remained there for what seemed a deliciously long time.

From my room, I ran to the playroom downstairs, where I turned on the record player and then shut it off. I ran with Golly to the kitchen, opening cabinets one after another. Just before suppertime, I led Golly on a grand tour of the neighborhood. From the wide cornfields behind our home to the steep hill before it, Golly and I staked our claim.

When I sat down for supper, I felt at last that I was really home. Remembering my father's promise, "No more doctors," I was sure I'd never leave again.

I slept soundly that night, exhausted and relieved that the nightmare in New York was over at last.

My father woke me up the next morning. He started with my feet, tickling insistently until I moved them back under the covers. Then he reached under my arms, awakening me with more tickling. Sitting on the bed, he picked me up and tossed me into the air. As I fell back into his arms, he tickled me once again.

This little ritual brought back for me all the warmth and happiness I'd known the day before.

Before he left for work, Dad pulled me up on his lap. Making sure I was looking at his ruddy face and focusing on his lips, he held my face in both hands.

"Welcome home, Boyji!"

In that special way mothers have, Mom knew I'd be ravenously hungry. She gave me two helpings of pancakes for breakfast. Her face, so drawn and worried-looking for so long, was aglow now, a soft smile permanently fixed on her face.

It was raining, just as it had been on the last day I'd spent here before the New York trip, a Tuesday I'd relived daily in my mind, wondering if I'd ever come back to this safe little house in this quiet little town.

Because of the rain, we played indoors, Robin and I, with Mom watching from her rocking chair.

After lunch, I napped for much of the afternoon.

My father took me into the living room that evening. Mom and Robin went upstairs. Dad's face looked more fixed than I could remember seeing it. His prominent jawline jutted out more than usual; I even thought his hawk nose was sharper than usual.

My father never was a man to beat around the bush. Nor was he one to put off 'til tomorrow what could be done today. That evening was no exception.

We sat on the old couch in the living room, its cushions showing the effect of years of heavy use. Turning on every lamp in the room to be certain his face was well-lighted, Dad beckoned me to his lap. He felt just like a favorite stuffed armchair.

"Boyji, there's something I have to tell you."

His eyes were wet; his face softer than just a few minutes ago. Stalling for time, he removed his bifocals and polished them with a tissue.

"Dr. Fowler told your mother something before you two left New York."

I stiffened at the mention of Fowler's name. Did my Dad mean I'd have to see more doctors after all? Even go back to Columbia-Presbyterian?

"Are you ready, Boyji? Are you a big boy?"

I shook my head. Whatever it was, I didn't want to know.

"I think you are," he said. "The sooner we look this in the eye, the better off we'll be."

I looked into his eyes, confused.

"Honey. Dr. Fowler said you'd never hear again."

I stared at him. Dad was crying now. Whatever it was that he was trying to tell me, it must be terrible, I thought. I'd never seen my father cry.

"Yes, I will," I said.

"I thought you'd say that," he told me. "I think you will, too. Mom says she just knows it. Someday, somehow you're going to hear again."

He smiled.

"But until then, we have to face up to the fact that right now you can't hear. It if means tightening our belts, well, that's just what we'll do."

I looked at his belt buckle.

"But I want you to know two things."

He raised two fingers.

"First, we're praying for you. We all know you need God's help. Your mother and I need it, too.

"Second, Mommy, Robin, and I are behind you every step of the way."

"Golly, too," I added.

He laughed. "Yes, Golly too."

The day before Halloween, a brand-new Paravox YMG hearing aid arrived from New York, together with a book called *Tim and His Hearing Aid*. I watched as my father opened the bottom of the aid and inserted a battery. Placing an earmold at one end of a long cord and plugging the other end of the cord into the side of the square metal aid, he hummed to himself. Satisfied, he motioned me to his lap and placed the aid on the coffee table.

Mom sat down on the couch beside my father. Looking at her, I remembered the time I'd thrown a hearing aid on the floor rather than try it on at Columbia-Presbyterian.

This time, in the privacy of my own home, was different. I sat quietly on Dad's lap as he put the aid in one of my shirt pockets, inserted the ear mold, and turned the volume on.

Suddenly, I heard my father's voice, alarmingly loud. I turned to look at him, my eyes wide.

"Is that loud enough, Frankie?"

I nodded.

"Yes," I said, and jumped in his lap, surprised at the sound of my own voice.

It had been six months since I had heard myself speak.

The rest of the afternoon, I wore the aid as I moved from room to room. In the bathroom, I turned on the spigots and was startled to learn that running water made noise. I slammed the door of my room and winced at the intensity of the sound. Once a train passed on the tracks across the street, and I felt a similar pain from the sound pressure. Gradually, I learned to adjust the volume control so that the aid allowed me to hear my own voice but was not set so high as to hurt my ears with sudden noises.

The next morning, I put on a harness for the first time. Worn under a shirt, it holds the aid. I turned the volume to the mid-level setting I liked and said: "Hmmmm. Hmmmm. *Hmmm*." Satisfied, I resumed dressing.

Even with the hearing aid, I was unable to hear sounds I did not expect. My parents practiced sneaking up behind me and making loud noises to accustom me to the idea of ambient sound. They found, too, that if I wore the aid for two hours at a stretch, I was less likely to object to it than if I wore it continually. I wore it daily for two hours in the morning and again for two hours in the evening; during the rest of the day, especially when playing outdoors, I never wore it.

A few weeks after the aid arrived, my parents took me to the Armistice Day parade downtown.

"I can hear it coming!" I shrieked, as the band made its way up Market Street.

Dr. Davison at Geisinger recommended a salt-free diet and more niacin pills, together with antihistamine capsules twice a day. After checking with Dr. Fowler by letter, Mom followed the suggestions.

For the first time in months, I never complained of dizziness or headaches.

"We have all calmed down considerably, thank goodness," Mom wrote to Dr. Fowler in mid-November. "Frankie hasn't had a tantrum since we came home in mid-October. And it seems that, severe handicap or not, once you learn to live with a thing, it is no longer so frightening as it seemed at first to be."

By Thanksgiving, I had forgotten about the five-week nightmare in New York. That morning, I arrived on the backporch to find Mom bustling from room to room, carrying cranberry sauce and corn on the cob. Dad was setting the table. Robin was pawing at a slice of cranberry. Even Golly was busy chewing at a piece of turkey.

A giant papier-mâché turkey sat at one end of the back porch table, a huge pile of sliced turkey at the other. Dad separated the white meat, which I loved, from the brown meat, which Robin preferred. When everything was ready, Dad motioned me to bring my plate and to help myself to the food. As I sat, the rest of the family paraded past me to fill their plates.

My spirits were high as I gorged myself on mashed potatoes, white-meat turkey, corn, and cranberry sauce.

That afternoon, we took the maroon Packard station wagon to visit my maternal grandparents at Walnut Dell Farm in Milton. I crinkled my nose at the familiar musty smell of the living room, clambered into the "secret" card room where I felt deliciously adventurous but perfectly safe, and visited with the fish in the basement tanks. Walking outside, I passed through a perfectly kept garden, devoid now of the flowers I knew bloomed in the springtime, to reach my grandfather's grass tennis court, rather in disrepair since it was used so rarely. Than I crossed to the other side of the farmyard to stand on the sloping stone bridge that spanned a small pond stocked with the biggest and goldest goldfish I'd ever seen. I spent almost two hours around the pond before Mom came to lead me to the car.

"Frankie," she said, resting a hand on my shoulder. "I think this has been our best Thanksgiving. I hope your hearing aid is just the beginning. I have a feeling that things are going to get better now."

A few days later, Dad arrived home for lunch to find me in the living room, looking at a picture book. Across the street, about ten boys my age were playing with a white soccer ball.

"Why aren't you over there, Boyji?"

"I don't know them."

40

*My father serving at Spring Lake, New
Jersey: Picture perfect form.*

*Outside the house at 150 Brown Street:
"Boyji on the biji."*

*In the living room: "I hope Charlie McCarthy speaks
better than I do!"*

"Sure, you do. There's Bobby. Pete's there. I bet you know half of them."

"Nah, I don't."

He looked at me strangely all through lunch.

That afternoon, it rained. I dragged Mom into the playroom and gave her a piece of paper and a crayon.

"Listen, Mom. Write the words."

She didn't say a thing as I placed "Never Smile at a Crocodile" on the small record player. I played it several times until she'd had a chance to write down all the words. Watching her lips closely, I asked her to sing the song. Her eyes were wet; the smile forced. But she sang.

Then I put the record on again. Lying flat on my back with the hearing aid against the speaker, I played the song a dozen times. Mom lip-synched the record for me, over and over. An hour after we started, I knew the song.

We did the same with two other records. By the end of the day, I knew them well enough to be able to pick up some of the drumming that set the beat for the songs. But I knew something else, as well: if my attention were diverted even for an instant, I would be lost, unable to find my way back into the song.

And I learned that unless I knew which song was going to be played, it was impossible for me to distinguish one record from another. This was true even when Mom put on "Tubby the Tuba," a record I'd learned more than year ago when my hearing still was useable.

But these problems did not deter me from learning songs. Music was something that tied me to the days when I could hear—and I refused to let it go.

Mom and I planned a special performance for Robin's birthday that January. She'd invited Beth and Margaret Crayton from next door, Pete Walters from across the street, and Diane and Bobby Spielman from the next block. As we ate the last of the angel food birthday cake, Mom turned on the record player.

"And now, ladies and gentlemen, I bring you the greatest singing sensation since Jerry Lewis!" she announced.

At her signal, I started dancing and lip-synching the words to "Never Smile at a Crocodile."

I didn't understand a word of it, but I'd memorized the song so well that my performance was a convincing one.

"You know," Mrs. Crayton said, "I really think he can hear it."

I felt like Christmas inside. For a few brief moments, I was just like everybody else.

Two weeks later, Robin and I both caught the measles. For me, it was the third time.

42

"This is unbelievable," Dr. Joseph Weightman sighed as he finished his examination of me in my bedroom. Dr. Weightman was our new family doctor. He had a practice with Bucknell University students and faculty at the college infirmary just up the hill from our home. "Twice is stretching matters, but three times is something I haven't seen in fifteen years of practicing medicine."

"Doctor, you've got to do someting," Mom pleaded. "I can't take this any more."

"Mrs. Bowe, if there were something I could do, I'd do it. All I can suggest is that you keep him warm and watch him carefully."

"What about streptomycin? That's what the doctor gave him the last time he had measles."

"He did? I wouldn't recommend that, Mrs. Bowe. We've learned that this so-called miracle drug has some unfortunate side effects. It does lower fevers, but it can also cause damage to some of the nerve cells in the head."

Mom remembered Dr. Fowler's words.

"Could that have caused his hearing loss?"

Dr. Weightman tugged at my covers for a moment.

"It might," he conceded. "I wouldn't rule it out. But I have no reason to believe it did, either.

"I doubt you'll ever learn for sure why his hearing has deteriorated. Even if you did find out, it wouldn't change anything. My suggestion is that you concentrate on helping him cope with what hearing he has left."

"I want him to get it all back."

"That's fine, Mrs. Bowe. I do, too. But that's in God's hands, not yours. Your job is to help your son do his best with the cards he's been dealt."

One evening a few days later, Mom joined my father in the living room. Seeing him sitting on the couch with his head in his hands, she asked: "What's wrong, honey?"

He looked up. "Frankie. I'm going crazy trying to get him to understand what I say to him. I have to repeat it, repeat it, and repeat it again. And sometimes, he still doesn't get it."

Mom nodded. "It's the same with me. The doctors at Columbia-Presbyterian said he needed to learn to lipread better."

"That's fine for them to say. But how do we do it?"

"I don't know, honey. The audiologists and speech pathologists I talked to there said that he has to learn it. It's an art, it seems. They did make one point I thought was interesting. They said it's very hard to lipread a word you don't know. I've been thinking about that. Is this one reason Frankie is having such a hard time?"

43

"What do you mean, Kitty?"

"Remember the words he knew at two and then at three? Those words I think he can lipread. He taught himself. But words he didn't know then, that he didn't learn through his hearing before it went bad, are words he doesn't know how to lipread.

"In fact, I don't think he's learned more than one or two new words since coming back here last October."

"But, Kitty, what you're saying is that he can only understand what we say if we talk baby talk."

Mom shook her head. "No. I've been thinking. If we can teach him new words, his lipreading will improve by leaps and bounds."

"You're talking in circles. How can we teach him new words if he can't lipread them?"

"Through reading."

"Huh?"

"By teaching him how to read."

Dad sat up straight on the couch, his hands on his knees. "By God, I think you've got something there, Kitty. Deafness doesn't prevent him from learning how to read. Hmmm. Yes, by golly, I think you're right. If he encounters a new word on paper, he can learn it. There's nothing wrong with his eyes. Then, once he knows it, he can lipread it."

"And the more he reads, the more words he knows, so the more he can lipread."

"There's just one problem, Kitty: how are we supposed to teach him how to read?"

Mom stroked her chin. "I have some ideas there, too."

"Kitty, if we can solve this problem, we can solve any problem. This is it. Think hard. Did you learn anything at Bucknell that will help you teach Frankie how to read?"

"Yes. I did. Remember all the books we read him, every night before he went to sleep? Books he knows by heart now? We can start with those. The words in those stories are words he's heard, words he knows. What I have to teach him is what they look like on the page."

"Then we'll show him what they look like on the lips."

"Right."

"Another thing. Hey, I've got an idea. What about putting labels on things around the house. You know. Curtains. Desk. Drawer. Cabinet. Refrigerator."

"Good idea."

"You know, Kitty. We'll lick this yet!"

When Dad tickled me awake the next morning, he showed me the labels he'd stuck all over my room.

" 'Mirror.' See, Frankie, this word says 'mirror.' I stuck it on the mirror. Tell me, Frankie, what is this?"

"Mirror."

"Ah, right you are, son. That's a mirror. M-I-R-R-O-R. Now, come over here. On your door, I've stuck a word. Let's see here. D-O-O-R. Door. This is a door. The word says 'door.' Frankie, what does this word say?"

"Door."

"Righty-right!" He gave me a slap across my back.

Dad pulled me over to the closet.

"Now, son. Look at this. C-L-O-S-E-T. Closet! And in here, would you believe it . . ."

I laughed. The sight of five-by-eight cards pinned to my clothes was startlingly funny.

". . . S-H-I-R-T and P-A-N-T-S. Shirt and pants. And down here, son, S-H-O-E. That's shoe!"

I picked up a shoe.

"Give me an S!" Dad shouted.

I looked at him.

"Come on! Give me an S!"

"Uh, S."

"Give me an H!"

"H."

"Gimme an O!"

I laughed. "O!"

"And gimme an E!"

"E!"

"What do you got? S-H-O-E! Shoe!"

I laughed again.

"YOU GOTTA SHOE!"

After breakfast, Mom started with the alphabet. It was the first of many morning sessions with the ABC's. Once she felt confident, about a month later, that I knew the letters, she started combining them into simple, familiar words, ones she knew I already understood. And every day, she'd ask me to read aloud the words taped onto the objects we passed on our way through the house.

Finally, one morning, something clicked.

"You're reading! You're really reading, Frankie! Let me tell your father!"

She called Dad on the phone: "He's done it! He's really done it this time. He's not guessing, he's not memorizing, he's not looking at the pictures. He's actually reading words!"

Mom's next step was to read me books she and Dad had read me over the years. She read them much more slowly than she had ever done before, conscious that I could no longer just listen to the story.

"I've got several problems," Mom said to Dad that evening. "First, I've got to be sure he can see my lips. Then, I have to be sure he can see the words on the page and the pictures if they will help him understand the story. Third, I have to figure out a way to be sure he understands the words I read. As if this weren't enough, I have to keep his attention, hold his interest in the story."

"But you're doing it?"

"I'm doing it." There was an unmistakable note of pride in her voice. "I sure am doing it," she repeated with a smile.

One windy afternoon in April, just after my birthday, a dozen of us were playing hide and seek in Bobby's front yard. Our base was the huge oak tree whose sprawling roots cracked the Spielmans' sidewalk.

Diane was "It" first. We all scrambled to find the perfect hiding place. From my position behind the oak tree, I saw Robin hide in the bushes on the side of the Spielmans' house. Bobby and Beth went past her to the rear of the house, while Pete headed to the other side. As I watched, Diane found all of them.

I saw her coming back to the oak tree and quickly hid between the tree and the Spielman's dark Ford sedan.

When I peeked out again several minutes later, Pete was pulling Bobby from the bushes.

I hid again, confused about why he was "It" before Diane had even found me.

A few minutes later, I noticed Bobby counting to ten, his head resting against the tree.

"Hey," I shouted. "Doesn't anybody want to find me?"

Bobby looked at me for a moment.

"Frankie, your mother's calling you."

"She is?"

"Yeah. You better hurry!"

I arrived home to find Mom reading a magazine on the back porch.

"What's up, Mom?" I asked.

"Oh, what a surprise, Frankie. I thought you were out playing at Bobby's house."

"I was. He said you called me."

She frowned. "No, Frankie, I didn't."

I rushed back to the Spielmans' house. But try as I might, I couldn't find any of them.

"I wish my friends were like Golly," I told Dad at the dinner table that night.

"She's a good friend," he agreed.

"Yeah. She doesn't tease me."

"That's true."

"And Golly doesn't care if my ears don't work."

Dad glanced at Mom before answering. "That's right. Though I'm not sure Golly knows the difference."

"She's always glad to see me."

"Honey, are the kids being mean to you?"

I nodded.

"Well," Dad said, his hand on mine, "if they're not nice to you, don't you be nice to them. Give them a taste of their own medicine."

I looked around for a medicine dropper.

"What I mean, son, is this. Children will be children. When you're older, things will be easier."

"I want to be older now."

"Can't say I blame you, son. But meanwhile, hold your chin high."

I did.

"That was a figure of speech. I mean, don't let them get you down."

"But, Dad, if they're not nice to me, and I'm not nice to them, nobody will play with me."

"That's their loss, son."

"I'll be awfully lonely, won't I?"

"Better that than let them push you around."

A few weeks later, Golly died under the coffee table in the living room.

"Mom, I can't wake Golly up!" I screamed.

In a moment, the whole Bowe family was gathered in the living room.

"I'm afraid Golly isn't going to wake any more, honey," Mom said, brushing away my tears with her hand.

"But she's my only friend!" I sobbed.

"I'm your friend," Robin assured me.

"No, you're not," I countered. "You're my sister."

No one said anything for a long, long while.

"Frankie," Dad told me gently, "I need your help to give Golly a proper burial. Are you a big enough man to help me shovel in the backyard?"

"You mean she's really dead?" I sobbed.

"I'm afraid so, honey. But we can give her the burial she deserves as your good friend."

"Will she go to Heaven?"

"I'm sure she will."

I looked down at the German Shepherd I'd shared so much with in two short years. "I'll see you in Heaven, Golly."

"Attaboy, son. Now let's get the shovels."

With kindergarten only a year away, Mom decided to start getting me ready.

She approached the task with all the fortitude and planning at her command.

"Now, Frankie," she began after breakfast one September morning. Her fine brown hair, baby thin, was gathered into the loose bun I knew so well. "Starting today, we're going to read at least one book every day. And I mean every day."

"I can read, Mom."

"I know you can, honey. But you've got a long way to go before you can really read."

I looked at her in confusion.

"Reading isn't just reading. It's understanding what you read. Even if you haven't seen the words before.

"Now, I have talked with some of the teachers at the South Ward School. They suggested some books. My professors at Bucknell gave me some ideas too.

"It'll be hard, but it'll be fun too."

I picked up the first book.

"Here's how we're going to do it. Frankie, We're going to make reading your ace in the hole."

I looked on the table for a hole.

"Most of the other kids in kindergarten and first grade won't be able to read by the time they start school, but you will. My hope is that reading will be your secret weapon. It'll give you a head start in the race."

"Do we race in kindergarten, Mom?"

"Uh. Sometimes, honey. But I'm talking about another kind of race."

"Oh."

"Now, I'm going to read 'The Three Little Pigs' first. Watch my lips as I read. I'll move my finger under the words so you can learn what they look like. When I finish, you read it. O.K.?"

I nodded.

" 'Once upon a time, there were . . .' "

"Mom, what does this word mean?"

" 'Upon,' you mean? It's just another word for 'on.' "

"Oh."

A few minutes later, we had five entries on her Master List of words I didn't know: world, seek, fortunes, lazy, and flute.

"This is going to be slow going, I can see that now. Five words in the first paragraph or so." Mom sighed.

"World" was defined for me as meaning the globe in our backporch. Mom spent about ten minutes showing me where we lived, and how the world moved around on an axis.

"But, Mom," I interrupted. "Where did the three pigs go?"

"They went out into the world. . . . Oh, I see the problem. I'm afraid this is one of the figures of speech my professors warned me about."

"Huh?"

"What 'went out into the world' means is that they left their mother's home and walked away somewhere."

"Mom, it says went out, but then it says went into."

"Uh. 'Out into' is just a way of saying they went somewhere."

"Oh."

"Now," Mom said, crossing out 'world' from her list. "The next word is 'seek.' This means look for."

"O.K., Mom. I understand."

"Good. Now 'fortunes' means money."

"They looked for the money. Right, Mom?"

"Right, son."

"Where was the money, Mom?"

"Uh." She put down her pencil. "This is what they call an idiom. The three pigs didn't actually look for money. They were trying to find a way to make a living."

"Like Daddy?"

"Right. Daddy makes a living for us by working. That's what the pigs were going to do."

"What work did they do?"

"Uh. Good question. The story doesn't say."

"Gee, Mom. This is hard."

"Well, honey it'll get easier."

We continued until lunchtime, but it didn't get any easier.

"How's my little scholar this morning?" Dad said as he sat down for lunch.

"O.K., I guess, Dad. Mom is teaching me how to read. After lunch, I'll read to her."

"Good. And tonight you can read to me, too." He smiled.

"Hey, Dad! Good idea!"

"We're going to look this right in the eye and not bat an eyelash until you learn to read."

I stared at his eyes.

"I mean, you're not going to give up, no matter how tough it gets."

"It's pretty hard already, honey," Mom said putting tomato soup and sandwiches on my placemat.

"But you just started, Kitty."

"I know. It's a lot harder than I thought it would be."

"I don't want any talk of defeat in this house, Kitty. Not from him and not from you."

Within a few months, I was making progress in my reading. My recitations did not make anyone in the family forget Edward R. Murrow, but at least my future no longer resembled the first little pig's.

"Now that any doubts we might have been so stupid as to have had that he can learn have been settled," Dad announced one night after supper, "the next decision is where he will go to school."

"Why of course he'll go to South Ward," Mom said.

"Not of course," Dad said, tapping a pencil on the coffee table. "There may be something better. I doubt it, but we have to look."

Our first stop was at Geisinger Medical Center. The ear-nose-throat specialist Mom consulted seemed surprised she was even considering the public schools.

"Mrs. Bowe," he lectured as we stood in a corner of the room I remembered so well from scores of audiometric tests over the years. "Mrs. Bowe, there's no question but that your son needs a special education. A very special one, in my opinion."

"No doubt. But . . ." Mom patted my head softly.

"You absolutely must begin facing the facts, Mrs. Bowe. You have to stop pretending that he's a normal child, because he isn't."

"I know that, but . . ."

"Good. Now there's a program over in Scranton that specializes in teaching deaf children. I recommend you look into it. And, of course, in New York there's Willowbrook. It's large, but it's probably equipped to deal with Frankie's needs."

"But if he goes to Scranton or New York, he can't be home with us."

"I realize that, Mrs. Bowe. But you have to face reality."

"I am facing reality. Doctor, have you been to this Scranton school?"

"My colleagues recommend it highly."

"And Willowbrook?"

"I've not actually been there, but . . ."

Mom turned to pull on my jacket. Her whole body was shaking with emotion.

"Doctor, with all the respect due you, how can you possibly tell me to send my only little boy to places you haven't even been to? Who knows what might happen to him there?"

"But, Mrs. Bowe. Nobody in Lewisburg knows the first thing about teaching a deaf child."

"We'll see if you're right about this as you are about Willowbrook. Come on, Frankie. We're going."

Two days later, Mom learned that he was right about Lewisburg. No one at South Ward had ever seen a deaf child, let alone taught one. There were no speech pathologists, audiologists, or language development specialists. None of the eight teachers in the school had even received any training in deaf education. No local, state, or federal law required local schools to accept disabled students. The South Ward School would not have to meet any of my special needs. There would be no interpreters in the classroom. The teachers would not have to learn any means of communicating with me. All the school would have to do, if it agreed to enroll me, was to give me a desk and chair to use.

"The principal agrees with the doctor," Mom explained to Dad that night over dinner. "She says Frankie would be better off if we send him to a special school."

"Did she name any?"

"Uh. No. She said Geisinger knows more about special education for deaf children than she does."

"Well, here's how I see it," Dad said, putting down his coffee cup. "Frankie's shown he can learn. You've shown that you can teach him. If he stays with us and goes to South Ward, we can help him after school. Right?"

Mom reached out and touched Dad's sleeve. With a loving caress, she said: "Right. We can do it."

"Then it's settled. Son, you go to South Ward."

"I can stay?"

"You sure can, son. You will stay right here. We're not letting anybody take you away from us."

"What if the school says they won't accept him?" Mom asked.

"They will, Kitty. I'm a taxpayer here. I'm paying the salaries of those teachers."

"But what if they really can't teach him?"

"We'll cross that bridge when we come to it, Kitty. But I have the feeling we'll never reach that particular bridge."

He took my hands in his.

"Frankie, it'll be hard. I know that. Your mother knows that. But as I told you before, we're all standing behind you on this. And I believe the hard way is the best way."

Whenever the subject of my attending regular versus special schools came up, Dad would respond with that same aphorism. For him, it was a philosophical tenet around which he would build my life. Dad never would permit me to escape from something I was supposed to do just because it would be hard. Indeed, he often placed me quite deliberately into situations he knew would be challenging for me. That it was the unanimous judgment of the doctors and educators the family consulted that I should go to a special school never troubled my father once he made up his mind to send me to South Ward.

For Dad, it was a closed subject: I would go to the public schools. If I failed there, he might consent to discuss special education. But until I failed, he would not permit the issue to be opened again. He had settled the question.

This was typical of my father. He solved problems and answered questions according to what made sense for him. Turning the idea around in his mind in the following days, he'd develop a theoretical rationale for doing what he had decided to do. This, in turn, would become a component of his life's philosophy. To challenge him on it, or even to suggest that the decision might be an incorrect one, was to attack the very core of his value system.

When he engaged in such thinking, his habitual posture was to be seated on the couch, always leaning forward on his elbows, nervously tapping on the coffee table, constantly shifting his weight. We, therefore, dubbed his way of thinking "The Philosophy of Toad." A green plaster toad appeared on the front porch, a small metal one on the hood of our car.

From that summer on, the idea that I would confront any problem I encountered head-on, without slinking away or being excused on the grounds of my deafness, became a cornerpiece of The Philosophy of Toad.

Chapter Four

Pete Walters and I were friends of convenience. We lived across the street from each other, were within a year of each other in age, and, at least before my trip to Columbia-Presbyterian, were both active youngsters. But as I began to change, becoming more withdrawn and fearful, Pete started to pick on me more and more.

"He's an Army brat," Mom consoled me one afternoon after Pete had raised a welt on my right thigh with a particularly brutal kick. "Mr. Walters is a sergeant, and he expects Pete to be tough."

"He is," I moaned.

"I don't know," Mom continued. "I think Pete takes more after his mother." Jean Walters, I knew, was as gentle a person as lived on our block. A soft, almost fragile woman with a bemused smile permanently fixed on her face, she seemed the polar opposite of big Bill Walters.

"Then why does he pick on me, Mom?"

"Probably because he wants to be more like his father, Frankie."

"He's that, all right."

"Well, the two of you better work something out. Because you're in kindergarten together starting next week."

Our teacher put a halt to the hostilities within a week.

"Mrs. Bowe," Mrs. Holter announced when Mom arrived to take me home Friday, "either Frankie goes or Peter goes. We have an afternoon session as well as a morning one. I can handle them if they're separated. But starting Monday, I refuse to have them together any more."

"Is it that bad?"

"That bad? Frankie destroyed a painting of Peter's, and Peter kicked down a castle Frankie made with his building blocks. I had to stop them from fighting three times already this morning. Yes, I'd say it was that bad."

I was moved to the afternoon session.

Separation from Pete didn't solve all my problems, however. I soon realized that singing songs comprised a major portion of what kindergarten was all about.

Disaster!

This was something Mom and I hadn't prepared for. It was not just that I couldn't sing; I didn't even know what songs the class was singing.

Mom attacked the problem with all the intelligence that had made her an honors student in high school and for two years at Bucknell.

53

Each week, she learned from Mrs. Holter which songs were planned for the following week. Then, at home, we practiced until I knew the songs by heart. And Mom taught me a trick I found invaluable.

The key to the kingdom of music, I learned, was to use the first minute or two in a song to figure out which one they were singing. This involved watching the teacher very closely; sometimes, I turned my head to watch a child whose lips were especially easy for me to read. Once I knew which song it was, I had to find my way into it. From Mom I knew that every song had what was called a "refrain," a verse that was repeated several times in the course of the song. When a refrain ended, there were only a few alternatives with which I had to deal. Either the class would begin the second verse, which I knew started with certain words, or they would launch into the third verse, the first few words of which I also knew from memory. By the time the class was halfway through any given song, I usually had located the right verse, the right line, and the right word, too. Then I'd join in the singing.

Sometimes, though, even this extensive detective process failed me. In those cases, I blandly mouthed some words without using my voice and hoped nobody caught me in the act.

Story hour was easier. Mom usually learned ahead of time which stories would be read and borrowed from the local library a week's worth of books. These we read slowly and carefully together, until I knew the stories.

The Little Red Caboose was an exception. I knew I was in trouble when Mrs. Halter called us to the library corner and pulled out a Little Golden Book I'd never seen.

"The little red caboose always came last," she read.

Now, if there's one thing Mom and Dad always told me, it was that I should ask if I didn't understand something. It was a lesson I took to heart that afternoon.

"The what?" I interrupted as she turned the page.

"Caboose," Mrs. Holter told me, pointing to a red car about to be swallowed by a cavernous tunnel.

"What's a caboose?"

Shirley hit me on the head. "Shut up! I want to hear the story!"

"Me, too!" chorused the crowd on all sides of me.

Roger turned my head to face his. "You're the caboose, Frankie, because you always come last!"

Shirley fell over Susan, laughing so hard she had to hold her tummy.

"I do not!" I insisted.

The teacher continued with the story.

"First came the big black engine, puffing and chuffing."

I raised my hand. "What's plugging and chugging?"

Four hands and three feet jabbed me in the back.

I turned to find Martha shouting to Susan, "Plugging! He said 'plugging.' Did you hear that?"

"Chug-a-lug, chug-a-lug!" chanted Larry. Soon the whole class was singing.

"Quiet, everybody!" Mrs. Holter insisted. "Now, Frankie, I want you to go over there and make a castle with the blocks. Later, you and I can read the story together."

I never did find out what was plugging and chugging.

In the mornings, while Pete was at kindergarten, I often played with Bobby Spielman. His older sister, Diane, was already in school; Bobby, I knew, would start the following September in Robin's class. He was eager to learn what school would be like. For him, school was exciting, wonderful, exotic; everything it wasn't for me.

"Did anything special happen yesterday?" he asked one morning.

"Nah."

"Did you go to a firehouse? See real firemen?"

"Nope."

"Well, what did you do?"

"We sang some songs, Bobby."

"Yeah? Which ones?"

"I don't know."

He was incredulous. "You don't know?"

"Something about winter and summer."

"Boy, it must be fun to sing with a whole lot of kids all at once!"

"I guess it is."

"Hey, you don't like school, do you?"

"It's O.K., I guess."

"O.K.? Just O.K.? Boy, you must be crazy?"

"No, I'm not."

"Yes, you are. Crazy! Wacko! Nuts."

That afternoon, Mom explained patiently what these new words meant. She also assured me that I was none of them.

As long as we stayed off the subject of school, Bobby and I got along all right. There was none of the Walters' physical activity in Bobby's home. Every time I saw his father, a medical officer at Lewisburg Federal Penitentiary, he was reading a magazine or newspaper. Bobby, like me, learned to read early. We spent many happy hours, at my house or his, reading picture books and playing with puzzles.

Toward late afternoon, I would amble down Brown Street from kindergarten and join Pete for games. Pete was not much for reading. Robin, too, who was three-and-one-half by now, played games with us. Sometimes, when they played records or talked with each other for example, I was left out; that didn't happen much, though, because we were all young and physically active.

One time a heated discussion resulted from Bobby's claim that he was the best reader in the room. I was particularly offended: not only was I older than he was, but I had given over many hundreds of hours by that time to the cause of learning to read. Pete also insisted he could read as well as Bobby. Robin, not to be outdone, put in her claim, too.

"Well, I'll prove it," Bobby declared. Pulling a book from under his jacket, he handed it to me.

"Here. If you're so smart, read this."

It was a book about animals at the zoo.

I opened to the first page. Facing me was a moose-like creature with small antlers.

" 'This is a,' uh, 'a ant-el-oop,' " I read.

Bobby whooped. "See! I told you!"

I tried again. " 'This is an,' uh, 'this is an ant-e-loop.' "

"Give me that," Robin said, pulling the book to her lap.

" 'Ant-el-lope.' " She frowned.

" 'Antel-ope.' Oh! 'Antelope!' " A triumphant grin replaced the frown. "It says, 'This is an antelope.' "

Pete nudged me with his elbow. "Even your sister can read it."

I turned to Bobby.

"What's an antelope?"

"Don't you know, stupid?"

"I'm not stupid!"

"Says you! Says you!"

That evening after supper, I asked Mom why even Robin could read words I couldn't.

"Honey, she's heard the word 'antelope' many times. All she had to do, or Bobby or Pete for that matter, is sound it out. Once she pronounced it correctly, she remembered hearing the word, so she knew what it meant."

"Even though she never saw it before?"

"Right. I'm sorry, Frankie, but most children use the 'sound it out' method of learning to read."

"I want to, too!"

"Well, for those words you remember hearing, we will. But I'm afraid it won't help you much."

"Why not, Mom?"

"Because sounding words out works only if you already know the words from hearing them. The only words you know that way are those you heard when you were one- or two-years old, before your hearing got bad."

I didn't feel too good.

"You also know the words you've learned by reading. So far, that's only a few, but it's growing every day. The problem is that Robin learns new words just by being alive. She hears words all around her. Even if she's not paying attention."

"Mom, how am I ever going to learn to read?"

"We'll do it, honey. Sounding it out isn't the only method in the world."

"Uh, Mom. Robin knows an awful lot of words."

"Well, yes, she does. That's part of the problem. That's one reason we're working so hard on building up your vocabulary."

"How many words does she know?"

Mom shifted in her seat.

"Well, Frankie, your father and I don't believe in hiding things from you. We believe you're better off knowing the truth."

I felt my stomach muscles tighten.

"But I don't know how meaningful this is going to be for you. Since you asked, I'll tell you. According to my professors at Bucknell, the average child Robin's age knows some five thousand or so. Now, Robin can't read all those words yet, of course. She just knows them."

"She'll read them, Mom."

I felt like the tortoise at the start of the race with the hare.

She nodded silently.

"How about me? How many do I know?"

"You really want me to tell you, Frankie?"

"Please."

"I guess a thousand, maybe two."

"Holy pajamas!" I jumped off my chair. "She's two years younger than me and already way ahead of me!"

"You'll catch up, honey. I know you will. But you understand now why we try to read a book together every day?"

I nodded miserably.

"Five thousand words! I don't even know how many five thousand is. Even Granddaddy isn't five thousand years old!"

"No," she laughed. "Not quite."

Robin and I spent much of that winter playing in the snow on the Bucknell campus. The hill was high and steep, an ideal sledding slope. She and I had round aluminum sleds called flying saucers that went down the hill with breathtaking speed. They were also very light, so we found them a breeze to carry up the hill. The only problem with the saucers is that they were difficult to steer on the heavily wooded hill.

One day I arrived at the house with a bloody nose and a scratched cheek.

"What happened, honey?" Mom asked after she put iodine on the cuts.

"I banged into a tree, Mom."

My mother didn't say anything, but when Dad got home that night he decreed that, henceforth, I would leave my hearing aid at home when I went out sledding.

"It's not that the aid is expensive, Frankie. It's just that I don't want you to cut your ear."

"But, Dad . . ."

"It's safer, Frankie."

Mom had a different solution in mind. "Shouldn't he just avoid sledding altogether?" she asked.

"Absolutely not," Dad responded. "Every boy his age sleds. So he sleds. Frankie's going to do everything he would do if his hearing were perfect. We're not going to protect him just because he can't hear. If we start doing that now, with something as silly as sledding, who knows where it will end?"

"But, Dad," I interrupted. "How am I supposed to hear without my hearing aid?"

"By lipreading, son. The aid helps, but not enough to be worth it when you might hurt yourself because you were wearing it."

Mom was silent.

"The rule in this house," Dad continued, "is that Frankie lives a normal, average, everyday childhood. If Bobby can do it, Frankie can do it. If Pete does it, Frankie does it. And there will be no more discussion of this issue in this house from this day on."

The Philosophy of Toad had struck again.

That spring we got our first TV set.

A DuMont, it was rather ugly and elephantine, particularly considering the tiny seven inch size of the screen. That screen was so miniscule that we had to sit directly in front of it to make out any pictures at all. There was also the matter of "snow," which no amount of juggling the control knobs could remove. For all of that, the DuMont was a miracle.

We watched wrestling, baseball, Roller Derby, and boxing matches. My favorite was Gorgeous George, the flamboyant wrestler. I could enjoy all of these sports programs with no difficulty at all, because they were action-oriented with little or no dialogue. "Superman," too, was fairly easy. I would watch George Reeves jump out a window headfirst and figure that he was on his way to save some damsel in distress. Who needed to know the conversation?

Other programs, though, were very hard for me to understand.

The dramas and musical presentations left me unmoved. But I was very upset to find that Clarabell and Howdy Doody were impossible to understand. Every motion of Howdy's wooden mouth was exactly like every other one. I was lucky, in fact, if I caught a dozen words of Buffalo Bob Smith or of anyone else during an entire show.

Because ours was one of the first TV's on the block, many spring afternoons found six or seven Brown Street children crowded around our living room. Mom always brought out milk and cookies, which we ate sitting on the floor.

Dad called us the Brown Street Irregulars.

The big favorite with our crowd was "The Mickey Mouse Club."

This program I found fairly easy to follow. In the first place, everybody wore shirts with their names printed in dark capital letters: Bobby, Cubby, Sherry, Doreen, Cheryl, Karen, Annette. And the camera focused full-face upon Jimmy whenever he talked to us or sang the theme song. Sheer repetition was another big help for me. I can still recite:

Mickey Mouse! Mickey Mouse!

Forever let us raise our banners high!

M-I-C

—See you real soon!

K-E-Y

—Why? Because we like you!

M-O-U-S-E!

The DuMont was notoriously unreliable. Almost every other week or so, we had to tell a disappointed contingent of Brown Street Irregulars that the set was broken. My father tinkered with it using every sharp instrument in the house. In those days, unfortunately, TV repairmen were nonexistent in Lewisburg. Finally, Dad gave up and purchased a new ten inch Philco.

The idea of going without a TV was, for him, unthinkable. Television was a gadget. He just had to have one, preferably the biggest and the best on the market.

A few weeks after the Philco arrived, I almost cured my family of the TV habit.

Watching them laugh at Ralph Kramer and Ed Norton, I demanded to be told what they'd said. My elbow-to-the-groin jab was almost as deadly as Norton's—and a lot more insistent.

Each time a Bowe cracked a smile, I demanded: "What's so funny? Tell me! Somebody tell me!"

It's a miracle Dad didn't throw the TV through the window. There were times, in fact, when I thought he might toss *me* out the window. One day, Dad announced a new policy: "In this house, we wait for commercials before we ask questions."

The message for me was that, like radios and record players, TV sets were part of their world, not mine.

It was a world I wanted desperately to enter. Watching "The Mickey Mouse Club," I marveled at how happy Tommy and Annette always were. Although I understood very little of what they were saying, I monitored their every movement with unflagging devotion. I wanted to become a Mouseketeer! For me, that represented the pinnacle of achievement: to be a normal, average, popular, happy, secure child.

And watching them, I fantasized, projecting myself into their adventures, blocking out for an hour the realities of my own life. I forgot the taunts of the kids on the block, my fears of school, and my sense of inadequacy.

Soon after I began watching the show regularly, I started having a dream about riding bicycles with Annette and Tommy. It was a dream I would have many times for years to come. Tommy was leading a group of boys on bikes, and Annette was heading a similar group of girls. I brought up the rear. Tommy's group headed up a mountain using one path; Annette's group took another route. I lost them both. The road I was on proved to be a winding one, shaped something like a pretzel within a pretzel. I could never come to the end or even return to the beginning. I had no idea where I was going, how to get there, or even where I was on the mountain. Then I saw Tommy's group and Annette's join at a fork on the road beneath me, all of them laughing. They never heard my cries for help.

For my birthday that year, Mom and Dad got me a toy firetruck (I still called it "bire tuck"), together with a bright red plastic hat and a black coat. I spent many happy hours in April and May pushing the truck along our front walk, engaging in fantasies that had me rescuing much of Lewisburg from the worst fires since Sherman pushed through Atlanta on his March to the Sea.

My sixth birthday was also memorable for the loss of my first tooth. We were eating corn on the cob that evening after the party. I took one bite out of the corncob, and my upper right molar helped itself out of my mouth.

I didn't touch corn on the cob for another five years.

"What do you want the tooth fairy to bring you in the morning?" my father asked after I'd recovered from my initial fright.

"How about a new pair of ears?" I asked hopefully.

My father smiled sadly. "I don't think the tooth fairy has ears in stock right now. I know she has quarters, though."

"How do you know?"

"I talked with her this morning."

That got me off the subject of ears.

"Oh, tell me about it!"

"Well, the tooth fairy says that only little boys and girls who are very good get presents. You have to be sound asleep when she comes or she'll just go to another child's house without leaving you anything.

"I'll tell you this, though. The tooth fairy told me she is very impressed by brave little boys and girls. I think she might have something special in mind for you since you're the bravest boy on the block."

I was so excited that I lay awake in bed very late that night. Apparently, it didn't bother the tooth fairy, because I found a bright shiny quarter under my pillow when I woke up in the morning.

I had no way of knowing whether or not I was doing acceptably well in kindergarten, since we had no tests or other measures of performance. Mrs. Holter did report to my parents regularly throughout the school year, though.

In April, she asked Mom to the school for a conference.

"Kitty," she said as they sat uncomfortably on chairs designed for children five years old, "as you know, I've had my doubts all along about Frankie's ability to make it here. Now that the year is almost over, I feel compelled to share my doubts with you candidly.

"I don't think Frankie is going to make it."

Mom refused to be shaken. "I'm sure he will. All he needs is a chance."

"I don't know, Kitty. I've tried to give him chances all year. But, you see, he misses most of what goes on every day. I don't mean a sentence here and there. I mean almost everything anyone says. I suspect he's lucky if he understands three or four sentences all afternoon."

"That'll come, Pat."

"Well, Kitty, I must say I admire your courage—and Frankie's. It must be hard for him. Why, the only time the other children talk to Frankie, usually, is when they want a toy or some blocks he's playing with. I think he is awfully lonely. I don't even know if he's going to be happy. I really think that he'd be much better off in a special environment."

"No. We've rejected that, Pat."

"Well, all right. I'll be reporting to Mrs. Ingwers, who teaches first grade, as you know. I'll tell her what has happened this year with Frankie. It'll be up to her."

"You mean it's her decision whether or not Frankie enters first grade?"

Pat Holter nodded. "Mrs. Ingwers will have to teach him, after all."

The rest of the school year passed quickly, and, before I knew it, summer was upon us. I really looked forward to the last day of school. Had I thought about it more carefully at the time, I would have asked the tooth fairy for permission to skip school. As it was, June arrived at its usual time that year.

My long-awaited vacation lasted exactly one month.

All of us in the Bowe family knew that first grade was looming just two months away. That would be the real thing, Dad told me. Kindergarten was just a warm-up.

"O.K., son," Dad said the morning after Independence Day. "You've had enough of a vacation; now it's time to start getting ready for school."

"But, Dad, I just got out!" I wailed.

"If you don't buckle down now, Frankie, it'll be too late."

I looked at my belt buckle.

"I *am* buckled."

Dad laughed. "I mean it's time to start studying. Starting this afternoon, you and your mother are going to read a book a day, just like you did last summer. This time, though, she'll also work with you on spelling. When I get home from work, I'll help you with arithmetic. If I find you haven't done your reading, though, I'll give you a spanking you'll never forget."

Dad's spankings were legend in our house.

"All right," I said glumly.

Mom took over after Dad left for work. First, we reviewed the alphabet in both upper and lower case letters. Then she said words that I had to write down. After half an hour of this, we started on my assignment for the afternoon: "The Ugly Duckling."

Mom sat at one end of the backporch table with a pad and pencil while I read. Each time I missed a word, Mom wrote it down.

Now, I don't know how other kids did it, but I spent a lot of time studying the illustrations in the book. Every time I saw a new word, I looked at the closest pictures to see if a clue was there that would help me. If that failed, I read the sentence again, trying to make sense of it from those words I knew. Sometimes, that helped. It was only when both tricks left me without any hint of the word's meaning that I told Mom to include the word on her list. Still, one paragraph into the story, Mom's list already had nine words: beautiful, spring, nest, snug, lay, very, still, waiting, hatch.

"I'm doing pretty well, Mom. I know more words than I don't."

"You're doing fine, honey. But don't get too confident. The words you know are used a lot, but the ones you don't know are very important."

To make her point, she cut up nine slips of paper and covered the words I had missed.

"Now, does the story make sense?" she asked.

I had to agree it didn't. "O.K., Mom, I'll buckle up."

"Buckle down, honey. The expression is 'buckle down.' "

An hour later, I slumped down in my chair.

"How many words did I miss, Mom?"

"According to my count, seventy-five," Frankie.

"Is that a lot?"

"Well, that depends. It is, and it isn't. What's important now is that we practice the words so you will know them next time."

It took the better part of the afternoon to go over those words.

The next morning, I read the story again. This time, there were "only" thirty-two words I still didn't know.

But I was coming to love this story. Hans Christian Andersen would have been pleased to find a reader identifying so strongly with his central character. All that year, whenever I'd feel depressed, I'd pick up "The Ugly Duckling" and dream of finding out someday that everything had been a terrible mistake and that I really was a normal kid after all.

That afternoon, my assignment was to read "The Little Engine That Could." I don't know if Mom was selecting these stories as much to build up my confidence as to bolster my reading skills, but she sure was succeeding. For the second time in two days, I found myself identifying with the character I was reading about, this time a small blue engine.

I took my mother's word for it that trains do sound like "chug," "puff," and "ding-dong." Still, the book was a sobering experience. Comparing the new list of forty-seven words I didn't know on the first reading with the original list from "The Ugly Duckling," I was dismayed to discover that only two words appeared on both lists.

"Mom, how many words are there?"

She smiled and shook her head. "I don't know, honey. A lot. Why?"

"Because I don't think I'm doing very well. This book has an awful lot of words the other one didn't."

"Well, that's O.K., honey. It means you're learning new and different words."

I walked over to the family dictionary, a tome that symbolized for me the task I had ahead of me. "How many words are in here, Mom?"

She picked it up and studied the first few pages. "It says 100,000, Frankie."

"Uh, what's a hundred thousand?"

She paused. "A lot," she said finally, putting an arm around my shoulder. "But you only have to learn a few at a time. It'll come. Don't get discouraged."

Several weeks before school was to start that fall, Mom met with Mrs. Elizabeth Ingwers, the South Ward first grade teacher.

She found Betty to be a warm and confident woman, enthusiastic about the challenge of having me in her class.

"Where there's a will, there's a way, Kitty," Betty smiled. "I know Frankie tries hard; I saw that in Pat's class. If he tries equally hard with me, as I know he will, he'll have a chance."

My mother was deeply relieved.

"But don't give up your struggle, Kitty. He has to make it this year. I know that if he does all right in first grade, his teachers in the second and third grades won't give you any problems about admitting him.

"This year is the key."

Just before I started first grade, I picked up the Walt Disney story, "Pinocchio."

It was enough to make me want to give up reading.

The first paragraph alone, I was sure, would send my mother gasping for breath.

The story opened with a description of an evening star shining down on a small village. The second sentence described how the star's beams painted the roofs of the town's humble dwellings.

I was already hopelessly confused.

"Shone," a new word, I skipped, but the rest of the first sentence made me envision a huge star crashing into a town like Lewisburg. I couldn't for the life of me understand how a house was supposed to be "humble." And how a star could paint roofs was beyond my ken. I tried conjuring up an image of a star balancing on a slate roof, brandishing a shining paintbrush, but it didn't work.

I spent the rest of the afternoon in my room, trying to understand how I was going to survive a whole year of real school. My father hadn't been kidding, I decided, when he said it would be tough.

At dinner that evening was one very despondent little six-year-old.

"Cheer up, Boyji," my father said. "You're going to make it."

"How?" I moaned.

"By taking it one day at a time, honey," Mom responded, her face soft and understanding.

"That's how they come, you know."

Chapter
Five

All summer, I talked myself into feeling confident. After all, I already knew how to read. I knew, though, that my classmates would catch up fast—and that I didn't have any more tricks up my sleeve.

I liked Mrs. Ingwers right away. Her crinkly brown eyes seemed to promise a wonderful, funny story every time she looked at me. She told me to sit in the front row, directly before her desk. Usually, she remembered to keep her face up and make sure that I could see her if she wandered away from her desk.

We began the year with a review of the alphabet. I smiled smugly upon learning that half the class didn't even know their ABC's.

Mrs. Ingwers divided the twenty-six of us into three reading groups and three arithmetic groups. My reading group started on the Scott, Foresman *Dick and Jane* series. These stories boosted my confidence even more.

Compared with the advanced literature I'd been reading all summer, the books were banal—and laughingly easy. Three whole pages were required to convey the fact that Dick was running somewhere. We then learned that Jane was running, too. Spot, the dog, and Puff, the cat, ran as well. Next, we were informed that Baby Sally also ran. It was a great feeling knowing that I'd finished a whole book without finding even one word I didn't know.

For the first time in several years, I had a glimmer of hope that my parents' high expectations actually might be grounded in reality. Maybe I would succeed in this ordeal called school.

It was comforting, too, to know that Robin and Bobby were just next door, in kindergarten.

One Monday morning, as I walked up the steps to the school building behind three of my classmates, Kermit, a boy I liked a lot, turned and said to me: "You look funny!"

All three of them laughed and ran into the building.

I had known from the first day of kindergarten that I was the only one wearing a hearing aid. I didn't like being so obviously different. But now Kermit's teasing made me determined to make myself look just like everyone else.

I quickly turned my hearing aid off and placed the cord and receiver in my pocket.

Mrs. Ingwers didn't notice anything all morning.

It was a good strategy I'd hit upon; I congratulated myself. I'd wear the aid when I was home. But as soon as I was out of Mom and Dad's sight, I'd take it off. That way, I'd always look just like everybody else but wouldn't get my parents mad at me.

At lunch, though, Mrs. Ingwers caught me.

"Frankie, you're not wearing your hearing aid!" she shouted, frowning. I shrugged.

She reached under my shirt, pulled out the cord, and inserted the aid.

"Frankie!" she said, holding my shoulders. "Why weren't you wearing it?"

"Nobody else has one. I don't want one either."

"Now, Frankie. Let's have none of that. Please keep your aid on. You know you can't hear a thing without it."

"I don't care."

Betty Ingwers determined to nip my revolt in the bud. After talking it over with Mom, she arranged for me to spend the next several weeks demonstrating the hearing aid to all the kids in the class.

"Frankie has a magic box," Mrs. Ingwers told the class one morning. "Yes, a real magic box. And Frankie's the only one who has one. This box is very special. It helps Frankie hear better."

I slouched in my chair.

"Frankie, please come up here and show us your magic box. Take it apart and show us how it works."

With reluctance, I lifted the aid from the harness and began explaining the function of its switches, cords, earmold, and receiver.

Even I had to admit that the thing was fairly complicated.

Then Mrs. Ingwers asked if I would let the kids see and feel the aid from time to time over the next couple of weeks.

I let Pete Walters listen to the aid first, since I knew him best. Susie Keister, from down our block, was next. David McCoy, a small, frail boy who almost always kept his right eye nearly closed (he later got glasses), said my hearing aid sounded like a dog whistle. Mary Snyder, a shy, timid girl who always looked as if she were about to burst out crying, handled my aid gingerly so as not to break it. And Mary Lou Nogel, the tallest child in the class and the most outgoing, flashed an ear-to-ear grin when she listened to her voice amplified through my aid.

"It's swell, Frank. You ought to be proud of this," she told me. I was intensely grateful to her.

Even Kermit was interested.

As Mrs. Ingwers had foreseen, the kids' fascination with my aid made me proud of it.

After every child had seen and handled the aid, Mrs. Ingwers showed me a special shelf in the cupboard.

"Frankie, I want you to bring a spare battery, an extra one, to school and keep it right here. If your battery ever breaks down, you'll have another one you can use. O.K.?''

I nodded.

Having disposed of my hatred of my hearing aid, Mrs. Ingwers turned to my voice. It was, she told Mom, very high-pitched, probably because I was so tense that the muscles in my throat were all drawn tight.

"I understand the tension, Kitty," she told my mother when Mom arrived to take me home one afternoon. "After all, he's under a lot of pressure. You can see it on that tight, white face; he almost never smiles unless you tell him to. Even his body feels rigid when you touch him. I feel for the boy. He sees the other kids, and he knows they learn faster and easier than he does.

"I'm talking to him, telling him it will be all right. I want him to believe in himself. That way, he won't beat himself, and he'll have a better chance.''

"Anything I can do, Betty?'' asked Mom.

"It will help a lot if I knew more about how much of what I'm saying is getting through to him. Why don't we do this?

"In the afternoon when he comes home from school, ask him to tell you what he learned at school that day. Write or type it up and send it with him the next morning. That way, I can read over your notes to see what he's learning, and you can follow his progress, too.''

Every school day for the rest of first grade, that's exactly what they did.

Mrs. Ingwers' remarkable patience calmed me considerably. "He's a much happier boy now,'' she commented on my report card at the end of the second nine-week reporting period.

After the New Year's break, the class started with a series of spelling lessons.

What I disliked most about these sessions was that Mrs. Ingwers called upon one child or another to spell a word. Since most of the words were fairly brief, they'd be spelled out by the time I figured out which word the class was on and which child was doing the spelling out loud.

But I was distraught to discover that first grade, like kindergarten, featured a lot of singing. This time, bogged down with other work, I decided not to try to participate in the singing. I didn't even bother learning the words.

One morning I found while dressing that the battery for my hearing aid was dead. This didn't happen often, since Mom placed a new battery on my bureau every school night to be sure I'd have a fresh one in the morning. She didn't do that on weekends, though, so it must have been a Sunday when I found my battery dead.

Robin was already up when I got downstairs. On an impulse, I put a record I knew on the record player and lay flat on my back as I used to do, with both hands on the speaker and my ear against it. Even though I turned the volume all the way up, I couldn't hear a sound. Mom and Dad, from the back porch, could hear it, though, something I learned when Dad rushed into the room to lower the volume. He found me crying.

"I can't hear it," I moaned.

"Well, of course you can't," Dad said indignantly. "You're not wearing your hearing aid. I'll say this, though: Your mother and I thought the entire Bucknell University marching band was here in the living room."

I laughed. "But, Dad I used to be able to hear it. Remember? Before the aid came?"

"Let's try it again, Frankie."

Such was a little boy's faith in his father, I really believed he could make me hear it this time. His magical powers must have been elsewhere at the moment, though, because nothing happened.

The next morning Mom told me I was excused from going to school.

I was delirious with joy until she explained the reason: we were driving to Geisinger to have my ears tested.

I had a new battery in my aid when the audiologist finished his examination. Facing me, he told Mom what he had found: "I'm sorry, Mrs. Bowe. His right ear is definitely worse than it was last time you were here. And, as you know, there's no hearing at all in the left ear."

"I see," Mom said, her eyes downcast.

"You mean I'm not getting any better?" I asked.

"No, Frankie. I think your hearing is getting a little worse every time you get sick. I want you to be a big boy. Try not to get sick any more. Stay out of puddles when it rains. Dress warmly."

I thought that over. "Will my hearing get better if I'm good?"

"No, Frankie," he shook his head. "I don't think it will. But you can do everything possible to make sure it doesn't get worse."

Before we left Geisinger, I had acquired a new, more powerful hearing aid. It was a little bigger than my first one, so I had a new harness too. And a few days later, a new ear mold came in the mail.

My ear had grown a bit, even if it didn't work any better.

When I returned home from school that Friday, it was with an important question for my mother.

"Mom," I began. "I can't hear things the same with this aid as I did with the other one."

"You mean it's not as good?"

"I don't know, Mom. I can hear the things I heard before, but now they sound different, somehow."

"Well, of course they do, honey. It's a different aid."

I shook my head. "But, Mom, which aid makes things sound the way they really do, the way you hear them?"

Mom's brows furrowed, her eyes narrowed, and she bit her lip. She looked just like she did when I came down with a cold.

"Neither one, honey."

"Huh? It has to be one or the other!"

"I wish that were true, Frankie. But each hearing aid makes sounds that are a little different from the way they really sound."

"Then I want one that makes them sound right!"

She covered my hands in hers. "Frankie, if they made an aid like that, we'd buy it for you."

"You mean I'll never, ever hear things right?"

"Well, honey," she said, "someday when you get your hearing back, I'm sure you will. But a hearing aid isn't going to do that for you."

I didn't talk to anybody all weekend.

By the spring break, the other kids had caught up to me in reading. I had hoped to stretch my head start out at least twice that long, but I had underestimated how quickly children who hear can learn anything they listen to.

And despite Mrs. Ingwers' best efforts to make sure I could see her at all times, I was missing much of what went on in the classroom.

The pressure was building.

Never a particularly patient person, I'd snap quickly now at the slightest imagined wrong. I remember one day that Mom came to talk with Mrs. Ingwers about the following week's assignments. While the teacher was out, Martha led the class in spelling a list of words. From my seat in the front row, I looked anxiously around me. Seeing Kay and Louise moving their lips, I moved mine, too. Within a few minutes, I'd lost my way. I didn't even know which word they were spelling, let alone how it was to be spelled.

Soon, Mrs. Ingwers returned.

"Martha's mixed the words all up, and they're all wrong," I informed her.

Mrs. Ingwers quickly calmed me down. The spellings, she informed me, had been given correctly.

That evening, Dad called me into the living room.

"Son," he began, after turning on the floor lamps all over the room and motioning me to a spot three feet in front of him. "Son," he repeated, "I've got some bad news for you."

I blushed.

"No, nothing you've done wrong, Frankie. This has to do with school."

I nodded.

"Mrs. Ingwers told your mother this morning that she thinks you are missing most of what goes on in class. Is that true?"

"I guess so."

"Yes or no?"

"Yes."

"Why?"

I shifted in my seat. Avoiding his eyes, I said: "Well, Dad, I do O.K. as long as she is right in front of me. If she turns sideways, or walks to another kid in class, I miss what she says."

"I see. And what about what the kids say?"

"I miss a lot of that, Dad."

"All of it?"

I looked into his eyes, expecting to see anger. Instead, I saw sadness. "All of it," I nodded.

Mom came in to join us.

"Well, son," Dad said, "I didn't expect it to be like this. I guess I thought lipreading was something you either knew or you didn't. When you're here, you lipread Mom and me really well."

"Robin, too."

"Yes, Robin, too. So I assumed you could lipread other people as well. Now I find out that it's not that simple. Here, we can make sure the lighting is right, that we face you when we talk, that you're sitting close by us. In school, that's often impossible."

"I'm sure Frankie is doing his best," Mom said.

"I'm sure he is, too. The question is: Is his best good enough?"

Mom was silent.

"Maybe what you need now, son, is lipreading lessons."

"Gee, Dad. More lessons?"

"We understand how you feel, honey," Mom told me. "You already have to work extra hard on your reading. But your father is right. If you can't lipread better than you do now, you're wasting six hours a day in school. Don't you get bored now, sitting there all day without understanding what's going on?"

I nodded miserably.

"Well, let's see what we can do about that," Dad said, standing up. "Kitty, do you suppose Geisinger could recommend someone to work with Frankie on his lipreading?"

Nothing I had known in six-and-three-quarter years of life was as boring as lipreading lessons.

Every Saturday afternoon, from early January through June, I sat across a table from a young woman who was studying at Bloomsburg State Teacher's College, about half an hour's drive to the east.

My teacher was a firm believer that good lipreaders read ideas instead of individual words. So she concentrated on getting me to lipread sentences. For hour after dreary hour, I would watch her mouth sentences that had nothing whatsoever to do with my life or with hers.

There would be ten or so sentences in a row, each differing only by one word. My job was to repeat each sentence after her.

The lessons featured such scintillating witticisms as: "Joe bought some nails at the store;" "Joe bought some snails at the store;" "Joe bought some pails at the store;" and "Joe bought some rails at the store." Never mind that some of these sentences didn't make sense (try this one: "Joe bought some jails at the store"). Halfway through these dreary sessions, I assure you I couldn't have cared less *what* Joe bought at the store.

Then there would be pairs of words; each word in a pair sharing all sounds save one. I had to differentiate between "string" and "spring," then "string" and "bring," "string" and "strung," and "string" and "sing."

We'd run through these fascinating words and sentences with my hearing aid off. Then we'd go through all of them again with my aid turned on.

My teacher would read them sitting down, and she would read them standing up.

"Now, we'll make it interesting," she said to introduce the next section of the lessons, one I dreaded. Turning her face to the wall, so I could only see her profile, she'd run through the miserable sentences and words yet again, asking me to repeat everything she said. Still in profile, she'd stand and move while saying a sentence or a set of words.

By March, we were working on homonyms, words that sound alike. "Bear" and "bare" for example not only sound the same, they also look the same on the lips. I learned that I'd have to hold the image of the word in mind while I watched the rest of the sentence in order to determine which of the homonyms I had just seen. My teacher called this "studying the context."

"If you miss a word, hang in there, Frankie," she reminded me time and again. "By studying the context, you can usually figure out what the person is saying. That's what I mean by lipreading ideas and not just words."

I was also told to "anticipate." Believe me, I had to anticipate to understand what she was saying when she said "anticipate." This particular four-syllable word has only one syllable clearly visible on the lips: the last ("pate"). "Anticipation helps you in many situations, Frankie," I was informed one particular Saturday afternoon. "Say you're in a restaurant. The waiter puts your hamburger before you and says, what?"

I shrugged.

"He says: "Would you like mustard or ketchup?"

"Oh."

"It's almost certainly that. Occasionally, a waiter might ask you if you want relish. Some might ask if you want steak sauce. But ninety percent of the time, the waiter is going to ask you if you want mustard or ketchup.

By knowing that, you're using your brains to anticipate what is going to be said. It makes lipreading much easier.''

"How does this help Frankie in school?'' Mom asked.

"I'd suggest that Frankie do his reading a day before everybody else does. That way, when the teacher (Mrs. Ingwers, isn't it?) starts talking, he'll be able to anticipate what she's going to say.''

I liked that idea. Slowly, piece by piece, a strategy for succeeding in school was taking shape.

Every day at home, my parents continued in an informal way the task of teaching me to lipread. They quickly learned some special techniques for testing my comprehension. Instead of making a statement, such as "It's a nice day today,'' which required no particular response from me, they asked a question. Not just any question; it had to be a question that forced me to give a substantive answer, more than merely a "yes'' or "no'' response. "What do you think today will be like?'' is an example. If my answer were inappropriate, they would know immediately that I had not understood the question. Then, too, they watched my face carefully whenever they talked to me, waiting for the expression on my face that signalled understanding. Mom and Dad learned how to say the same thing two or three different ways until they saw my features clear in dawning comprehension.

All of this was easier for Mom than for Dad. It took great patience, a trait my mother had in abundant supply. Dad, on the other hand, was eager to complete any activity as quickly as possible and with a minimum of fuss. He surprised me time and again by showing remarkable patience with me, rarely showing the temper for which he was justly famous in our house.

One day, Dad showed me why he was able to muster so much patience with me. I was building an edifice with my erector set on the dining room table. For several hours, he and I constructed floor after floor of an imposing tower. It was a task requiring great concentration, for each piece had to be secured precisely before another could be placed over it. By the time the building was half built, I was tiring.

"Dad, let's just put a roof here.''

"That wouldn't look right, Frankie.''

"I know, Dad, but it's good enough.''

"No, it's not, son. If you're not going to do it right, don't do it at all.''

I sighed and went on building. Fifteen minutes later, I again suggested terminating the effort.

"Dad, it's good enough now.''

"Are you really proud of this, Frankie?''

"Uh, yeah. At least it's half-way done.''

"Is that all you want?''

"Dad, a lot of it is good.''

"Look, son. If you stop here, you have done half of a job. If that's all you're going to do, you might as well not have done any at all."

"How come?"

"Because if you're not going to do your best, don't do anything at all."

This, I learned, was another tenet of The Philosophy of Toad. My father stuck with a task until he had completed it to his satisfaction, regardless of how long it might take. When he placed a fish tank in our living room, he outfitted it with every option available. When he built a stand for the tank, he devoted almost as much time to the mathematics of designing the stand as he did to the mechanics of constructing it. But when the fish tank and the stand were completed, they were, in his words, "Done and done right."

Almost every spring while I was growing up, the banks of the Susquehanna River, less than 300 yards behind our house, flooded as snow melted in the Allegheny Mountains to the north of us.

Most times, the flooding was minimal. The water would creep slowly across the corn fields behind our home but stop about midfield. A few times, however, the flood waters reached our backyard.

That spring was one of those times.

I was fascinated by the flooding. With Bobby or Pete at my side, I'd sweep the water with a stick, skip stones across the flat surface and marvel at the ever-expanding concentric circles I made, and float boats made from leaves and sticks along the edge of the water.

One Tuesday after school, I walked straight to the water behind our home without first stopping at the house. I found the flood receding somewhat, with mud spread in its wake. Picking up several sticks and a few corn stalks, I began constructing a mud castle. No sooner had I built the walls than I created a moat around them, with a bridge made of leaves spanning the moat. I filled the moat with flood water by dragging a stick from the water's edge to the castle and letting the water trickle into my moat.

Two hours must have passed. The sky was darkening above me. I knew it would rain soon.

Just one more road, I thought, then I'll go home.

At that moment, I lifted my head to see Mom, Dad, and Robin running toward me.

"Look, Dad. I made a castle. And here's my moat. Just like a real castle."

I looked up to his face, expecting to see pride and approval. Instead, his features seemed drawn tight, his jawline shaking. Mom's face seemed pale. She was breathing rapidly.

Dad took me by the hand without a word and led me back to the house.

73

We walked awfully slowly. I kept glancing from my mother to my father for some sign of what awaited me at the house. But I saw none.

Mom sent me up for a bath. When I came down to the living room, I found my parents staring angrily at the TV.

"What's wrong?" I asked.

"Sit down, son." Dad's face seemed set in stone.

He turned on the floor lamps as I took a seat at his side.

"Frankie, you almost caused your mother a heart attack today. She spent an hour looking for you. Your mother was frantic. She called me at the office. I've never heard your mother so frightened."

"Am I going to get spanked?"

"Is that all you can think about? Do you realize what we went through this afternoon? Your mother and I went to half the houses on Brown Street. We went across the railroad tracks to search all over the Bucknell campus."

Mom was sniffing softly into a handkerchief.

"I couldn't call you, Frankie. You wouldn't have heard me."

I noticed Robin coloring in the back of the room, near the piano.

"I'm sorry."

"You better be. Now you listen to me, son. When you come home from school, you come home. Here. You report to your mother. You tell her where you want to go. Then, and only then, do you go off. Is that understood?"

"I promise not to play out there any more."

"No, Frankie, that isn't what I want. I want you to play out back, across the tracks, anywhere you want to play. The worst mistake we could make with you is to treat you like a baby and watch your every move. We're not going to make that mistake. You're going to have a normal childhood if it kills your mother and me. But you will, you absolutely will, tell us where you go."

I nodded.

"Am I making myself clear?"

"Yes."

"Now get out of here."

"You mean I won't get spanked?"

"'Frankie," Dad said, his face breaking into a smile for the first time that evening. "Frankie, if you don't scat in exactly five seconds, you sure will."

I scat.

Chapter Six

Almost daily, groups of boys played baseball in the Bucknell field across the tracks from our Brown Street home. I was determined to join in, despite repeated rebuffs. One late August morning, like so many others, I walked over and called to the biggest boy there, who was pitching.

"Hey, can I play?"

He ignored me.

"I live over there," I added, pointing to the house.

The group might as well not have heard me.

I sat to watch them play. After about half an hour, I gave up and returned home.

The next day, I saw them again. This time, I brought a bat and a ball.

"Hey, guys. I've got another bat. You can use it. You can use my ball, too."

They ignored me.

The next day, a Wednesday, I watched the field from my room. As soon as a group of boys, ten this time, started walking onto the field, I rushed across the tracks.

I noticed right away that this group was different from the other one.

"Hey, you guys! You need more players. I'll be glad to join one side."

"Who asked you?" a redhead with a Yankee's sweatshirt retorted.

I looked from one boy to another. "I just thought you'd have more fun if you had more guys."

No one answered.

I sat by the tennis courts, watching them. After the first inning, I tried again. "Hey guys. Let me be the catcher. I can catch for both teams."

"Stop bothering me!" snapped the redhead.

"Aw, let him. It can't hurt," rejoined the pitcher.

So I became the catcher.

After supper, Robin and I went up to her room to color. I made a picture of a baseball field with green grass, an orange fence, a tan bat, and players wearing red-on-gray uniforms.

Robin's picture was of a princess.

"When I grow up," I informed my little sister, "I'm going to be a great baseball player. I'm going to be the next Babe Ruth. What are you going to be?"

She fixed her light blue eyes on mine.

"A princess," she answered.

"You can't be a princess." I was quite matter of fact about it. "You aren't the daughter of a king and a queen."

"I can, too," she insisted.

There followed a volley of "No, you can't" and "Yes, I can."

Finally, she said: "If I can't be a princess, you can't be a great baseball player."

I treated this assault on my masculinity with the aplomb required of all great baseball players. I decked her with a right cross.

As she turned to the weapon called upon by all princesses and other damsels in distress, my parents came bursting into the room.

My father hauled me into my room and slammed the door behind me.

Shaking me by the shoulders, he said: "I don't ever want to see you fighting with your sister again!"

With my jaw jutting up into his, I replied: "I don't have to listen to this," and promptly shut off my hearing aid.

My father dropped both his hands from my shoulders and stood before me, stunned and speechless for, I was confident, the first time in his life.

We stared at each other like matador and bull for a few moments.

Then Dad placed me stomach-down on his lap and started to spank me.

"Hey, Dad. Please, Dad, not so hard."

He turned me around.

"Why not? You hit your sister pretty hard."

"But, Dad. You can't hit me hard. You see, I can't hear."

For the second time in ten minutes, he was speechless. Finally, he shook his head.

"Frankie, I'd hit you just as hard if you could. Your hearing has nothing to do with this. And you've just given me another reason to spank you. I don't ever want you to use your hearing as an excuse."

When he finished, I knew his reputation as a spanker's spanker was richly deserved.

School wasn't much fun that fall. There were two big reasons: borrowing and carrying.

All through September and October, I puzzled over the mysteries of borrowing. Take the following lesson we got one morning:

I was in my front-row-center seat when Mrs. Clinger, our teacher, wrote two numbers on the blackboard, 31 on the top and 15 just below it. She placed a minus sign before the 15 and drew a line under the number.

"Now, we're going to subtract 15 from 31. Who knows what to do first?"

She called on Cathy, who sat in the third row near the door.

The South Ward School

With Robin: "Mister Tiger sleeps in the bathroom!"

Mrs. Ingwers, at left, and my first grade class: Pete Walters is the towhead fourth from right, top row; below him and to his right, someone smiles with the sure knowledge that there are just a few more weeks of school.

I turned to see what Cathy was saying. I missed it, so I turned my attention back to Mrs. Clinger.

"Right, Cathy," she said.

While I was wondering what was right, the teacher drew a line through the 3 in 31. She placed a small 1 just above and to the left of the 1 in 31.

Turning to face the class again, she asked: "Who knows what eleven minus five is?"

I raised my right hand. "Six," I said.

"Right, Frankie. I'm glad you understand."

I didn't. Where had that little 1 come from?

The teacher turned to the board and wrote a 2 just above and to the left of the 3 in 31.

She said something I missed. Then: "Right, Mary Lou." And she placed a 1 beside the 6.

"Thirty-one minus fifteen is sixteen. That's what borrowing is all about."

She moved on to the higher mathematics of "132 − 54," with the comment: "Now, we're going to borrow two times. Linda, why don't you tell me what to do?"

Mrs. Clinger turned to face the blackboard and kept her face to it as she completed the exercise.

"There. One hundred thirty-two minus fifty-four is seventy-eight."

I didn't have the heart to admit I still didn't understand "31 − 15."

Carrying was more of the same. Try as I might, I couldn't understand how it worked.

Our teacher used the same numbers to illustrate carrying. We started with "15 + 16 = 31."

"Now, who knows the answer?"

I scribbled furiously at my desk. First, I added the five and the six to get eleven. Then I added the two ones to get two. Finally, I combined my answers to arrive at 211. I distinctly remembered Mrs. Ingwers' injunction in first grade: "Add the numbers in the right column; then add the numbers in the left column; now put them together." But this time the answer didn't make any sense.

I still didn't understand carrying when the teacher asked David to explain how to do "78 + 54 = 132." With her back to me, she nodded as David said whatever he said. Somehow, the answer came out right: 132.

I knew I was missing something.

I finally admitted defeat, swallowed my pride, and asked Mom for help.

"Oh, no, you don't!" She said in mock horror. "Numbers are your father's domain, not mine."

Dad patiently explained borrowing and carrying. The fact that I could see his lips as he worked through the problems made all the difference. We were done in an hour.

"Ah, ha!" I shouted. "So that's what it's all about."

Second grade was also special because of Cathy Young, Davy Crockett, and Little League baseball.

Small, freckle-faced, shy, Cathy lived in the small white house next to our South Ward Elementary School. Every morning for much of second grade, I joined her family for breakfast (my second of the day) and walked her the fifteen feet to school.

I know it doesn't sound like much to you now, but the fact that someone cared enough to be my friend meant a great deal to me at the time.

Cathy's sparkling brown eyes rarely were raised to meet anyone's gaze, but she didn't hesitate to look straight into mine. Sometimes, she even held my hand as we walked to school.

Cathy didn't say much. But she didn't have to. If I talked about being afraid of Kermit, Cathy would nod sympathetically and confide that she didn't much like him either. There was a world of compassion in those nods and little confidences. Cathy made me feel that no matter how difficult things might get, someone would be there who would suffer with me and stand by my side until they got better.

I found myself looking forward to going to school. The few minutes I shared with her over breakfast made the rest of the day bearable.

With Cathy, I felt I could discuss the really important things in life, such as what my classmates were saying and thinking. They were a special group to me. They were smart; they were popular; they were, above all, normal, average, typical children. Cathy, I knew, was my conduit to understanding them. She was easy to lipread. Just as important, she was one of them. My hope was that if I knew how they thought and what they said, I could become more like them. Nothing was more vital—or more elusive—to me that fall.

One morning in October, Cathy and I sat at her breakfast table. I'd been thinking a lot about my future. The kids in school, I was sure, had much greater expectations for their lives than I could ever have. It was with a rather morbid curiosity that I asked her about her own dreams.

"What do you want to be when you grow up?" I asked her over toast and jelly that morning in the crowded kitchen of her house.

"Oh, I don't know, Frankie. A mother. A wife. Maybe a teacher or a nurse."

That didn't sound to me like the momentous career I was sure she'd have.

"Don't you want to do something important?"

"Not especially. I don't think anybody does. It's not important to be good at something. I mean, too good. Nobody likes eggheads."

"Eggheads?"

"Smarty two-shoes," she laughed. "You know. What matters is being a good sport, part of the team. You don't want to stick out too much. You don't want to be different."

I was silent. I didn't want to tell her I already was different, and there wasn't a thing I could do about it.

"What about you, Frankie?"

I hadn't expected the question. "Well. I guess, I want to be liked, too."

"Everybody does."

"Yeah. I'm no different from anybody else. That way, anyway."

"Well, drink the orange juice. We'll be late for school."

That afternoon, I asked Mom a very significant question.

She was reading a paperback novel on the front porch as I came home.

"Mom, is it more important to be liked or to be good at something?"

"Well, honey," she said, putting the book aside. "Why do you ask?"

"Because Cathy says what matters is to be part of the team. She says none of the kids at school want to be too different."

"That's fine for Cathy. I'm glad for her."

"Yeah, but what about me? I'm already different. I stick out like a sore finger."

"Sore thumb. It's 'like a sore thumb.' Well, I've always felt that if you're good at something, people will admire you. They'll like you because you're special."

"What can I be good at?"

"Anything you like, dear."

"Really?"

"Really. I wouldn't lie to you, Frankie."

At that moment, I felt ten feet tall. Maybe she was just being nice to me, but I didn't care. I needed that encouragement.

"I wish more people were like you, Mom."

"Oh, Frankie. I do, too. It's the times, I guess."

"The times?"

"Yes. A lot of things are happening in the world, in our country. I don't know how long it will be this way, but right now the thinking of a lot of people is 'don't rock the boat.' "

"The boat?"

She shook her head. "When am I ever going to remember that we use expressions all the time that don't mean what the words say? 'Don't rock the boat' means don't step out of line." She scratched her forehead. "I'm sorry, Frankie. I'm so used to talking this way. What I mean is people don't want to stand out too much."

It didn't make sense to me. These people could do anything they wanted to do.

"Mom, if I were normal, I'd do great things. I'd build great buildings. I'd write great books."

She patted my hands. It was a gesture she often used to reassure me that everything was all right.

"I know you would, Frankie. Dad and I are very proud of you because you're like that. That's exactly how your father thinks. He couldn't care less about rocking the boat or looking different. We're trying to raise you to be that way, too."

Mom looked at the romance novel she'd been reading before I came home.

"You know, Frankie, this reminds me. The other day when Dad and I were sitting out here, taking a break, I told him about a book I was reading called *The Man in the Grey Flannel Suit*. You ought to read it some day."

"I will, Mom. What's it about?"

She smiled. "You'll find books wonderful, Frankie. You can live so many lives through books. It's my favorite thing in life, reading is. Well, the book is about a man named Tom Roth. Tom's not a man I like; your father would detest him. Tom's a clock-watcher."

"A what?"

"Oh, darn. It's so hard to talk without using those expressions. A clock-watcher is someone who works from eight to five. At five o'clock, on the button, he goes home. He only works because he has to. He only does as well as he has to. Tom says somewhere in the book that all the great inventions have already been made, that there's nothing interesting or new in life. In the book, he's rewarded for being like that. Everybody likes him. He's offered a promotion. He turns it down, because it would mean he'd have to work harder, and he doesn't want to do that."

I shook my head. I vowed then and there that if I were ever offered a promotion, I'd accept it in nothing flat.

"Anyway, Frankie, that's how a lot of people think. Your father says they're only half alive. I think he's right."

She paused. "Maybe another part of all this, I don't know, is that people are afraid of communists. In Washington, last spring, a Senator from Wisconsin stirred up a storm with charges that important people in our government were Reds. I guess that's another part of the 'don't rock the boat' philosophy."

I nodded.

"I'm glad you're asking, Frankie. For the longest time there, you lost that curiosity that was so wonderful in you when you were small. I hope you'll ask Dad and me more questions."

"What was I like?"

Her gentle, light-complected face softened into a smile that reminded me of chocolate pudding. It was a special smile, one that I treasured. The smile seemed to say: "Every time I see you, I feel again all the joy you've brought into my life."

She patted my thighs. "A regular devil, you were. Always into everything. You just had to know what things were made of, how they worked." Taking my hands in hers, she added: "We love you just the way you are. We always will."

In mid-December, the Walt Disney television program began a series of "Davy Crockett" stories. Every Wednesday night that winter, Robin and I sat mesmerized as Fess Parker singlehandedly opened the great frontier of the West with a little help from a coonskin cap and a rifle called Old Betsy.

I was a little slow in catching on to the monumental significance of Davy Crockett.

When I returned to school after New Year's, I was startled to find that almost every boy and girl in school brandished powder horns and coonskin caps. There were Davy Crockett T-shirts, Davy Crockett sweatshirts, Davy Crockett pistols, and Old Betsy rifles. There were even Davy Crockett lunch boxes and Davy Crockett bicycles.

Because I hadn't come equipped with my Davy Crockett paraphernalia, the crowd turned on me during recess.

"An Indian! There he is! Indian! Come on guys, let's get him!"

I beat a hasty retreat. During our lunch break, I ran all the way home to get my cap and rifle. It was more important to me than the tuna fish sandwiches Mom prepared for lunch, more important than my hearing aid, more important, in fact, than anything in the world at that moment.

It didn't matter any more that January afternoon that I couldn't hear. My coonskin cap made me just like everybody else.

For my eighth birthday, March 29, 1955, my parents bought me a new baseball glove, together with the usual assortment of books and toys.

"Son, this year you're playing Little League baseball," Dad announced. "As soon as the weather warms up a bit, we'll start practicing for the tryouts."

True to his word, we did.

In April, Dad took me to Daniel Green Field at the other end of town. Pete Walters came with us.

I passed the tryouts and was selected for the "Cardinals" team sponsored by Baker and Baker, the local garbage disposal firm. We were issued red-on-gray uniforms with large letters across the chest spelling out "B&B."

Pete didn't pass, because his eighth birthday didn't fall until the season would be almost over.

I was elated.

It didn't matter to me that the reasons for my passing the tryouts were hardly achievements of stupendous magnitude. I was selected because I was a male of the species and because I was fully eight years old.

Two things happened that afternoon that hadn't happened to me before in my whole life. A group had accepted me, and I beat somebody at something.

Second grade, I decided, would go down in history as my greatest year.

At last, I was what I'd always wanted to be: an average, mundane, typical small-town boy. Just like everybody else.

My father had been an outstanding athlete in his youth, so good that he turned professional in both basketball and tennis while still a teenager. And that was against the top competition in the country's largest city. So it was not unreasonable for Dad to expect at least a minimum of athletic prowess in his only son.

That's what he got: the minimum.

Frail, nervous, and frankly too eager to please, I didn't make anyone forget Honus Wagner that year.

In baseball, right field is where the team's weakest performer traditionally is placed. I was B&B's third-string right fielder.

My idea of contributing to the Cardinals' offensive firepower was to crouch low at the plate and pray for a walk. I considered the at-bat a success if I escaped alive without getting beaned by a fastball.

My father knew I couldn't be that bad, so he put the problem down to a lack of self-confidence.

"Frankie's going to play this game until he learns it," he lectured to my mother. "One of these days, I don't care if it's three or four years down the road, he's going to learn how to do something right out there. That'll give him confidence. Once he gets confidence, there's no telling how far he can go."

How far I could go was the furthest thing on my mind the day we played an exhibition game at the Federal Penitentiary.

The other team had the biggest pitcher in Lewisburg Little League that year, a fearsome left-hander who was so imposing that I almost asked the coach to let me spend the game on the bench.

When he finally put me into the game in the third inning, I learned what real fear is.

Trotting out to my position in right field, I found myself less than fifteen feet from two dozen "lifers." I tried desperately to locate some guards, just to reassure myself that they were there. I could see none. I was terrified, so certain the prisoners were just waiting for the right moment to leap over the short fence that separated us to kidnap me that I spent more time watching them out of the corner of my eye than I did concentrating on the game.

The lifers got their opportunity when a two-out fly came right toward me. Legs shaking, glove over my head more to ward off the anticipated thugs than to catch the ball, I somehow managed to get it.

I broke the world record for eight-year-olds running to the bench that afternoon. I was "scared straight" long before the TV program of that name was ever screened.

Except while I was on the baseball diamond, I spent most of my after school time alone. Loneliness was something I was getting used to; it was safe, free of the tension of communicating, a time when I could sort things out. With our new Golly by my side, I spent countless hours walking around the Bucknell campus, grateful for the quiet.

I had just set out on a walk one Saturday morning when I saw smoke rising from the tiny wood house of the poorest family on Brown Street. Soon, a crowd surrounded me. I saw my sister's horrified face. "Why them?" she asked. I was silent. I could no more explain a world in which fire ravaged the weakest among us than I could anything else in my confused life. I stood for a long time after everyone else had gone, watching the smoking embers of what was once a house.

A few days later, as we were playing catch in his yard, Pete told me he'd hitchhiked to Rolling Green Park, an hour's drive away, the previous afternoon.

I was astonished that he was allowed to go on a trip by himself. I was also jealous.

"Your parents don't love you if they let you do that," I told him. Mrs. Walters was standing right beside us. She didn't say anything.

When I repeated the story to Mom over supper, she didn't react as I had expected her to.

"Frankie, parents love their children in different ways. I'm sure Bill and Jean Walters were very careful about Pete's trip."

"Then, I want to go on a trip by myself, too."

Mom ignored me.

"Frankie, I want you to go right back to the Walters' house and apologize to Mrs. Walters."

That was a new word for me. On her lips, it looked like "a-polish-eyes." I was too downcast and confused to ask her about the word.

Five minutes later, I rang the Walters' door. While I waited for the door to be answered, I carefully polished my eyes by making them water.

Jean Walters answered the door. "Mrs. Walters, I a-polish-eyes," I stammered, and ran off before she could say anything.

Every day, all summer long, three or four girls went swimming with Robin. There wasn't a day in June, July, or August that she didn't have an invitation or two to do something with a group of girls.

There wasn't a day all summer when I had such an invitation.

Since I couldn't very well order anyone to invite me to play with them, I seized upon swimming as the key to normality.

It was then that I learned that one of the absolute "No's" imposed upon my parents by all the doctors they had consulted was that I was not to swim. The theory, it seemed, was that my ears might get infected by swimming-pool water.

I didn't take well to this edict.

"I want to go swimming."

"You can't, Frankie," Mom sighed. "You know that. I've already explained that the doctors . . . "

"Are afraid my ears will get infected. I know." I slammed the book she'd been reading on the table.

"Look, Mom. Believe me, if my ears got infected, they'd be doing me the first favor they ever gave me. Mom, the way my ears work, an infection isn't going to hurt. It might even help. At least, I'd know they were there!"

She shook her head. "I'm sorry, Frankie, believe me, I am. But that's something that is absolutely ruled out. There's only one exception . . . "

I almost leaped out of my chair.

"What's that?" I shouted.

"Well, I'll let your father explain it."

I ran to the living room to find my father feeding the fish in the tank over our new Zenith television set.

"Hey, Dad. Mom says there's an exception to the rule that I'm not allowed to swim."

"Sorry, son. I feel as I'm sure your mother does. We just can't risk an infection."

"The exception, Dad! What is it?"

"Oh," he nodded. "You're allowed to go swimming . . . "

"Whoopee!!"

"Let me finish. Only to learn how to take care of yourself in the water. My estimation is that this will require about ten lessons. One hour per lesson."

"Lessons? Robin doesn't get lessons."

"Yes. But she's learning because she's in the water everyday, and your mother is usually watching her."

"I'll learn the same way!"

"You'll do no such thing." My father seemed determined to nip my revolt in the bud. "Every Saturday morning for the next couple of months, you and I will drive to Milton. There you'll have a private lesson. Once the instructor is satisfied that you can save your life if you fall off a boat or something, the lessons stop." He paused. "We may have to give you refresher lessons every year or so, but that'll be the extent of the swimming you're going to do."

All I could say was: "Gee, Dad."

"Not that I expect you ever to have to use these lifesaving skills. I hope you'll be smart enough to stay out of small boats. But your mother and I will sleep better at night knowing that if you were stupid enough to fall into the water, you'd at least know enough to float until help came for you.''

They may have slept well that night. I sure didn't. Second grade, I told myself, better not be my greatest year or I'm in big trouble.

Chapter Seven

I knew I was in trouble when I first saw our third grade reading books. One glance through the text told me that the vocabulary was advanced far beyond my level.

"Isn't there some mistake, Mrs. Lewis?" I asked during recess period on the second day of school.

Florence Lewis' motto, repeated many times during the school year, was: "Look for the good, and love one another." Her hobby was collecting insects; she also had an impressive collection of shells and coins displayed in cases throughout the third-grade room. I liked to talk with her alone in a quiet moment. Face to face, just a few feet away, we were much more successful in communicating than we were during class.

"What do you mean, Frankie?"

"Aren't these fifth-grade readers or something?"

"Why, no, of course not."

"You mean, they can read this?"

"They? Oh, your classmates. Oh, yes, I'm quite sure. Don't you think you can?"

I shook my head slowly. I knew as I knew nothing else that there was just no way I was going to be able to handle these stories.

"Frankie, your question points to a real problem. The average child I teach in third grade has a vocabulary of some 30,000 words. That child will pick up thirty or thirty-five words a day, each and every day, seven days a week. Some of it will come in this classroom. To be honest, though, most of it won't. These kids will learn from listening to their parents at the dinner table, from watching television, and from talking with each other.

"Their hearing is always 'on.' They don't even have to pay attention, really."

I thought about something that had happened that morning. Mary Lou Nogel had been looking out the window when the teacher surprised her by calling upon her to answer a question she'd posed. I was awed when Mary Lou immediately answered it.

"I think I know what you mean," I said quietly.

"They could be tying a shoelace," she added, "or leafing through a book, or playing with a pencil. It doesn't much matter. If they hear what I say, they understand it. It's that way at the breakfast table, in front of the radio, and on the baseball field.

"What I'm saying is this: you're very likely far behind your classmates. I daresay your sister in second grade is probably ahead of you in many ways. Right?"

I shook my head vigorously, then nodded reluctantly.

"I'm willing to help. But you'll have to do your share."

I nodded. "But how?"

"By reading, Frankie."

"Reading?"

"Reading, reading, and reading some more. I don't know how much hearing you've got, but I don't think it's enough for you to be able to learn through your ears. You'll have to do it with your eyes. By reading you might be able to pick up those thirty-five or so words every day that you're going to need. Otherwise, you'll just fall further behind with every passing day. You don't want that, do you?"

I shook my head.

"I'm afraid, Mrs. Lewis."

"Don't be. Here's what I suggest. Why don't you borrow a book from our library every other day or so? Read it, bring it back, and borrow another one. The other kids won't be doing this. It might help you catch up with some of them."

So began my library career.

Mrs. Lewis was certainly right that the other kids weren't burying their noses in books as I was beginning to do. Again, it made me different. Just how different I wasn't long in discovering.

I was the only child in third grade who skipped recess to read a book. It was no big loss for me. The other kids played in groups of three or four; I was a group of one. I wasn't missing anything important on the playground. I was, I devoutly hoped, gaining something in the classroom.

One afternoon in late October, I checked out of the library a book I'd wanted to read for some time. *The FBI Story* interested me because of all the talk in school about communists. Stories about "Reds" were everywhere that year. The kids talked about it, comic books showed hero FBI agents beating suspected communists senseless, and teachers talked of J. Edgar Hoover in terms that were tinged with awe.

It was my dream that year to become an FBI agent when I grew up. I wanted to help Mr. Hoover save the country from dreaded communism.

As I turned into the alley on my way to Third Street, three boys emerged from the shadows.

"Stop right there, Bowe." I recognized Larry, one of the biggest fourth-grade students in the school. With him were two boys from my class.

"Huh? I'm going home."

"No, you're not. You're staying right here with us." Larry smirked knowingly at his two colleagues.

"What do you have there? A book? A real book? I ain't never seen none of those things before. Have you, Lar?"

"Nah," he answered. "Only bookworms got those things."

"Hey, Lar! This is *The FBI Story*. Bowe here wants to find out all about the FBI!"

"Why don't we teach him a thing or two," smiled Larry.

"Sure. Help his education."

"Yeah. Give him some real-life education about the tactics of the FBI."

I wanted to get out of there. "Look, guys. Please give me my book back."

"He says he wants his book."

"Yeah. Isn't that too bad?"

"Too bad, Bowe. Too bad." Larry threw my book down the alley.

"Want your book, kid?" he added. "There it is."

"Help yourself," John taunted.

I lunged for the book.

At that moment, all three of them jumped on me. Larry's companions grabbed me by the legs while he pushed my face into the gravel of the alley.

They lifted me to my knees. Larry let loose with a devastating right cross that buckled my body against my legs. One of his friends, I didn't know which, caught my back and pushed it up again. This time Larry used a left hook to send my sprawling against the fence that lined the alleyway.

I staggered home fifteen minutes later, my face bloody, and my right ear throbbing. My nose felt as if it had been squashed and stuffed with cabbage.

Two days later, it happened again. I didn't even know these two boys. But they sure had heard of me.

"Hey, Bowe!"

I turned to see two boys following me down the alley.

I started running as fast as I could. I was plenty fast, but they were faster.

When I picked myself up from the ground, the bigger of the two of them stabbed my chest with a forefinger.

"Heard about you today. Troublemaker, aren't you?"

"Huh? Who are you?"

"Never mind. Let me show you something."

He took out a comic book; one I'd never seen. The cover showed two scruffy-looking men holding jackknives at the throat of a man wearing a red jacket.

"Look at this, Bowe," the bigger boy told me. "This is what we do to troublemakers around here."

I felt sick to my stomach.

He flipped the pages to another picture. Both of them were wearing broad grins.

I was now shown a man brandishing a white-hot poker. Another man was cowering in the corner.

"That's what we're going to do to you if you don't stop making trouble."

"But I'm not making any trouble! What are you guys talking about?"

"You can go, Bowe," the bigger boy told me. "Just as soon as I show you one last picture. We want you to know what's in store for you, don't we?"

His friend nodded.

I found myself looking at a man strung up by his wrists to a tree, with a gang of other men standing around him, whips in their hands.

"We don't like your kind, Bowe."

The bigger boy closed the magazine.

"Go now. Just remember: next time we won't let you off so easy."

I was shaking. My skin felt clammy and cold. I could feel my heart beating a thousand times a minute.

I didn't budge an inch.

Finally, they laughed and walked back to the school yard.

I decided I'd better play at recess, just so I wouldn't look so different. The strategy didn't always work. I remember one surprisingly warm November morning when I walked to the playground for recess.

I found George and Jimmy playing catch at one end of the grounds.

Walking up to them, I asked: "Can I join you?"

George shook his head. "We don't want you, Bowe."

Jimmy shrugged.

I walked over to the swings, but they were all occupied. After a while, I gave up and returned to the classroom.

More often, I played alone on the swings or with some baseball cards.

I also stopped asking questions in class. I knew that if I spoke up, the whole class would know I hadn't understood a word all day. Instead, I waited until a break in activity, lunch, or after school to ask Mrs. Lewis to explain things I hadn't understood.

And I didn't take any books out of the library at school that year.

But I wasn't about to give up completely just because some boys at school didn't like me. I had enough sense to recognize that that would lead to certain failure.

So I went to the Himmelreich Memorial Library on Market Street after school every Friday. It was the beginning of a love affair that would continue for almost ten years. That library was my home away from home. From my first day there, the librarians welcomed me as though to a family.

"Oh, yes. You're Kitty's little boy. We all know her here. She's one of our most faithful customers. Of course, we'll give you a library card."

A minute later, I was the proud owner of a real library card.

"The card lets you check out any book here except the reference books. You can take out up to ten books at a time."

I felt as if I'd just been given the keys to the kingdom.

One of the books I found there was a Boy Scout handbook. My attention was drawn immediately to the section on communicating with deaf people.

There was a whole page of small drawings showing how the letters of the alphabet, and some numbers, could be made on the hands. The handbook explained that "sign language" was used by deaf people. With it, they could understand anything somebody said. Scouts were urged to learn to "talk with their hands" as a good deed.

I didn't care about the Scouts. But I did care, a whole lot, about why I'd never been told about sign language.

Here it is, I thought: the real keys to the kingdom.

I checked the book out and rushed home.

Mom was making pumpkin pie in the kitchen.

"Look at this, Mom! People can talk with their hands!"

I noticed her stiffen in front of the stove. She didn't turn around to face me.

"Hey, Mom!"

She didn't answer.

I tugged at her apron. "Mom? Did I do something wrong, Mom?" My ears felt hot.

Finally, she turned. Her small brown eyes were wet.

"No, honey. You didn't do anything wrong."

"Well, then. Come on! Look at this Boy Scout Handbook!"

She shook her head.

"Frankie, that's something you're going to have to discuss with your father. I don't want to hear another word about it until he gets home for supper."

I was baffled. Mom had never acted this way before.

It seemed an interminably long time before my father got home. I didn't understand what was wrong with sign language. Mom's reaction made me fearful of bringing the subject up at dinner.

Mom must have told Dad about my Handbook, because as soon as he stood up from the dinner table, he turned to me.

"Son, bring me that book." His face was fixed as if chiseled from stone.

I didn't want to give him the book.

What was going on around here?

Finally, with a sense of foreboding, I handed over the book.

After looking at it for a few moments, Dad said: "Come on, son. Let's go in the living room for a talk."

I glanced at Mom, saw nothing there, and followed him.

Dad turned on the floor lamps, sat down in his favorite seat on the couch, and sighed.

"Frankie, sit down."

I didn't.

"Frankie," he repeated. "I said, sit down."

I sat.

"O.K., Frankie. I knew this day was going to come. Since it's here, we have to deal with it."

I had no idea what he was talking about. All I had done was find some pictures in a library book. Why had my parents suddenly become so remote and cold?

"Frankie, every doctor your mother and I talked to, every last one of them, put the fear of God in our hearts when they talked about signing. If there's one thing I remember loud and clear from all those visits it is this: 'Don't let Frankie learn signs.' "

"But, Dad! Why?"

"Because if you learn to sign, you won't talk. You won't learn to lipread. You'll only be able to talk with those few people who know that hand language."

I couldn't believe what I was seeing on his lips.

"Frankie, we didn't bring you up to toss you into a ghetto."

"But, Dad!"

"That's the last word I'm going to say on this topic. I've told your mother not to talk about it either."

I felt cold, very cold.

"But, Dad! Listen, Dad! If I learn signs, I can understand everything I see. Don't you understand? It would be so easy. It would be—yeah, that's it—it would be like you hear everything so easy. I could see everything so easy too."

"I've told you before, and I'll tell you again. We've had to make a lot of hard choices in your life. A lot. But this is one thing everybody, and I mean everybody, warned us against. I don't know why, to tell you the truth, but they were so urgent in condemning signs that there must be a good reason, a damned good reason.

"If someone, even one person, had recommended that we teach you to sign, I might consider it. But, Frankie, no one did. No one!

"We were told, I can't think how many times, that our choice was this: either we bring you up in the hearing world, which happens to be our world, or we give you over to the deaf world. That means giving you up. You mean too much to us to do that.

"Besides, and I really believe this: the hard way is the best way. We've made our decision. We're going to bring you up the way we have been. After you're grown up, you can join the deaf world if you want. Not until then.

"Now that's all I'm going to say about this sign language business."

The next day, I took the Boy Scout Handbook back to the Himmelreich Library.

Every Saturday and Sunday that winter, Dad played tennis in the Bucknell gymnasium. Hank Peters, the college tennis coach, arranged for Dad, Donald Ross, Walt Thompson, and several other members of Dad's tennis group to use the basketball court when the university did not need it. They'd measure off a tennis-court sized area on the polished wood floor, set up a net, and enjoy two or three hours of fun and exercise.

Dad brought me with him most of those weekend mornings. I usually took a book with me because I felt guilty if I didn't spend my time learning the words I knew my classmates would be learning without even trying.

As conscious as I was about how difficult school was for me, I was keenly aware how lightly the men Dad played with seemed to treat work. It was as if nothing was particularly hard—or important—to them.

I remember one time Dad and I went to Donald Ross's photography store on Market Street. Don wasn't there, so someone else helped us get film for Dad's Polaroid.

"Dad," I asked as we got into the Buick. "Where's Don?"

He smiled. "Don's store is making money. He doesn't need it much. So he spends more time playing the stock market at the broker's across from the five-and-dime than he does working."

I noticed, too, how other men in the neighborhood never seemed to be as preoccupied with worries as I was. I looked in vain for even one man who seemed to be driven by ambition. Fathers seemed to have all the time in the world to play with their children, take the car out for a Sunday spin, and mow their lawns. Mothers thought nothing of going to the supermarket with their hair in curlers. They didn't seem worried about anything either.

As I got to know Dad's tennis partners better, I noticed that none of them talked about wanting a promotion. I knew from Dad that Walt Thompson was an insurance agent, yet I didn't once notice him talking about insurance with the tennis group.

It was all very strange. These people had nothing wrong with them. They could do anything they wanted to. Why, then, did they seem so content, so complacent, so comfortable? I thought back to Mom's comments about Tom Roth. Were these people like Roth? Were they just satisfied with life as they lived it, more interested in enjoying themselves than in getting ahead?

I noticed some of the same things about other people in Lewisburg. No one seemed to work too hard. Yet most had nice homes, one or two cars, television sets. They had enough money, it seemed, to buy whatever they wanted. None seemed worried about losing a job; all that year, I didn't once hear anyone talk about someone in Lewisburg getting fired or laid off from work.

None of us thought twice about walking right into someone else's house; doors were never locked. Friends from Milton and Sunbury would barge right into our house, shouting from the living room: "Anybody home?" And there was little sense of privacy. When Robin had a coughing spell in front of the Crayton's house one afternoon, Mrs. Crayton came over the same evening to ask if there were anything she could do.

I contrasted all of this to my own experience. I knew, now, that I was different. I wondered, urgently, whether my life would ever have the carefree quality I saw all around me. Or would I always lug a book to the gym, uncomfortable about "wasting" several hours doing nothing particularly important?

Would I always be different?

Figuring out the way normal people lived was almost a full-time occupation. It seemed important to me to understand how they did things and why they did them that way. Of all the dazzling differences between my life and theirs, none was so painful as the divergence between my social life and Robin's.

Almost every day, Robin would be invited to do something with her friends; she spent more time playing in her girlfriends' homes than she did in our house.

I was acutely sensitive to the fact that I never got those kinds of invitations.

Beth, Joyce, and a half-dozen other girls would breeze into the living room and call out for Robin.

Beth and Joyce always said, "Hi!" to me before going to play with Robin. Some of the other girls didn't.

I remember countless afternoons I spent reading a book in the stuffed armchair in the living room while Robin spent hour after hour playing with her girlfriends upstairs. I would still be in the chair when they would sail down the stairs, gaily making plans for the morrow.

After a while, I couldn't take it any more. I started reading in my room, coming down only for a drink or some cake.

Mom and Dad knew I was uncomfortable.

"Why don't you come down?" they asked one afternoon, coming into my room.

"I'm O.K., Mom. It's all right."

"But, honey, you don't have to spend all your time cooped up in your room."

I didn't say anything.

"Frankie," my father said, sitting on the edge of the bed across from my chair. "Are you worried about being different?"

I looked at Mom. "You aren't mad at me?"

Dad shook his head. "No, of course not. But, son, this is important." He paused, collecting his thoughts. "Frankie, has it ever occurred to you that they are the ones who are different? Not you?"

"Huh? How can that be? They're all normal. I'm the black bear around here."

Mom patted my hands. "Black sheep, honey. And no, you're not."

Dad nodded. "Your mother's right."

Mom kneeled at my side. "Frankie, I know you're unhappy right now. Believe me, I suffer with you every minute you go through this agony."

"But it is important, terribly important, that you realize one thing. Someday, when you've won at this crazy game we call life, you're going to feel pretty super, aren't you?"

I nodded. "If I win, Mom. If."

"Well, yes. 'If' is a big word. But you think you will, don't you?"

I nodded.

"If you don't son," Dad interrupted, "you might as well give up now."

"You will win, honey," Mom continued. "Your father and I believe that with all our hearts. But let me tell you what I came up here to tell you. When you win, you'll have every right in the world to be the proudest boy, the proudest man, on the face of this earth. For you'll have done what they all said was impossible.

"Just think how wonderful that's going to feel."

Dad chimed in: "Mom's right, son. As for Robin, Beth, and the rest of them, much as we love Robin and like Beth, their victory will be much smaller because they started so far ahead of you. If they do the things you will do, they're only doing what is expected. There's nothing particularly remarkable in this day and age for a boy or girl to graduate from high school. It's done all the time.

"For you, though. Just think how you're going to feel when you graduate."

Mom stood up. "My professors at Bucknell called it deferred gratification. You put off your happiness in order to make it greater later on."

Dad walked over to pull me to my feet.

"Now, let's go downstairs and join the world, Frankie. You have nothing to be ashamed of—and a great deal to be proud of."

Their little chat cheered me greatly. I remembered their words time and again when my problems seemed too great for me to cope with and when my hopes sank in the face of evidence that I had a long, long way to go.

On some magnificent day, I knew, I'd throw up my hands in laughter and shout: "I did it!"

One Monday morning, as I walked up the steps to the school building behind two of my classmates, Kenny Blair, a guy I liked a lot, turned and said to me: "You, freak!"

"No, I'm Frank," I responded before I could react to what he was saying.

They laughed and ran into the building.

It wasn't until I got home that afternoon that I learned what the word "freak" meant. I immediately ran to my room and slammed the door shut.

When Dad came home that evening, he found me there.

"I don't care what you say, Daddy. You can spank me if you want. But I'm not going to school any more."

To my surprise, Dad didn't argue.

"O.K., son. If that's the way you want it."

"That's the way I want it!"

He turned to leave the room.

"Uh, Dad," I called. "What will happen to me if I don't go to school?"

"Think hard, Frankie. What do you think will happen?"

"Well, I'll fall behind."

"That's true."

"And I guess I won't get into fourth grade."

"That's true, too."

"But, Dad, even my friends are turning against me. If Danny called me a bad name, I wouldn't be so upset. But why was Kenny so mean?"

He sat on the bed.

"Well, Frankie. Children can be pretty cruel sometimes. Are you sure he's your friend?"

I nodded.

"Well, all I can say is what I'd do if it were me they were teasing."

I smiled for the first time that evening. "Tell me!"

"I'd beat them up until they said 'Uncle'!"

"Uncle?"

"I mean, until they took the word back."

I laughed.

"Why don't you try that tomorrow?"

I shook my head. "I can't. He's bigger than I am."

"Well, son, we'll have to do something about that, won't we?"

"What?" I couldn't think of any way to grow up real fast.

"Tonight, I'll make some phone calls. If you promise to go to school tomorrow, I may have a surprise for you when you get home."

I couldn't wait to get home the next afternoon. Mom didn't say much as I watched "The Mickey Mouse Club," waiting for Dad to come home. Whatever it was that my father had in mind, I didn't think Mom was going to like it.

When Dad arrived, it was with a huge boxing mask and four gloves.

"I've arranged for a student at Susquehanna University down the river to come up every week to teach you how to box."

"Wow, Dad!"

"Wow, what?"

"Just wow!"

My training started that Saturday morning. First, we ran a mile around the campus. Then I learned how to put on the gloves and the mask. I felt a lot braver with the mask on my head and two big gloves on my hands, but progress was painfully slow.

First, I learned a left jab. Then it was a right cross. With a small boxing bag Dad installed on the back porch, I practiced my new moves. I also spent hours in front of the mirror in my room, jabbing until my arm felt as if it would fall off. After I got the fundamentals down fairly well, I learned defense, starting with how to block a jab by feinting with my head and countering with a jab of my own.

Pete Walters soon was brought into the Bowe training camp. Tough as he was, Pete was a little smaller than me. I felt supremely confident as we held our first sparring match.

I lasted five minutes.

"Stop it, Dad!" I yelled.

That was when I learned the importance of confidence.

The three of us sat at the back porch table. "Frankie," Dad lectured, "Pete won because he wasn't afraid of you."

I nodded.

"You lost because you chickened out."

I nodded again.

"You have to be confident, Frankie. You have to believe in yourself. Otherwise, you'll never win, not at boxing and not at life."

"Come on, Frankie," Pete said. "Let's play ball across the street."

After we'd played ourselves out, I decided to confide in Pete. He was the most physical of my few friends, and I knew that the kids in school were afraid of him.

Thank God, Pete rallied to the cause.

"Anytime somebody picks on you," he said after I'd outlined the situation, "you just tell me. I'll see that they don't do it again."

His promise was the only thing that kept me from quitting school at that very moment.

The pressure of keeping up in school, the daily reminders of how popular everybody else was, and the difficulty of lipreading people other than those I knew very well combined to turn me into something of a recluse.

I slept late in the mornings. I was slow dressing for school. On Saturdays and Sundays, I sometimes slept to one in the afternoon. There didn't seem to be any especially good reason to get up.

I spent the dinner hour with a book at my side, not looking up more than once or twice during the entire meal. Right after supper, I'd head upstairs for a long, hot bath. Soaking in the tub, I'd read my latest book.

I especially liked novels. They served two important purposes. First, they were easy to read. The vocabulary of the average novel was, I found, much lower than that of the average nonfiction text. Second, they satisfied a desperate need of mine: to find out what people say when they talk to each other.

My lipreading talents were restricted to comprehending the utterances of people I knew well, who were standing in good light, facing me directly. As soon as a third person entered the conversation, I almost invariably got lost. And what they said to each other, as opposed to me, I just about never knew.

One question that never got answered in any of these novels was: Why do people talk about the weather?

I popped the question to Mom one morning over breakfast.

"Because, honey," she said, "it's something to talk about."

"Yeah. But, look. You can't do anything about the weather. I can't do anything about the weather. It is what it is. So what's the point in talking about it?"

"Frankie, sometimes people choose a subject that is a safe one."

"Safe?"

"Safe. Noncontroversial. I know if I ask you about the weather, you won't mind. It's not a personal question. It's not like asking what your opinion is about, oh, Richard Nixon. It's a good, safe topic of conversation. That's why people talk about it."

"But, Mom, isn't the purpose of conversation to communicate?"

"Yes, honey, of course. But there are ways of communicating besides words."

"Huh?"

"Let's say you and I had just met. I hope we become friends. I want to be sure I don't offend you or upset you with anything I say. Now, since I don't know you, I don't know what topics to avoid with you. You might be a Democrat, in which case talking about Nixon's virtues wouldn't be a good idea. You might be a Catholic, in which case discussing the world population problem wouldn't be smart. So I choose a perfectly harmless little topic like the weather. With me so far?"

I nodded.

"Later, when we get to know each other, I'll know what I can say to you without giving offense. But until I do, it's smart for me to stick to subjects like the weather."

"Gee, Mom. I never knew there was so much to talking to people."

She laughed. "Well, no wonder. You hear so little conversation."

I thought about that for a few moments.

"Mom, how do I sound when I talk to people?"

She responded right away. "You sound just fine, honey."

"Do I pronounce words right?"

"Oh, yes. Dad and I are really proud of that. Haven't you noticed it yourself?"

I shook my head. Speech was something I'd not given any thought to until just then.

"Here's what you do. You read something in a book, a magazine, or a newspaper. Occasionally, you lipread it on someone's lips, but not often. For some reason, it's very hard for you to lipread words you don't know. Anyway, it's mostly through reading that you encounter a new word. A little later, you use it in conversation."

She laughed.

"Sometimes, you get it right. English does, every now and then, follow its own rules of pronunciation. Often you don't, though. You say the word in a sentence, and it takes Dad and me a moment to know what you've said. Once we understand you, we tell you the correct pronunciation.

"I'm really pleased with how well you've handled this. We only have to tell you once."

I smiled. Speech was turning into an interesting topic.

"Hey, Mom. I remember one time I walked into the kitchen and said: 'What does eta-kwette mean?' You told me to get the *Daily Item* newspaper for you. I thought you were ignoring me until you pointed to that newspaper cartoon called 'Etta Kett,' you know, the one about the teen-aged girl. You told me to say the name of the comic strip. I did and you said: 'Frankie, that's how *etiquette* is pronounced.' "

She laughed at the memory. "That's how it's been ever since you were three years old."

"You mean my speech is normal?"

She smiled. "It's very good, it really is, Frankie, for someone who hasn't heard his own voice since he was a toddler. You know yourself that people understand you when you talk.

"Those 'W's,' for Weak, and 'I's,' for Improving, that you keep getting from your teachers when they grade you on speaking clearly and distinctly show that you still have a way to go. But even they don't strain and struggle to catch your words. How do you feel about it?"

I grinned.

"Good, Mom. It's nice knowing that there is one thing I do pretty well."

In Little League that summer, I was graduated from third-string right fielder to second-string second baseman. Pete made our squad and became

B&B's first baseman, a slot he held for the remaining years I spent in Little League. We were becoming real friends, not just friends of convenience. Pete and I spent hours together on the tennis courts across the street, on the baseball diamond, and in each other's rooms.

Pretty soon I noticed that I almost never played in our B&B league games. Even newcomers like Pete played at least three times as much as I did.

My father noticed it, too.

He came with me one afternoon for practice, talked with the team's coach for a few minutes, then watched our practice session from the stands.

Riding home with him that evening, I noticed he was being awfully quiet.

"Hey, Dad," I asked. "Did you find out why I never play any more?"

My father nodded, but said nothing.

I waited for my answer. With my father, you always got an answer; not that you always liked it, but you were guaranteed to get an honest answer if you would just wait for it.

"Frankie," he said eventually, "your coach is afraid of playing you. He thinks you will get hurt, and it will be his responsibility."

I pulled both feet up on the seat. "That's not true! I won't get hurt any more than anybody else!"

He nodded.

"Dad, does this mean I'm not going to play?"

Dad raised his bushy eyebrows in a gesture of futility.

"I can't force him to play you, Frankie. He's the coach."

"Goodbye, summer," I mumbled.

My father didn't say anything.

Later that summer, Pete led me down Brown Street to what we called "Fraternity Row," a set of Bucknell frat houses. It was a fairly cool, overcast day.

"Shhh!" he whispered as we walked to the rear door of one of the houses.

"What are you doing, Pete?"

"Quiet! I think they're all gone for vacation. We're going to have some fun."

For the next two hours, I felt just like the Hardy Boys. We had a deliciously dangerous time exploring the darkened rooms of the frat house. I felt a sharpening of my senses of touch and sight as I tiptoed from room to room, opening drawers in search of hidden treasures.

Pete and I emerged triumphant just before sundown, with a fistful of pencils, a pocket brimming with paper clips, and three whole pads of yellow writing paper.

"Do you really think we should?" I asked Pete, having a sudden attack of conscience.

"Sure! It's their fault if they left the door unlocked."

That was good enough for me. We fled.

Twenty minutes later, I was cowering behind the window in my room, certain the Lewisburg police would be pulling up any second now, sirens going full blast, to arrest me for larceny and worse.

In another fifteen minutes, I convinced myself that I'd be in much better shape if Mom and Dad were on my side when the cops arrived.

Within the hour, I'd confessed the whole shameful deed to my parents.

"It's wrong to steal," Dad reminded me.

I returned the pilfered merchandise and ran home as fast as humanly possible.

"You know, Mom," I told her at dinner that night. "Crime really doesn't pay."

"That's right, dear," she said, smiling.

"Because," I finished, "you're so scared about being found out that you don't ever dare use your stolen stuff!"

One afternoon, Danny Weller, the local tough, accosted me as I walked to baseball practice.

"I hear you're a freak," he sneered.

"Look, Danny. Who cares whether I'm a freak or not? What did I ever do to you?"

"That doesn't matter, freak. What matters is what I'm going to do to you!"

I searched everywhere for Pete, but he was nowhere to be found.

"Come on, Danny," I pleaded.

"Oh, I'm coming all right!" And he did.

Half an hour later, I dragged myself home. My right ear was bleeding, I had two bloody nostrils, and my right cheek featured a shiner. My arms didn't feel too good, either.

"Oh, Frankie! What happened to you!" Mom shrieked when I walked into the house.

"What didn't happen to me?" I bawled. "Everything happened to me!"

That night, my father hit the table so hard every dish on it jumped four inches.

"Dammit, nobody's going to push my son around like that!"

"Pushing wasn't all he did," I said, egging him on.

"You know what I mean. Now, we're going to have to think of some way to deal with Danny."

"You do it," I suggested.

"I know!" Dad shouted. His face took on a look I didn't recognize.

"What?"

"We'll invite Danny here tomorrow."

"You're crazy, Dad!" My father just smiled. In desperation I turned to my mother. "Mom, isn't he crazy?"

"Just leave it to me, son," Dad told me.

No matter how hard I tried, I couldn't get another word out of my father that night.

For some reason, I never did find out why, Danny Weller agreed to come to our house the next afternoon.

Dad took him out to the back porch without a word. Putting boxing gloves on both of us, he led us into the back yard.

"Now, Danny," he began. "I know what you did to Frankie the other day."

"Me? I didn't do anything!"

"Don't argue with me, Danny. Now, here's what we'll do. I'm going into the house for a drink. No matter how much screaming I hear out here, I'm not coming back until I finish that drink."

I felt like running away from home. How could my father do this to me?

"By the way, Danny," Dad continued. "I believe in fair fights. I want to be as fair with you as I can. So does Frankie."

He paused dramatically. Both of us were watching his every move.

"It's only fair that you know this before Frankie gives you a beating you'll never forget."

I gasped.

"Danny, Frankie's been taking private boxing lessons from an expert at Susquehanna University. Well, forewarned is forearmed. I'm going for my drink now."

Danny looked at his gloves and at mine.

"Mr. Bowe," he said.

"Yes, Danny?"

"Take these. I, uh, don't want to."

With that, he ran around the house and was gone.

I let out a war whoop.

"Son," Dad said, resting his hand on my shoulder. "Son, sometimes if you can't beat 'em with your hands, you gotta beat 'em with your brains.

"Now I am going to have that drink."

Chapter
Eight

One late August Saturday, Dad drove me to Baltimore to watch the Yankees play the Orioles. The Yankees were close to clinching the American League pennant by that time, but I found this insufficient reason to explain the casual indifference I sensed on the field. Yogi Berra, normally their catcher, played first base that day. My idol Mickey Mantle joked easily with the Oriole catcher each time he came to the plate. The other Yankees seemed equally relaxed. Still, they won.

It was a powerful and long-lasting memory I carried back to Lewisburg: these men were so incredibly talented that they could win without really trying.

I got the same impression on another trip we took before school started that fall. This one was to Spring Lake, New Jersey, to the Bathing and Tennis Club at which Dad had spent his summers as a youth. My father was still a top player, but Maureen "Little Mo" Connolly, the club pro and former world champion, handled him with ease.

I marveled less at their shot-making than at the easygoing camaraderie I saw on the court. Little Mo did not appear to be concentrating on the match at all; rather, the attitude she conveyed was one of playfulness more suited, I thought, to an informal practice session than to a performance before hundreds of spectators.

It was all very confusing to me. As a nine-year-old, I associated excellence with grim determination, not with easy nonchalance.

"That's what it means to be a pro," Dad informed me when I asked about this apparent contradiction. "A pro makes it look easy. What you didn't see out there, and you didn't see in Baltimore either, is the long grueling hours of practice that were necessary to produce that level of excellence."

I thought that over for a while.

"Dad," I asked over supper, "does what you said about being a pro mean that someday it will be easy for me, too?"

He faked a right to the chin. "Right, my boy. You sure are right. Someday, you'll pick up a book and breeze right through it. Someday, you'll toy with people on the tennis court, dazzling them with your artistry, and all without breaking a sweat.

"It's the getting to that point that's tough. That's why I keep telling you that all the effort you put into it now will be worthwhile."

He paused. "I remember when I was fifteen or sixteen. All the boys around me were piling into jalopies and bombing all over town. But I knew that if I didn't practice my tennis, somebody somewhere would be practicing. And when the two of us met on a tennis court, he'd win.

"When I thought of it that way, it didn't seem so much of a sacrifice. Eventually, the game became easy for me, and I became a champion.

"In fact, right here in Spring Lake, at the Monmouth Hotel, I was club pro before I was out of my teens. I played with Bill Tilden, Don Budge, and George Lott. My worst defeat, I remember, was by Don McNeal, national champion in 1937. He really taught me quite a lesson.

"To play on that level, you have to work very hard. The same thing is true in life."

Dad reached for my hand. "I have the feeling that someday you're going to know what I'm talking about from your own first-hand experience."

Dad's words gave me a boost that carried me well into fourth grade.

A few days before school was to start, the local paper carried a front-page picture of Pete Walters staring gloomily at a desk. He sure didn't look as if he wanted school to start. I took him a copy of the paper, with a note attached: "Pete, I know how you feel!"

My most vivid memories of the year with Sara Eyer are of my struggles with the reading she assigned us every evening.

If anyone had asked me that fall to define "hell," I would have replied unhesitatingly that it consisted of assigned reading. My personal Hades on earth was a set of story books about some mythical family, the adventures of which I have mercifully forgotten. Five nights a week all through fourth grade I had to read about this miserable family and answer a dozen or two dozen questions about them.

The ordeal was so troubling for me that Mom and Dad cleared out part of the living room area to create a study corner for me to use.

Every night after dinner, I placed the story book, a writing pad, and a dictionary on the desk, turned on the desk lamp, and started the dreary assignment. Three hours of sheer agony followed. I was lucky if I finished one paragraph without reaching for the dictionary. More often, I'd need it three or four times for each paragraph, a dozen times or more per page.

Not that the dictionary was much help; the synonyms and antonyms it offered looked as strange to me as did the words I was looking up.

One evening during the third week of school, Mom sat at my side as I tackled the assignment. I knew that she wanted to help me. I knew, too, that for her the reading would be as easy as glancing over a newspaper story.

But this was my assignment.

The first new word I encountered that night was "consume." I reached for the dictionary. This seven-letter word, the dictionary advised me, meant "squander, as of money or time." A second meaning offered was "engross or absorb—*v.i.*" A third was "waste or destroy."

The only synonyms I recognized were the last two. The problem was that these two words, "waste," and "destroy," meant two different things, neither of which seemed right for the context in which the word appeared in my story. So I turned to the dictionary again, this time in search of the meaning of the word "squander."

That eight-letter word, I learned, meant "spend wastefully, *v.t.:* prodigiality, *n.* wasteful expenditure."

So far, so good, I thought; "consume" meant "waste." But "waste" didn't look any more appropriate in the sentence now than it did the first time I tried it there. So I looked to the dictionary once again, this time searching for a definition for the word "engross."

I found four definitions for this seven-letter word: "absorb," "occupy completely," "copy legibly in a large hand," and "monopolize [goods in the market]."

"Absorb" I already had from the definition of "consume." I was going around in circles: "absorb" meant "absorb."

I looked over at Mom. Sitting on the edge of her chair, one hand under her chin, she seemed about to interrupt me but apparently thought better of it and said nothing.

In desperation, I turned to "copy legibly." Now, where had this come from? Oh, yes, from the definition for "engross." But how could "absorb," a synonym for "engross," mean "copy legibly"?

So I looked at the third definition: "monopolize." This ten-letter word, my dictionary enlightened me, meant "obtain a monopoly of." Now I was really going around in circles. A second meaning of "monopolize," I learned, was "assume exclusive possession or control of." This sent me to locate the meanings of "exclusive" and "possession."

By now, I'd expended fifteen precious minutes on one single word in one paragraph of a ten-page story.

Hopelessly confused, I copied down all the definitions I had found and tried each one in the sentence. None of them worked.

"Uh, Mom," I mumbled. "I'm not getting anywhere."

It was clear that she was as exasperated as I was.

"Try 'use-up,' honey."

"But, Mom, that's not anywhere in the definitions I found."

"Try it anyway, son."

I did—and it worked.

Five nights a week I endured this madness, determined not to call upon my mother for help more than twice in any evening.

What disturbed me most was the discovery that figuring out the meaning of a word in one context often didn't help me when I ran into the same word in another context. Eventually, I resigned myself to the fact that there was a reason the dictionary offered three or four different meanings for each word it listed.

Sometimes I stayed up until 11:30 at night with this stupid family; more often than not, I headed up for bed thoroughly discouraged, with much of the assignment undone.

The haggard look of despair on my face soon started arguments between Mom and Dad.

One evening I wandered to the front of the living room and collapsed on the couch.

"I can't do any more," I groaned.

My father refused to admit defeat. "Sure you can, Frankie. It'll get easier as you go along."

"Oh no, it won't!" I shouted. "I've looked ahead. It gets worse and worse."

"Take a break," Mom put in. "You'll feel better when you go back to it."

"What I need is a long, long break." I rubbed my eyes. "I've got a headache. I'll be right back. Gotta get some aspirin."

When I returned, Mom's eyes were wet, and Dad was staring at the TV with his face immobile.

I was startled. "What's wrong?" I asked, looking first to Mom and then to Dad.

"Nothing, honey," Mom assured me.

I knew she was lying.

"Dad! What's going on, Dad?"

"Son," he answered. "Your mother and I had a little argument. But it's over now."

I knew who had won that argument. In our house, my father always won.

"Mom, tell me. What was it about?"

"Oh, honey. I just want it to be easier for you."

"Frankie," my father said, rearranging the glasses on the coffee table. "Frankie," he repeated, "I know it's tough. But by going through this now, you'll be better prepared for fifth grade and then for high school."

I couldn't doubt the accuracy of his assessment.

"Your mother wanted to make it easier for you by helping you do these assignments," he went on. "She thought it would help you. I told her that wasn't the answer. If we give you too much help now, you won't be able to handle your work later on."

"It's O.K., honey," Mom patted my hands. "Why don't you go back to your reading?"

"You sure?" I asked her.

"Sure, I'm sure. Now, you better finish your assignment."

I went back to my desk. Half an hour later, though, I gave up the ghost and retired for the night.

The championship team: Coach Bowe is upper left, his pitcher lower right: "Wittes or no Wittes, I'm gonna strike him out!"

Doubles championship in Williamsport: Coach Bowe is upper right, his protege to his left: "One of these days, Dad!"

First date at Eagles Mere: "Hey, Dad, what do people say on dates?"

I arrived at school one morning to discover that South Ward had just engaged the services of an itinerant speech therapy teacher. Lois Garvin would be at our school one day each week. I was scheduled to see her for half an hour during study-hall period every time she came.

The first time I saw Mrs. Garvin, an unhappy looking woman in her thirties who had a streak of white running through the middle of her brushed back black hair, she gave me a list of about thirty words and told me to say each one out loud. I read them into the microphone of her tape recorder.

When I arrived for the next week's lesson, Mrs. Garvin informed me that my "S" and "R" sounds needed work.

I was delighted that only two letters out of twenty-six were less than adequate.

She then told me we would be working together on these two sounds for the next several months.

I'm sure Mrs. Garvin was a wonderful person. I'm sure, too, that her methods of helping children improve their speech were sound according to the state of the art at the time.

I also know that she'd probably never worked with a deaf child before.

Mrs. Garvin's approach was to have me read several dozen words into a tape recorder. The words were neatly typed on one side of a piece of paper. One row, I noticed, contained words that had the "R" sound at the beginning, middle, or end; the other row featured similarly placed "S" sounds.

I read the words.

Mrs. Garvin then rewound the tape.

"Frankie, now I want you to listen carefully. You'll hear that you are rolling your 'R's.' That's what we will have to work on first.

She played the tape. I took her word for it that I was rolling my "R's."

In our third session together, she played the rest of the tape to illustrate for me how I was mispronouncing the "S" sound.

I stopped her after fifteen minutes.

"Mrs. Garvin, I quit."

She stared at me.

I pulled myself to my full nine-year-old height of almost five feet.

"Mrs. Garvin, these words you want me to read don't make any sense to me. There's just a list of them. They don't tell a story or anything.

"And I'm sorry, but I can't understand a thing on those tapes."

She motioned for me to sit down, but I refused.

"Mrs. Garvin, if I could hear my 'S' and 'R' sounds, I wouldn't be making them wrong."

I turned around and walked out.

I never had another speech lesson in my life.

It wasn't long, though, before I found myself faced with another set of lessons.

My parents, bless them, shared the great American belief that being good parents meant providing your children with the benefit of "lessons."

The particular lessons they had arranged for me, however, didn't strike me as especially helpful for my development.

"Piano lessons!" I screamed when Mom broached the subject. "You've got to be crazy!"

I could see her fighting the urge to laugh. She succeeded. I found myself staring into the fixed smile of a very determined woman.

"Frankie, you're going to have a normal childhood. Robin has piano lessons. So you're going to have piano lessons."

After five lessons, I decided that being "normal" wasn't such a great goal after all.

I discovered the first advantage I'd ever experienced to being deaf: I didn't have to listen to myself play the piano.

I begged Mom to let me quit. It was like talking to a stone wall. After one particularly futile argument, I began to wonder who it was who was deaf in our house.

Dad was no help at all; the brother of a virtuoso concert pianist, he was hopelessly biased in favor of my continuing the lessons.

I used every argument at my command. Nothing was too remote to serve as a weapon in my battle against piano lessons.

"Dad! Look, Dad! Spring is coming. I've got to practice baseball or I'll flunk out of Little League this year! You don't want that, do you?"

He was unmoved. "There are six days a week to get ready for Little League. You can spare one for the piano."

"Mom! Hey, Mom! I'm falling behind on my reading assignments! If I could only do them on Tuesday afternoons instead of going to piano lessons, I'd catch up in no time at all."

"I'm sure you'll be fine, darling. It's only an hour a week."

One Tuesday, I hit upon what I was sure would be a winner.

"Hey, look, Mom! My battery is dead! I can't hear anything at all!"

She said exactly what I thought she'd say. "Let's get a new one so we can go to your piano lesson. It's getting late."

We walked up to my room together. Try as she might, Mom couldn't find any extra batteries.

"That's funny," she mumbled, shaking her head. "I could swear that I put a new box in your drawer just the other day."

I was all sympathy. "Gee, Mom. That's really too bad."

"Well, it's getting late. Hurry up and get your coat on."

"Huh? You mean we're going to piano lessons?"

"Of course, honey."

"But, Mom . . ."

"After I drop you off, I'll go to Rea & Derick's to get you a new box. Now let's go."

I had to admit defeat.

"Uh, Mom," I said, reaching into my dresser drawer. "Here are the batteries. I hid them."

My piano lessons didn't end until school closed for the summer.

I confided to my teacher that I couldn't wait for the lessons to end. To my surprise, she agreed with me right away.

"Huh? You mean you play baseball in the summer, too?"

"No, Frankie. But as soon as these lessons are finished, I'm not coming anywhere near a piano for three wonderful months!"

My desire to escape piano lessons didn't extend to other aspects of music. I still treasured the chances I got to learn new songs.

One afternoon in early spring, Robin sat with me for several hours, transcribing the words for a song popular that year: "Soldier Boy." Then she played it for me, her hands moving under the words, until I had memorized the song.

This was typical of Robin. If she saw that I had noticed her playing or singing a song, she volunteered to write it out for me. She never complained about the tedium she must have felt—or the time it took away from her social life.

I was deeply appreciative.

"Robin, you're a swell sister," I told her after we'd played "Soldier Boy" about fifteen times.

"You know, Robin. With all these birthday parties, pajama parties, and everything else you have, it really means a lot to me that you'll take an hour or two to help me out."

"Oh, don't mention it, Frankie."

"They must be a lot more fun than sitting like this writing words out for me."

"Oh, I don't mind, Frankie."

"You know, Robin, I often wish I could have a social life like yours. It must be exciting. I wish some of the guys would invite me to do things with them."

"Nah, it's not that much, Frankie. And only girls have parties."

I felt much better all of a sudden.

"Only girls?"

"Only girls."

Robin was a model of patience with me. There was one thing she did complain about, though.

Soon after I learned the words to "Soldier Boy," I sang it several times a day, usually in the evenings while doing my homework.

She walked into my room one morning.

"Frankie, what do you want for your birthday?"

I thought about it for a moment.

"How about some tennis balls, Robin?"

"Great! I'll get you some nice Wilsons!"

I smiled.

"There's just one thing, though, Frankie."

I waited.

"I want my birthday present now, even though my birthday doesn't come until next January. Will you be so kind? Let me have my present way ahead of time?

I was feeling generous. "Sure, Robin. No problem. What's the present?"

She looked at me with an expression of urgent earnestness on her face. "Don't sing."

In the days that followed my promise not to do any more Enrico Caruso imitations, I learned to my astonishment that hearing people can hear the most amazing things.

This discovery started when I walked down for breakfast one morning to find Mom scrambling some eggs for me.

"What took you so long, Frankie?" she asked.

"Oh, I was just thinking, Mom."

"I'm asking because I heard you pacing back and forth up there."

"You heard that?" I gasped.

"Oh, sure. I also heard you pour some water into a glass."

I stared at her. The enormity of what she'd just told me was too much for me to comprehend.

Another time, my parents were on the front porch when I walked into the kitchen. Within a few minutes, Mom breezed into the room, opened a cabinet, and brought out the peanut butter jar.

"Is this what you're looking for?"

"How did you know?" I asked when I recovered my powers of speech.

"Oh, I just heard you opening and closing the cabinet doors and figured you were hungry."

"You heard that from the front porch!?"

"Well, yes, Frankie. Ears work like that."

She returned to the front porch.

I decided to test this phenomenal ability of theirs.

Picking up the tea pot, I filled it with water. I turned on the gas under the right rear burner and waited until the water started to boil.

I knew it was boiling, because I could see the steam emerging from the spout.

Holding my peanut butter and jelly sandwich on a plate, I walked casually onto the front porch.

"Well?" I asked. "What was I doing back there?"

Dad looked over at me.

"Son, I think you're a little young to start drinking coffee."

"Is there *nothing* you people can't hear?" I demanded.

Dad found me reading in my room one Saturday afternoon in mid-March.

"Good news, son! I've been meeting with the men who run Lewisburg Little League. They're planning this year's season."

I put the book down.

"Remember last year you hardly ever played? Well, you weren't the only one. Lots of boys went to all the practices, suited up for all the games, and almost never got to see any action. I can understand that on the professional level, but for eight- to twelve-year-olds it doesn't make much sense.

"This morning, I rammed through a new rule. Starting this year, every boy has to play at least one inning in every game."

"Whoopee, Dad! That's great!" I shouted, hugging him. Now that I knew I'd play at least a little, I started looking forward to Little League again.

As it turned out, I didn't need the rule.

That summer I made first-string third baseman.

In the third inning of our first game, all three batters hit ground balls straight at me. I retired all of them with pinpoint throws to first.

In the fourth, on my second trip to the plate, I hit a fast ball 300 feet deep into center field. As I rounded first base and headed for second, the center fielder leaned way over the fence and grabbed the fly.

I returned to the dugout, but with an elation that took a week to wear off.

I didn't hit another ball that far for the rest of the season, but I did turn in a respectable performance at third base. It was good enough to warrant proud smiles from Dad as he took me to Tastee-Freez for milk shakes after each game.

And I became friends with Mike Burgee, our catcher. Mike lived next door to Kenny Blair, another guy I liked. We spent a lot of time together that summer, piecing together gigantic picture puzzles and going to the Bucknell campus to watch the college baseball team.

One day as we were tackling one particularly massive puzzle, Mike told me his cat was about to give birth to a litter of kittens, and one of the kittens would be mine if I wanted it. When the litter was born, Mike selected the whitest of them all, named it Whitey Ford, and then declared that I could pick one of the remaining kittens.

It chose me. Yogi Berra climbed up my arm as we sat watching the litter, settled herself at the back of my neck, and promptly went to sleep.

My neck got awfully stiff that afternoon, but it was worth it.

When it was time to bring Yogi home, my mother was at Geisinger Medical Center recovering from a minor operation. So I sent her a letter, addressing it with the nickname I thought Dad used for Mom:

"Dear Sistikins:

"May I please get Yogi this Wednesday when the Burgee's come home? Send back anser: [ ] Yes [ ] No.

"I have been doing crazy things since you Left. Like playing tenis last night. Well. I have to say Good-by to you now—Because we are going up town to mail you.

"But just rember. I love you. Frankie."

When I took Yogi Berra home a few days later, she was already a friend, but Golly didn't like this new intruder.

I delighted in the feeling that someone was jealous of my friendship. They were only a dog and a cat, but I didn't care.

Yogi Berra turned into a remarkable cat. If Golly or one of Pete Walters' dogs chased her, she would stop in her tracks, bare her teeth, and raise her paw with a sharp nail extended. That would make the dog limp away, tail between his legs. Then Yogi would start washing herself, completely at peace with the world. Yogi was my friend all through elementary and high school. When she finally died, I didn't have the heart to replace her. There could only be one Yogi.

In fifth grade, my class moved to the North Ward school building at the other end of town. There we joined with the fifth grade students from that school to form an enlarged class body. It was a year made remarkable by Becky Hinish and Sputnik.

Becky came into my life just as I finished reading *Tom Sawyer*. The daughter of a local clothier, whose store on Market Street featured the best men's fashions in the area, Becky was tall, thin, and very smart. I worshiped her from afar and daydreamed about saving her from some cave somewhere much as Tom had saved Becky.

I don't know if Becky noticed my existence. If she didn't, it was hardly her fault; I didn't say more than a word or two to her all year long.

One Friday in October, an announcement over the school intercom system stopped all activity. I didn't learn why until the next afternoon when I read the Saturday edition of the *Daily Item*. I knew right away that I was in deep trouble.

This particular catastrophe took the form of a sphere the size of a beachball that circled the earth once every 96.2 minutes. The beeping ball was the Soviet Union's "Sputnik." I learned that it had been launched the day before, October 4, 1957, and represented a "grave challenge to America's leadership." There was, the papers reported over the next several days, a "missile gap" of serious proportions. Then, a week after the original launch, the Soviets put Sputnik II into space.

The *Daily Item* story about the second beeping ball ruined my year.

"Oh, no!" I gasped.

"What's wrong, honey?" Mom asked, reasonably enough. We were sitting on the back porch.

I told her. "There's a story here that has interviews with school leaders from the area. They agree on one thing: the schools have failed. One of them is quoted as saying that Lewisburg is going to have to improve very fast to catch up with the Soviets."

"Well, good," Mom said, missing my point altogether. "That means your education will be better."

"But, Mom! You don't understand! It's already so hard I can barely keep up. Here they are saying school will be twice as rigorous, whatever that means, as it is now. Twice! Can you imagine!"

"I'm sure it will be O.K.," Mom said. Ever the peacemaker, she usually used that response for any situation she wasn't in a position to change.

"Oh, I wish I'd never heard of Sputnik," I groaned.

Reading further, I learned that the Lewisburg public schools planned to stress mathematics and science more than ever in the years to come. The news deepened my gloom; I didn't feel very confident in either subject. The paper's lead editorial argued the merits of a twelve-month school year. And then came the kicker: there'd be a special emphasis upon foreign languages.

I had so much trouble with English that the thought of having to learn another language as well filled me with a nameless dread.

I had less than two years of a reasonable pace of life remaining before I had to face all these projected changes in junior high school.

It came as no surprise after the Davy Crockett craze of a few years back that the stores that Christmas were filled with space toys. But at least one Lewisburger didn't want any.

The Sputnik story didn't ruin my appetite for the news, though. I had discovered with delight in the middle of fourth grade that being deaf didn't matter at all to me while I was reading, as long as I knew enough words to understand the newspaper stories. All winter and spring, I had devoured every word of the *Daily Item*.

Much in the news those days was the recession of 1956. I also learned about the uprising in Hungary, and about America's helplessness in the face of the Soviet Union's brutal suppression of that revolt. I read the serialized "I Led Three Lives" by Herbert Philbrick, about a man who had been an FBI informer while serving as a member of the Communist Party. I read the comics, the advice columns, and the features. One I remember dealt with a question much on the minds of Americans that year: What to do if an atomic bomb were dropped and your neighbors wanted to get into your bomb shelter but you only had enough food for your own family. I read about the Cincinnati Reds changing their name temporarily in response to growing anxieties in the Midwest about communism. And I learned something about what America was watching on television. "Good night, Chet" and "Good night, David" were said to be among the country's dearest expressions.

There was a lot of local news, too. I learned that milk was the number-one product of the local farms, bringing in some $2.3 million in sales for 1957. Unemployment in the area hit an all-time high that year, with 394 people jobless, a statistic so alarming in Lewisburg that it rated a front-page story. The marriage-divorce rate, I learned, was 10 to 1.

I knew by this time that the Lewisburg area was overwhelmingly Republican, so I wasn't surprised to read articles about the GOP candidates for various offices with nary a mention of Democratic candidates. In fact, some Republicans ran unopposed, something not too surprising when one realized, as the *Union County Standard Journal* reported, that in the 1956 elections only one Democrat had won any local or county office at all, and that in a major upset.

All through sixth grade, I did a great deal of reading.

Reading was becoming a pleasure. As long as I didn't have to understand every word and answer a dozen questions about what I was reading, it was an activity well suited to my limitations. I didn't have to ask anyone to explain what I couldn't lipread. And reading relieved me of the necessity to act as if I were enjoying myself as a member of a group.

I settled down on the back porch for supper each evening with the newspaper or a book at my side. I seldom said more than a dozen words to anyone throughout dinner.

After supper, I retired to my room to read some more.

I continued to favor novels because there, and only there, I learned what people said to each other, how they talked, and what expressions they used.

I must have read three dozen novels that fall and winter, hungrily absorbing all I could about the behavior of those mysterious people whose ears did more than hold up their glasses.

Mrs. Sauvain, our sixth-grade teacher, was warm, pleasingly plump, and perpetually optimistic. I needed all the cheer she could give me because all through sixth grade I worried about what I would face in seventh grade.

Every story I heard about junior high school seemed to make it more awesome. Instead of one teacher, the kids had at least six. Six different teachers, all with their own particular speaking styles!

My twelfth birthday that March 29 was a special one.

Dad assembled some of the guys from the B&B baseball team for a "baseball party." After the game, we all went to the local movie theatre.

As soon as everyone was seated, Dad took me out, and we joined Mom and Robin in the new Buick.

I was on cloud nine; this was going to be my last day as a deaf person, for we were going to a "faith healer." This amazing person was going to do something called "laying on of the hands." And I would walk away able to hear just as well as Robin could. That was something I'd eagerly awaited for nine years.

As we entered the small rural church building where the service would be held, I told myself that from this day on I'd be a normal, average, everyday 12-year-old. Nothing could come closer to heaven on earth.

Mom had been very excited all week.

She started by reading me excerpts from Emily Gardiner Neale's *A Reporter Finds God Through Spiritual Healing*.

Next came interminable lectures about my behavior.

"Frankie," she intoned, her face looking very serious and very happy at one and the same time, "You've got to be good. I know you're frustrated and anxious, but you've got to put all that out of your heart. If your heart is filled with bitterness and hatred, there won't be any room in there for God to come in and heal you."

I was bewildered. "But Mom, I *am* good."

She shook her head slowly. "I know you are, most of the time. But sometimes, you know, you hit a smaller child on the head. Sometimes you lash out at people. Just the other day you hurt me very badly with something you said. Now I know it was your idea of humor, and that you were thinking about my knowledge of English and about my weight problems, but it's not nice to tell your own mother that she reminds you of an unabridged dictionary in more ways than one."

I sighed.

"Frankie, I know all you're doing is acting out your own sense of frustration. I don't blame you; I really don't. But now that we're going to see Canon Best, it's important that you open your heart wide for God to come in and heal you. You want to be healed, don't you?"

I nodded.

"Well, you can be, and you will be. Just give God plenty of room to come into your heart and make you well."

My father came in and sat down beside me.

"Frankie," he told me, his hands on my lap. "we're going to try this. Your mother believes it will help you. Frankly, I have my doubts. I think that if God wants to cure your ears, He'll do so, without any magic ceremonies or laying on of hands or special waters. But Mom may be right, and I don't see how it could hurt. So we'll just have to see."

Canon Best was magnetic, a persuasive and absolutely confident personality.

116

"Frankie," he began. "Repeat after me: 'God can do anything.' "

"God can do anything."

"He can heal my ears."

"He can heal my ears."

"Because God loves me."

"Because God loves me."

"Now, Frankie. Water is a symbol of life. I'm going to sprinkle water on your ears. Then I'm going to hold your head in my hands and call upon the Lord to heal your ears."

I bowed my head.

Ten minutes later it was over.

On the way home, I turned down the volume of my aid as an indication of my faith that God would restore my hearing.

There was just one problem: the laying on of hands didn't work.

I left just as deaf as I'd come.

Mom held onto her faith that somehow, someday something was going to help me. But I was crushed. I dreamed every night for weeks about walking along the shore, gazing out at the deep roaring ocean. But I never saw myself plunging in.

My final year of Little League baseball began a few days after our visit to Canon Best.

Dad coached the team that year and turned me into a pitcher. He was determined that on the mound, if nowhere else, I would find the confidence in myself that he believed would make all the difference for me.

With Dale Byrd still the team's main pitcher, I worked alternate games, usually against weaker opponents.

But Dad's relentless practice sessions with me began to pay off; I won most of the games I pitched that summer.

Our chief opponent that year was Flying A, led by John Wittes, their best pitcher and clean-up hitter. In our first clash, in June, we held them to only three hits. I picked up the victory, with Jerry Erb taking over for the final three innings. Dale Byrd hit the league's first grand slam home run of the year as we won, 16–5.

We won the first half of the season.

I was feeling pretty confident as I headed off for summer camp during the mid-summer break.

Finally, I had the doctors' permission to do a little swimming, although I was warned about getting too much water in my ears. The chance to be on my own was intoxicating. The most appealing part of camp, though, was that I wouldn't have to witness, day after depressing day, the whirlwind social life of my sister Robin.

117

"Dear Mom and Dad,

"I *love* it here at camp, and I mean it. It's great swimming at the Pool, and I passed the test. Freddie and I are real pals. Uncle Bob is going to try to get a ball game up. Last night, he had a real magic show for the whole camp and boy, was it swell. I don't miss Robin at all.

"Everybody's feeling good. It is a swell place and I want to come back each year. Write soon.

"Love, Frank"

"Dear Mom,

"We are having a great time here. I just got home from swimming and will go to dinner and evening activities tonight. I hope Robin is feeling well, and I also hope that Daddy is feeling well. Uncle Bob is going to do some more magic tricks, and we are going to do some skits.

"See you soon.

"Love, Frank."

"Dear Mom,

"We had a. big dance last night from 8 to 9:30 and then went swimming to 10 PM at night. I will see you on Sunday.

"Love, Frank"

When I got back from camp, baseball picked up where it had left off. This time, though, Flying A was flying high, with Wittes seemingly able to do no wrong.

It was three weeks before we met them head to head. When we did, it was sweet; I pitched a four hitter, and Jerry Erb hit a grand slam homer as we won, 8–4.

We had our troubles with some of the other squads, though, and Flying A did well enough in the second half of the season to earn a shot at us in the playoffs.

I was nervous as I dressed for the playoff game. The Flying A squad was no pushover.

John Wittes, I knew, was the leader of their team, the clean-up hitter, and a tough, no-nonsense type with trouble written all over him. With a .429 batting average, he was one of the most feared hitters in the league. I knew I'd have my hands full with him.

Mom and Robin were in the stands as we took the field.

My sidearm fastball was working well that day. For four innings, I fashioned a no-hitter.

True to baseball tradition, nobody mentioned it.

In the fifth inning, Flying A strung together two walks, a fielder's choice, and a hit by Warren Snyder to take a 2–1 lead.

The Cardinals roared back in our half of the fifth, with Mike Burgee, Jerry Erb, Dale Byrd, and me all getting hits.

As I took the mound in the final inning, protecting a 5–2 lead, we were all very nervous. First baseman Pete Walters kept kicking his base and slamming his left hand into his oversized mitt. Mike Burgee, the catcher, kept moving his hands in a "calm down" motion as I stared at each Flying A batter. Jerry Erb and Dale Byrd paced nervously in left and center field.

A bobbled grounder to third put Wayne Bromfield on first.

I struck out the next batter.

One out. Two to go.

A walk and another error filled the bases.

Mike joined me on the mound.

"Calm down, Frankie. You can do it!" he urged.

Craig Rothermel bumbled a liner to second, recovered too late, and missed catching Warren Snyder at first. Now it was 5–3.

I struck out the next batter, for two outs. But the bases were still loaded.

I knew that Wittes was in the on-deck circle as I faced the next Flying A batter. Just knowing that Wittes was waiting was enough to unsettle me. I walked the batter on four pitches.

As the guy on third base trotted home with Flying A's fourth run, Dad came to the mound for a conference. Mike joined us.

"Wittes is up now, Frankie," Dad told me.

I didn't need to be reminded.

"Frankie, Billy represents the tying run. He's on third. You can't afford a walk now. A hit and it's all over. You've got to bear down."

"Come on, Frank!" Mike said. "You can do it!"

I looked at Dad's worried face.

With a determination I'd never felt in myself before, I told him: "Wittes or no Wittes, I'm gonna strike him out!"

Dad patted me on the back. "Way to go boy!"

As he walked back to the dugout, I stared at Wittes. He was flexing his muscles, supremely confident.

Mike crouched behind the plate, balanced himself, and called for a fastball down the middle.

I made it, for strike one.

On the next pitch, which was supposed to be a curve, I threw the ball a foot over Mike's head. He was a big guy, so the ball must have crossed the plate about seven feet in the air.

Mike signalled for a change-up.

It fooled Wittes, who swung vainly at the ball.

Now it was two strikes, one ball.

I took a deep breath. Mike was signalling for another change-up. I shook him off. He asked for a curve, but I shook that off too. Finally, Mike called for the fastball.

119

With a wary glance at Billy Stevenson on third, I let go with the hardest fastball I knew how to throw. It just nicked the outside of the plate as it sailed into Mike's glove.

"Strike three!" shouted the umpire. "You're out!"

"We did it! We did it!" Mike yelled, jumping up and down.

On the way home that night, I turned to Dad.

"You heard me out there, didn't you, Dad? I said: 'Wittes or no Wittes, I'm gonna strike him out!' And I did."

"Son," Dad said, an arm over my shoulder and his eyes wet with joy. "Today, Frankie, you became a champion."

I woke up the next morning to find on my bureau an 8 × 10 picture of our championship squad. On the back of the photograph was a note from my father:

"Frankie—I'm very proud of your spirit, the way the team means everything, and your never giving up. It means a lot to me. To pitch as you did in the playoffs shows you are able and willing to take on any job for the good of the team—and most of all, you did a real good job.

"When you grow old and put in your work what you do in baseball now, you will understand Daddy better.

"We just like to put all we have in everything we do.

"Love, Dad"

Chapter
Nine

Lewisburg Joint High School stood at the corner of Market Street and Route 15, a highway leading north to Williamsport and south to Harrisburg. The school drew students from a half-dozen elementary schools in the Lewisburg, Winfield, Vicksburg, and East Lewisburg areas. A large, two-story building, it had a gymnasium, a cafeteria, and a playing field for baseball, football, and track.

On the first day of school in September, 1959, some 950 kids entering the seventh through twelfth grades assembled on the field waiting for the school doors to open.

The first few days were dominated by hushed whispers, passed from one seventh grader to another, about the star of us all, a lanky left-hander named Bob O'Dell. Bob's father, the Bucknell University football coach, walked with a noticeable limp. The son had copied the limp out of admiration for his father.

Within two weeks of the opening of school that fall, more than half of all the seventh- and eighth-grade boys in the school were limping.

The good news was that the word "egghead" was back in favor. In these post-Sputnik times, academic excellence was smiled upon. The fact that I was obviously studying hard didn't cause my popularity to sag. I have to admit, though, that there was not much of it to sag.

The bad news was that seventh grade was all it was cracked up to be.

I had girded myself to face the task of trying to lipread six different teachers. Two weeks before school started I learned, to my deep dismay, that I'd have eight, not six, different courses: English, history, mathematics, social science, art, industrial arts, gym—and music!

It was hard enough trying to cope with my teachers' eight different speaking styles. To make matters worse, unlike my elementary school teachers, these faculty members often read aloud from their notes.

Now I know this doesn't sound like much of a problem to you. It didn't bother me much either, until I noticed two things.

First, people who read aloud tend to talk a lot faster than do those who are reciting something from memory or just talking extemporaneously. And, second, people who are reading out loud look down at their paper, not up to meet our eyes.

I got more exercise bending down in my seat trying to see my teachers' lips as they read from their notes and moved around the room than I did in our thrice-weekly gym periods.

Then there were the teachers who made this bad situation worse.

I'm sure Mr. Wilson was a kind and thoughtful person, much admired in the community. I'm sure, too, that he was a fine social studies teacher.

I also know he drove me crazy.

Not only did Mr. Wilson lecture from notes; he gave tests from notes. His notes.

Standing in front of the room, he'd boom out a question. Thirty pencils would hit lined paper. The thirty-first would go up in the air.

"Mr. Wilson . . ."

"Now, Frankie. You know our rule: No questions about the questions."

After six weeks of this, I sought out Mrs. Deck, one of our school guidance counselors.

It was the first time I asked for special treatment in junior high school. It was also the last.

"Frankie, I'm sorry. But the administration is not about to interfere with the way a teacher runs his class," Mrs. Deck advised me.

That was the end of that.

Understanding why I had to take two full years of music in seventh and eighth grades was another matter altogether.

If I hadn't been able to comprehend the rationale for my having piano lessons, at least I'd been able to ascribe it to a child's ignorance of the wisdom of his parents.

Our junior high music teacher, a Bucknell graduate who was pursuing a master's degree while teaching at Lewisburg Joint High School, did everything Mr. Wilson did. He lectured from notes. He tested us from his notes. And he declined to give us assigned reading.

If ever there were a time when I was ready to give up my efforts to compete with normal kids, this was it.

I just could not lipread the man. His drooping moustache, tiny mouth, and bad teeth made the task of catching even two words in any given class period an impossible job. That he didn't use a regular text book meant that I couldn't bone up on the book to pass the course. And the oral tests were, to put it mildly, an exercise in dread anxiety.

In my first six-week marking period I received an "F" in music. The socially approved reaction would have been shock. Frankly, I *was* shocked: my grade was actually as high as 43!

The second grading period I made some progress. By borrowing the notes of good students like Cathy Young and Becky Hinish, I managed to eke out a "D − ." Of the ten questions our teacher asked on the six-week examination, I'd only understood four. Fortunately, those four counted for a lot of points, enabling me to earn a passing grade.

Marking period by marking period, I slowly did better.

If you stare at one person's lips for several hundred hours, as I did, allowing nothing to distract your attention for even an instant, you'd learn to lipread that individual a little, too.

Eventually, I earned a "C +" in music for the fifth grading period.

The final marking period's examination consisted of listening to a classical record in class and writing an "interpretation" of it. Cathy told me, when I jabbed her arm anxiously, that "creativity" would be rewarded in the grading of our compositions.

I smiled.

Victory! There was no question in my mind that my interpretation just had to be the most creative in the class.

And it was. My final six weeks' grade was "B."

My seventh grade homeroom teacher was Mrs. Webster. She was also my English teacher. A warm, relaxed, and always happy person, she called me "My Beau."

She was big on puns.

People who are happy are easier to lipread: their lips move confidently and smoothly, their faces display their emotions, and their bodies slide from gesture to gesture to emphasize shifts in meaning. So it was with Lois Webster. I could imagine her arising each morning to the joy of the day; certainly, when I first saw her in homeroom every school morning, she looked genuinely delighted to see me. Everything between Mrs. Webster's fine grey hair and her mobile chin, but especially her crinkly, bemused brown eyes, contributed something to my understanding of her words.

One day Mrs. Webster gestured excitedly for me to come to her desk. It was homeroom period before the first classes of the day were to start.

"You'll never believe what the latest rumor circulating Lewisburg High School is, Frankie!" she gushed.

I confessed that I was sure I'd not heard it. In fact, I was quite confident; I was resigned to being the last person to learn about any rumor. It was a fact of life.

"Ah, Frankie. You'll love this!" She pulled my face close to hers. "Kids are complaining to the principal that one seventh-grader is listening to a transistor radio all day and ignoring the teacher!"

"That's terrible," I said.

"No! No, silly! That's you!"

"Me?"

"Yeah! Isn't that just great!"

Mrs. Webster also figured in one of my real eye-openers of seventh grade.

Every week, as our English teacher, she gave us a vocabulary test based upon a list of words we'd received the previous week.

I felt as if I were back in fourth grade again, with those dreadful readers.

Whoever invented vocabulary tests, I vowed silently, won't live another day once I catch up with him. Or her. I was as coldblooded about this as Sherman was in Atlanta.

The big difference between the tests of seventh grade and the reading in fourth was that the words on our vocabulary lists appeared out of context. There was no surrounding message to help me figure out the words' meanings. To top it all off, I'd never seen any of these words in my life.

Every week, I spent untold hours, Monday through Thursday nights, cursing Samuel Johnson for inventing the dictionary. I wasn't at all surprised to learn that the synonyms for the multisyllabic words on Mrs. Webster's lists were just as strange to me as were the words on which we would be tested.

My grades in these weekly trials by torture were dismal: "62," "48," "32," and, my high for the first month, "64."

In desperation, I used two dictionaries in October, then three in November.

Nothing helped.

"The trick," I informed my mother, "has got to be to locate the right dictionary. If I only knew which dictionary Mrs. Webster is using, I'd get all A's!"

"I'm sorry to disappoint you, Frankie . . ." Mom began.

"Yeah, I know," I sighed, returning to the task.

One day during our homeroom period, Wayne Bromfield and I stopped at Mrs. Webster's desk to pick up the test papers from that week's vocabulary test.

I asked Wayne how he'd done.

He looked at Mrs. Webster and replied: "98."

I gasped.

"How'd you do it, Wayne?"

He shrugged.

"What dictionary did you use?" I asked, desperate for something to explain his extraordinary success.

"I didn't."

I was speechless.

"I already knew these words," he finished.

I stared at Mrs. Webster as Wayne walked back to his desk.

I spoke very slowly: "He already knew these words."

There were some good times, too.

I remember the seventh-grade talent show we gave for the patients at the Seilinsgrove State School, ten miles south along the Susquehanna River.

124

Russell Fairchild, the class comedian, was chosen to give a skit. Nancy Fisher, our best singer, was picked to sing a song. Since I didn't have any particular talents that were obvious to anyone, I was selected to be the M.C., master of ceremonies. My job was to read from a set of 5 × 8 cards, announcing each act.

The show proceeded smoothly. What struck me most sharply was the fact that I did not once get nervous. And that has been true of speeches I've given since, all over the world. An audience won't talk during a speech or a performance; I don't have to worry about lipreading. Being in a small group of three or four people can make me nervous. But lecture audiences, even as large as five or ten thousand, never bother me.

I remember the skit that David Epler, son of a local farmer, presented. He played the role of a retarded vendor. It was the first, and one of the last, references to handicapped individuals in my school career:

WOMAN: Now, all you gotta do is hold this cup of pencils and shout: Pencils, two for a nickel! Pencils, two for a nickel! Even a retarded man like you can do that!
EPLER: What do I say if they don't want any?
WOMAN: Then you say: If you don't somebody else will. (Departs)
EPLER: Pencils, two for a nickel!
MAN: What do you got there?
EPLER: Pencils, two for a nickel!
MAN: Are they any good?
EPLER: If you don't, somebody else will.
MAN: How'd you like a punch in the face?
EPLER: If you don't, somebody else will.
MAN: (Punches Epler).

I may have been comfortable as an MC but I was miserable on the other side of the lights.

The school auditorium was the scene of mindless tedium for me every time we had a school assembly. I discovered in the very first such gathering that it is virtually impossible to lipread a mouth that is hidden by a podium and a microphone, regardless of where in the auditorium I might sit. For hour after dreary hour, all through my six years at the school, I sat bored out of my mind while this activity or that took place in the auditorium. I knew better than to complain about this being a total waste of my time; the administrative problems of having a child unsupervised in some room while the rest of the school was in the auditorium weighed more heavily with those in control than did my desires. Eventually, I hit upon a solution of sorts: sit toward the very back of the cavernous room and read a book.

Leon Uris' *Exodus* consumed much of spring recess and early May assemblies. When I finished this novelization of the birth of the State of Israel, I felt an exhilaration greater than any I had known since we won the Little League championship. I identified totally with the Ari Ben Canaans of the world—scorned, oppressed, beaten, and killed—who let no one stop them from living the lives they wanted to live. The fact that they won despite overwhelming odds gave me courage to fight my much smaller, more frivolous, battles for a life worth living.

Eagles Mere is a Pocono Mountain resort area featuring a beautiful lake, mile after mile of wooded hiking paths, a respected summer stock theatre, and one of the most popular tennis tournaments in the junior circuit.

It was also the site of my first date, in July of 1960.

I had just won my quarter-final tennis match one afternoon when John Myers informed me that he'd fixed a double date for us with two of the girls in the tournament. We'd be taking them to the Eagles Mere Playhouse that evening to see "Long Day's Journey Into Night," the Eugene O'Neill play.

After showering, dressing, and splashing about a gallon of Jade East all over my face and neck, I sought out my father for some advice.

I knew that John and our dates had learned a great deal about the unwritten rules of social conduct that were still Greek to me. Starting with casual conversations over cokes, chats in the hall, bull sessions with their peers, and group dates, they'd picked up the subtleties of social intercourse that still eluded me. I wanted to avoid the mistakes that were normal for someone in sixth grade but that would be inappropriate for someone about to enter eighth.

"Hey, Dad," I began as we sat at the dinner table. "What do people say on dates?"

The question took him by surprise. "What do they say?"

"Yeah, Dad. You know, those 'intimate whispers' Robin is always talking about."

He looked at my mother. I had the strange feeling he wanted to burst out laughing.

"Well, son. You tell her what she looks like."

"Huh?" This didn't make sense. "But, Dad, if she's anything like Robin, she spends about six hours every day looking at herself in the mirror."

He smiled. "Every woman wants to be told how she looks. It's impossible to tell a woman that too often."

I took his word for it.

Debby sat on my right during the first scenes of O'Neill's play. What happened on stage I can't tell you. I was observing Debby's face with a sculptor's care and planning my lines for the intermission I knew would come quite soon.

As John led his date to the lobby for a soda, I turned to Debby.

126

Leaning toward her as casually as I could, I whispered sweet nothings into her ear.

"You know, Debby, you look exactly like Pal, the palomino I rode this morning before my match. She's a nice horse. I can see uncanny resemblances in the slope of your nose, the shape of your eyes, and wave of your hair with Pal's handsome features."

Debby was silent, pondering, I was sure, the profound wisdom of my words. A few minutes later, she reported a sudden sickness and departed the theatre.

When she hadn't returned for the closing acts, I left. I could no more lipread the actors on the stage and follow the action than I could fly! It seemed pointless to sit through a play I didn't understand when my date was not there to enjoy it.

Twenty-five eighth graders, out of a class enrollment of 190, were selected for a special algebra course instead of having another year of mathematics. Bob O'Dell and Wayne Bromfield were there, of course, as were the other stars of our class. For some reason I couldn't understand, I was assigned to this honors course as well.

The reality of competing head-on with the *crême de la crême* of normal kids, though, proved too much for me.

I understood my lessons, all right. The assignments we did for homework caused me no problems. But I froze in examinations, unable to concentrate.

These are among my most vivid memories of junior high school: leaning over on my desk, my head down, so Donna Murray behind me could see Mrs. Delcamp's writing on the blackboard, although this meant, of course, that I could not, and positioning my legs around the sides of my chair exactly as Wayne always did.

I revered these kids. They were another, higher, race of beings, lower perhaps than the gods but at least as high as the angels.

By mid-year, I was struggling along with a D − average.

One afternoon, the gloom was just too much to bear. I reported to the administrative office to explain that my hearing aid battery had gone "dead," and, unfortunately, I would be unable to continue in my class.

Mrs. Deck would have none of that. After a quick phone call, she assured me that my mother was on her way to the school with a fresh battery.

I slumped in the wooden chair, praying for Mom to have a flat tire that would delay her arrival until algebra class ended.

Mrs. Deck must have sensed my despondency.

"Is something wrong, Frank?" she asked while we waited for my mother.

I blurted it out: "Yeah, there sure is. I just can't keep up with these honors students in algebra. I'm way over my head."

She shook her head. "I'm not so sure you are, Frank. All of us here think you have what it takes. We're rooting for you to make it."

When Mom arrived with the battery, I didn't mind that algebra class was still in session. But, important as this boost Mrs. Deck gave me was, it did not last long. The next day's algebra test showed me I was still unable to overcome my fears of the other honors students.

One afternoon in gym, I twisted my right knee playing soccer. The sprain was a bad one, necessitating a three-day absence from school.

As I lay on my bed at home, I felt an incredible sense of serenity. The relief I felt at having escaped from the competition at school was enormous. This must be, I thought, what religious exaltation is all about.

By Friday morning, though, the knee had healed. With a deep sigh, I re-entered the battle.

Glenn Limbaugh burst into my life just before my 14th birthday in March, 1961. Slightly taller than my 5'6", with brown hair swinging freely in the breeze, Glenn leaped from a light-blue Triumph TR-3 convertible, grabbed a racket, and loped gracefully to the court where I was practicing my serve.

"Hi!" he boomed. "Let's have a match!"

I had never seen anyone filled with such sheer exuberance, so much pure joy at being alive.

We played two fast sets.

"I'm hungry!" he announced. "Let's get some milkshakes!" Without waiting for an answer, he led me back to the TR-3. With a raucous roar, the small sports car blazed down Seventh Street and careened in at the local Tastee-Freez.

Two chocolate shakes in our hands, we rumbled on to my house on Brown Street. Glenn jumped from the car, shouted greetings to my parents sitting on the front porch, and ensconsed himself at their side.

It was as though he had been a member of the family for years.

Two or three times a week thereafter, until he left two years later for Dickinson College in Carlisle, Pennsylvania, Glenn visited with the Bowe family. Invariably, he would screech the TR-3 to a halt in front of the house, barge in the front door, and let loose with a booming: "Anyone home!"

I was awed that such happiness was possible on earth.

Mrs. Deck called me to her office shortly after all of us in eighth grade had taken standardized achievement tests.

"Frank," she began, with a smile that invited me to join her, "remember what I told you earlier about the high expectations all of us here have for you?"

I nodded, pleased to recall the confidence her words had given me when I had needed it so badly.

"Well, Frank, now we know we're right. Your test scores are way out of line with your grades since you came here last year. There's a lot of potential that you've not yet tapped. In fact, the difference between how well you should be doing and how well you are doing is so great that I need to ask you about it."

I shifted uncomfortably in my seat.

"Well, having eleven different courses this year probably has something to do with it, Mrs. Deck."

"I realize that, Frank, but all your peers have the same number of courses."

I was silent.

"Frank, you've got to come to some decision about what you'll do next year. As you know, we have a commercial program here, for students who want to go into business. We have an industrial arts program, for those interested in craft work. We have a home economics program. Then there is the general program, that gives you a taste of a lot of different things. Finally, and most difficult, is our college-preparatory academic program.

"The decision has to be made this year, Frank."

I nodded.

"Your grade point average to this point is 77. Now, a C+ normally doesn't indicate ability to do good academic work in high school. But if you're willing to try, we're ready to let you have a shot at it."

"Do you really think I can do it?"

"Frank," she responded, "I want you to know something. You have the respect and friendship of all of us here, the faculty, the staff, and the students."

I wanted desperately to believe that she was leveling with me. It must have shown on my face, because she pressed the point.

"We know that it's harder for you than for the others. And we admire your courage in facing up to that challenge. You have more friends than you know, Frank, maybe more than you'll ever know."

I was elated as I discussed the choice with my parents that evening.

"Son," Dad said, "this may be the most important decision you will make in your life."

"I know, Dad. And I've decided."

He looked up at me in surprise.

"I know it'll be hard, but I'm going for the academic program, Dad. It's the best education I can get, and I want only the best."

"You realize, honey," Mom broke in, "that the academic curriculum is going to be very competitive. Bucknell's presence in the town creates intense pressure upon the high school to produce outstanding results in the college preparatory program."

I nodded.

"You sure you want this?" Dad asked.

"I'm sure."

He reached out a hand to shake mine. "Son, I've waited a long time for this day. My son is becoming a man."

For three days in early July, I underwent an intensive Summer Testing Program at Bucknell University's counseling service center on the hill across the tracks from our home.

Allen Ivey, the center director, and John Haddon, a counseling intern, administered the tests.

First they tested my listening ability. I sat at a table across from Haddon, my hearing aid on but my eyes closed. Mr. Haddon spoke some words I was expected to repeat. Within two minutes, he gave this up as impossibly difficult.

The balance of the testing was done with me watching his lips as he presented the test instructions. They started with a Weschler intelligence test, moved on to a battery of differential aptitude instruments, administered some achievement tests, and gave me a set of interest inventory assessments.

I especially remember the vocabulary test. Mr. Haddon showed me a long list of words and asked me to define each one. I made it through the first eight. The hardest word I knew was "belfry," which I explained was the place where the bell was on churches.

Every other word on that lengthy list was new to me.

One week later, my mother deposited Dr. Ivey's report on my lap as I sat reading the *Daily Item*.

"You might want to look at this," she said casually.

I read the report, first with a sense of dread born from too many disappointments with tests, and then with trembling fingers, my heart beating a thousand times a minute.

I absolutely could not believe what I was reading.

"Hey!" I screamed, running to the back porch where Mom and Dad sat drinking iced tea. "Listen to this! Dr. Ivey says that my performance on the tests was depressed because of my hearing loss. He says my vocabulary is only average. Well, he's sure right about that. But then he goes on to say that even with this vocabulary weakness, I'm going to be able to do anything I want to do in high school and beyond!"

"Anything!" I plopped on the end chair at the table, staring at my parents in disbelief.

Mom smiled as she set down her glass. "I guess you made the right decision to enter the academic program, Frankie."

"Are you kidding! Mom, if this is true, it means that I can compete with Wayne and even with Bob O'Dell. I won't beat them, but I won't be laughed out of school either."

Over the next two months, I picked up the Ivey report at least once every other day. Each time I did, I saw something in the seven single-spaced pages of test results that I hadn't noticed before. Slowly I was beginning to believe that the report might actually be true and not just a wishful dream.

On the weekend before I was to enter ninth grade, I played three hard sets with the captain of the Bucknell University tennis team. Don Warren was eight years my senior and the best player the University had.

It was the first time I'd ever beaten him.

"Frankie," my father told me when I arrived home that evening, "I always thought that all you needed was confidence, belief in yourself. You've got it now. You're ready for anything life can throw at you."

He handed me a towel.

"All these years, I worked on your baseball and tennis. I figured that since your body, except for your ears, is O.K., sports would be easier for you to master than schoolwork would be. Once you excelled on the diamond or on the court, I hoped that confidence would transfer into the classroom.

"And here you are, confident at last."

He shook his head.

"But, I'll be damned, you did it the other way around. You got your confidence in book work and used it to excel in tennis. To be frank with you, I feel pretty ridiculous.

"Still, I couldn't be prouder. Ever since I started teaching you to play the game, I've dreamed of the day you would beat me."

He smiled. "That day isn't here yet, but I can feel it coming. It's going to be the happiest day in my life."

Three weeks later, I beat him.

Chapter
Ten

Few books have changed my life. Ayn Rand's towering novel *The Fountainhead* is one that did.

Reading it during the "lazy, hazy days" of late August, I found myself transported into a world I never had dreamed could exist. That anyone could live as Howard Roark lived I had not imagined. All my life, I had aspired to be average, normal, accepted.

Roark did not.

Surrounded by medley of mediocrity, Howard Roark played a theme of thunderous egoism. He refused merely to exist; rather, he exalted and excelled. The architect lived a life dominated by dreams—and he refused, even for a moment, to be diverted from those dreams.

And Rand showed how difficult a struggle he chose. So great were the demands of an egoistic lifestyle that others in the book similarly endowed with drive and intelligence could not bear the burden. The sculptor Steven Mallory was forced to his knees; the publisher Gail Wynand could not rescue his integrity after a lifetime of denying it; Henry Cameron died defeated. Dominique Francon did not dare to be herself.

And Rand showed the vanity of professed selflessness, the final emptiness of Peter Keating's reliance upon others to define the values of his life and of his desire that he be, not great, but thought to be great; not daring, but perceived to be daring; not strong, but believed to be strong. In Keating, and more viciously in Ellsworth Toohey, Rand attacked the entire concept of altruism, of a life lived for others.

That theme of the book gave me pause: altruism was, after all, firmly entrenched in the America of 1961; it was the basis for the Peace Corps, for work in Appalachia, and it was a precept of all of the major great religions. I could not accept this portion of Ayn Rand's philosophy.

But the balance of Rand's monumental work I found life-giving in a wonderful and profound sense. I was reminded of my father's injunctions: "The hard way is the best way," and "If you're not going to do your best, don't do it at all."

I could see now, all at once, that great things were possible. And having grasped this strange notion, I could not let go. Indeed, it seemed that anything less than a life driven by dreams would not be worth living . . . certainly, not after the pain through which I had persevered to be able to live at all.

I understood, at last, what integrity really meant.

And I discovered, with a sense of wonder, that work could be a mission, that there was such a thing as a fire that would not be denied.

I closed *The Fountainhead* as one bids farewell to a close and dear friend. Something made me look for the publication date—and I realized, with astonishment, that Rand had written this book before anyone outside Nazi Germany knew what was happening at Buchenwald and Auschwitz. Yet she explained the holocaust better, I thought, than anyone I had read who had the benefit of hindsight. I had never been able to understand how thousands of people could have cooperated with the Nazi high command in the systematic destruction of six million lives. Roark's climatic speech at his trial lept from the pages for me as an explanation of the phenomenon of Nazi Germany. It is a lengthy oration in which he states that the most dreadful butchers were the most sincere; that they, and the people they led, really did believe that men must be sacrificed for other men; that the perfect society may be reached through the guillotine and the firing squad because such murders are, after all, committed for an altruistic purpose— life may be better for those who survive; and that the inventors among them must be stoned and scorned, lest they upset the delicate balance of society. Yes, I thought, it is true: the great masses of people do reject original thinkers, those who have the courage most people never know. But whose life, finally, was more worth living: the man who remained true to himself or the one who bent to fit the mold?

I knew I was no Roark. The ideas I found so alluring were not dreams by which I could drive my life. No, much too much remained to be done just to reach an acceptable level of achievement, to catch up to my peers, to acquire the tools I would need. But as I placed *The Fountainhead* back in my bookshelf, I thought it would not be long before I retrieved it again. I knew that someday I would awaken the dream and follow its beckonings wherever they might lead.

That fall I began my first of four years of Latin.

It was not a course of study I began with eager anticipation. Between the Scylla of French and the Charybdis of Latin, I was caught by the school's foreign language requirement.

The choice was not a choice at all.

French was taught at Lewisburg Joint High School through "the conversational method," with daily use of headphones. This, no one needed to tell me, was absolutely out of the question as far as I was concerned.

All through the first six-week marking period, I grumbled and fumed. "Here I am," I commiserated with myself, "having enough trouble acquiring the English language. Before I have the half of it, what do they do? They throw another language at me!"

I wished again I'd never heard of Sputnik.

Then one afternoon, as I worked to translate a selection from Cicero's orations, I realized with astonishment that I was in fact mastering English *because* I was learning Latin.

I was stunned by the idea.

Rushing upstairs to my bookshelf, I pulled down Ayn Rand's massive novel and set at once to copy down the words I did not understand. One by one, I then "decoded" them using their Latin roots.

"Superfluous," one of the words I had copied, could be split, I saw, into the Latin word for "above, over" and *fluo, fluere* meaning "to flow." I understood immediately what the word meant—and knew I'd never forget it.

Next on my list was "implore." I had difficulty seeing how it differed in meaning from "deplore." Again, Latin acted as a beam to understanding. *Ploro, plorare,* I knew, meant "lament, wail, cry aloud for grief." The Latin prefixes, *in-* for "towards" and *de-* for "from" sharply differentiated the words. "Implore," I now know, meant to beg someone *to* do something, while to "deplore" was to beg someone *from* doing something.

The Latin prefix *in-* carried a second meaning: "without, not." It is this meaning, together with *sto, stare,* "to stand," that illuminates the meaning of the word "instability."

Another set of words that caused me trouble was "emerge" and "submerge." Once again, Latin gave me the answer. *Mergo, mergere,* meaning "to dip, plunge into" suggested being in a solution. The prefix *ex-*, meaning "from, out from" combined with *mergo* to mean to come out from within, while the prefix *sub-*, meaning "underneath," lent to *mergo* the sense of going into something.

"Equivalent," I learned, was based upon the Latin words *aequus,* for "equal" and *valeo, valere* for "to be worth, to be strong."

Even so difficult a word as "vivacious," in fact, was easily understood from the root word, *vivo, vivere,* for "to live."

English was beginning to make sense.

Pete Walters returned that year from an extended stay in Germany with his father. I was delighted to have him back, but things were not the same. A year behind me in school now, his interests and problems were different from mine.

As is the case with any adolescent, I wanted desperately to be accepted by my peers. This proved to be extremely difficult. No group sought me out, so I sought them out, one group after another. Nothing worked. Typical of the problems I encountered were my difficulties with Wayne Bromfield's clique. These guys always gathered around Bromfield in the cafeteria to exchange jokes and stories about the faculty and staff.

Joining them one late morning, I watched as Wayne told a joke. Almost without laughing, Russ Fairchild responded with one of his own. I nudged Tom Hess.

"Hey, did you hear the one about the overworked maternity ward doctor who finally became overwhelmed and put up a sign over the ward door that said: 'Make war, not love.'?"

Tom smiled slowly and indicated Wayne.

It was a polite way to tell me that Wayne had just told that joke.

In the course of an average day, at the most two classmates would say something to me, beyond a nod of the head or a mumbled "Hi." Most times, it would be the same two: Charley Boyer, son of the local Western Auto proprietor, and Chuck Vollmer, whose father had died in the Korean War shortly after his birth. They lived across the street from each other on the far end of town, but their twosome never minded becoming three.

What little I did in high school aside from my studies, my tennis, and my immediate family, I did with Charley and Chuck. When Boyer took his lessons for a pilot's license, he was kind enough to bring me along to introduce me to the wonders and terrors of twin-propeller-engine Piper Cubs. When Vollmer headed for the Bucknell golf course for a round, he was good enough to let me play with him.

It was a joy to return home from these sojourns to respond to the routine parental inquiries of every other 14- or 15-year-old boy:

"Where did you go?"

"Out."

"What did you do?"

"Nothing."

Not that my parents had much cause for concern. I made the honor roll five out of six times that year.

I'd like to say a word about my sex life.

The word is: nonexistent.

Not that I didn't try, you see, but the unfortunate fact is that every girl in Lewisburg I asked for a date absolutely had to babysit that precise evening.

In desperation, I turned to the only source I knew I'd understand: books.

Twixt Twelve and Twenty, by Pat Boone, together with assorted teen advice books by the likes of Abigail van Buren, gave me a great deal of information I had absolutely no need for and precious little I absolutely had to get.

I learned twenty ways to fend off hysterical girls clawing over each other to touch me. I learned the twelve signs by which to determine when puppy love becomes true love. I learned, too, how to keep a necking session from becoming what the books euphemistically called "too serious."

136

What I didn't learn is how to make a girl listen to me when I used one of the fifteen "sure-fire" lines guaranteed to land me a date.

American boys, all the books told me, tend to marry the girl next door. I was, I thought, more fortunate than most; the girl who lived, literally, next door, was beautiful, popular, sophisticated—everything I was not.

When, as a tenth grader, I developed a crush on Beth, all I had to call upon in the way of experience to guide me was one-half of a date with Debby in Eagles Mere.

It doesn't take a genius to describe what happened when I tried to get a date with Beth. But I'll call upon Virgil anyway. The famous simile in the twelfth book of the *Aenied,* his powerful poem presenting what many critics view as the highest expression ever achieved of the Latin hexameter, describes my feelings when it was all over:

Ac velut in somnis oculos ubi languida pressit nocte quies, nequiquam avidos extendere cursus velle videmur, et in mediis conatibus aegri succidimus, nec lingua valet, nec corpore notae sufficiunt vires aut vox et verba sequuntur—

Or, to put it in much more mundane English (I suppose it is rather a crime to translate something this elegant): "As in a nightmare, when an unnerving calm presses us down, in vain we try to run, in the midst of our exertions we collapse exhausted, nor does our tongue have strength, nor our body its familiar power, nor does speech come—."

What brought me to such a deplorable state of being? Well, a combination of things.

First, learning from the Sunbury *Daily Item* that a movie I knew I'd enjoy, "Son of Flubber," was playing in area theatres, I determined to take Beth to see it when it came to Lewisburg's own Campus Theatre.

Second, while bedridden with measles and a high fever in mid-January, I watched from my window as a hated competitor, Jim Lakes, brought Beth back from a date.

Third, I learned that she, too, had become sick and was home recuperating while I was still recovering from the measles.

Problem: how do I invite her? I can't very well telephone Beth, since I can't hear. Nor can I run into her at school, since we're both home sick. If I wait until we're both well, I probably won't have the guts to ask her face to face. Besides, by that time, someone else will have asked her to see "Son of Flubber."

Solution: slip a note to her into her mailbox.

Which I did. Together with a two-page letter explaining why I would enjoy taking her.

Thereupon, two households erupted in furor. Beth's parents were up in arms, complaining to my parents, who ascended to my sickroom to give me a tongue-lashing.

Little did I suspect what was up when Mom walked in and planted herself firmly at the foot of my bed. I did become suspicious, though, when Dad walked in to stand at her side.

"Frankie," Mom began.

I could tell right away something was wrong. Very wrong.

"Frankie, people just don't do things like this."

"Like what, Mom?"

She held up an envelope. "Like this, Frankie."

My ears were burning.

"How'd you get that?"

"Frankie, you don't get in this deep without even one date. Beth had no idea this was coming. Out of the blue you send her a love letter and ask her to go out with you. I can't tell you how embarrassed we are, how upset her parents are, and how startled Beth was to find the note."

I was in no mood to continue the discussion.

It was then that I thought of Virgil.

Barely a week later, such being the vicissitudes of adolescence, I emerged from the depths of despair to the peak of excitement.

A page from the diary my mother kept that year tells the story:

"Kids had first day of spring recess today; just two days off school, but nice. Robin went uptown as usual, and so, for a change, did Frank. That is, he went to Chuck Vollmer's and together they went to a bowling alley. Frank won with a score of 149. They walked to Donehower's Sporting Goods store and talked with old man Donehower about boxing equipment. Then to J. J. Newberry's for a coke, where they saw Margie Boyer and Bonnie Spearman. So Frankie walked Margie as far as the movies.

"Came home and said: 'Now, that's what I call a day!' "

My father's heart began giving him severe chest pains a few days after his 45th birthday March 1, 1963. In one day, he had four separate angina attacks. The following day he entered the cardiac care unit at Geisinger Medical Center, attended by Drs. Zimmer and Johnson.

Dad called me to his side after the doctors had stepped out for a moment.

"Frankie," he said, his face grey and strained, "I've tried to be a good father for you. I think I have been. I sure hope so. If anything should happen to me, it's your job to take care of your mother and your sister."

I didn't want to hear this.

"Dad, you're going to be fine. Nothing will happen," I insisted through the tears.

"No, Frankie. Heart attacks sometimes are fatal. I hope I got here in time. But I may not have. That's why I want you to listen to me now. I'm depending on you to carry on if I go."

Why did he have to be so damned consistent? Even at what might be the very end, he had to be totally honest with himself and with us. He didn't want sympathy—and he wasn't about to give it to himself either. The facts had to be faced, by all of us, and the sooner the better.

He was able to do it; I wasn't.

I fled from the room to the sun porch at the end of the fourth-floor hallway.

Mom joined me there.

"Frankie," she said, pulling my face from the cushions of the couch where I'd collapsed, "I know it's a shock. All I can think of is how *good* your father is, how he doesn't deserve this. I'm thinking about how glad I am that we spent so much time together, that we did what we wanted to do. Your father never was one to do what others wanted him to do; now, at last, I'm glad. To follow the crowd would have wasted so much of his life. This way, at least, he lived the life he wanted to."

"Mom. You're talking as if he's already dead."

"I'm sorry, honey. These are the things that go through your mind at a time like this. I have so many regrets—but so many satisfactions, too. And I'm glad he had that long talk with you. It's so like him, almost as if he had a premonition and wanted to give you what he could of himself."

We were both crying unabashedly as we sat on the worn sun porch sofa.

At length, she raised my face with her chin.

"He'll make it, Frankie, I just know he will."

During my father's six-week stay at Geisinger, my sister and I didn't give Mom much rest. Robin contracted a bad case of tonsillitis, and I got the flu. Then our family doctor told Robin she'd have to lose about twenty pounds, and placed her on a strict, 1000-calorie diet.

I wasn't very sympathetic when Robin complained about the rigors of staying on her diet.

"To hear you," I blasted her one afternoon when I found her crying in frustration, "people would think you're the one with a handicap around here. Well, let me tell you, Robin. Nothing you're going through can hold a candle to what I live with every day of my life."

It took Mom to separate us. "Please, let's not fight," she begged. "We have enough trouble in this house without the two of you going at each other."

A few days later, I failed my driver training examination. Mr. Weiss at the state police office explained to me that my left eye was far too weak and that to pass the test I'd have to be fitted with eyeglasses.

By the time I arrived home, my mother knew I had failed the test, but she didn't yet know why. The tension she was under caused her to leap to the conclusion that I had done something wrong, and she erupted in anger. After about an hour of screaming, she quieted down enough for me to explain that I hadn't even stepped into a car. The only thing wrong was a problem with my vision.

139

She immediately made a 180-degree turn from anger to intense concern.

"Did you say your left eye, Frankie? Oh, no! I hope this doesn't have something to do with your nerves."

"Huh?"

"You know. Your left ear doesn't work at all; the right one has to carry the ball. Now the same thing is happening to your eyes."

All of us were greatly relieved when I finally had an eye examination and learned that my left eye had become lazy during my protracted periods of reclining on a sofa or in bed reading novel after novel, at a time when I was growing very fast physically, spurting from five-eight to six feet in less than a year. It had nothing to do with my nerves or my ears.

Mom told me she was embarrassed about her outburst and showed me an entry in her diary by way of explanation: "I feel as though, if one more person in the family even sneezes, I would shatter into a million pieces and never get back together again."

The day after Dad returned from Geisinger, I was fitted for my first pair of glasses. The next day our dog Golly died.

It was a bad spring all around.

Dad made a swift recovery and soon started to work again, first just a few hours a day, but soon nearly full time. He still didn't want any sympathy. So pretty soon, the household returned to normal. In the back of my mind, though, was always the thought: I'm lucky I still have him. Some day, maybe very soon, I won't.

"Normal" in our household that summer meant work for Dad, keeping house for Mom, reading for me, and a merry-go-round of social activities for Robin.

As the proud big brother with a new driver's license, I chauffered her to dances, parties, slumber parties, the swimming pool, the movies, and more dances. Usually, Beth, Joyce, and one or two of Robin's other friends joined us in the car. Before getting out, they told me what time to pick them up. I returned home, read the newspaper or a book until the appointed hour, and then brought them back.

Robin insisted that I stay with them at one dance, at the fire hall in Winfield, about a ten minutes' drive downriver from our house.

As I walked in, I could feel the wooden floor vibrating. At the opposite end of the room sat five boys a few years older than I was, all of whom looked as if they needed a bath and a haircut.

When I mentioned this to Robin, she shut me up. "You're just jealous!"

The cavernous room was dim. Although the dance was just beginning, the air was already cloudy with smoke.

I stood by one wall watching small clusters of four or five kids standing in semi-circles talking. Every once in a while, pairs of them would wander to the middle of the room and begin to writhe their bodies in what I knew from Robin were the day's popular dances. After about five minutes, they'd return once again to a small group and stand for another half hour, moving their bodies slowly to the rhythm of the music.

Since every song sounded like every other song to me, which is to say that they all sounded like an approaching locomotive, I soon turned my hearing aid off. I had a bad headache when Beth and Robin reappeared at my side two hours later to say they'd like to return home.

One afternoon, Robin burst into the house looking as though she'd just won a million dollars. In her hands was the record jacket for "Meet the Beatles."

I was dumb enough to ask who the Beatles were. The only answer I got was a look of stunned incredulity.

I looked at the jacket copy. It advised me that one would have to be deaf, blind, and isolated on a deserted island out of communication with the world to be unaware of the Fab Four.

"See?" Robin said in triumph.

I nodded dumbly.

"Do you know who the Rolling Stones are?" she asked, taking the record back.

I had to admit that all I knew was that I'd read somewhere an expression to the effect that rolling stones gather no moss.

"Humph! Well, Mick Jagger and Keith Richard are just out of sight!"

I tried to edify my ignorant little sister with the biological and physical facts that rolling stones did in fact gather moss, but she was off.

Even so staunch an establishment organ as *Time* magazine endorsed the Beatles, calling them the most important innovators in popular music.

Before I could ask anybody to write out the words of some Beatles songs for me, I learned that a boy in my class with whom I'd been friendly had just been hit by lightning at the local swimming pool. Randy Mase had been one of the last to leave the pool area when rain began and a lightning bolt had hit him in the head. Our gym teacher, Mr. Raber, had administered mouth-to-mouth resuscitation. A week later, Randy's fate was still uncertain, but we did know this much: he was paralyzed from the neck down.

By the time school had started again in the fall, I learned from Mom that Randy's mother was asking for volunteers to come to the Mase home to help in physical therapy sessions in which each of his limbs was exercised.

"I want to go," I told my parents.

"Why, Frankie? Were you two close friends?"

"No. But I just have the feeling, Mom."

My mother shook her head. "Frankie, they say the prospects are very dim. There's no assurance at all that even with thousands of hours of physical therapy Randy will ever be able to live anything like a normal life. Are you sure you want to get involved in something like that? It'll be very hard for you to do."

I nodded. "I know, Mom. But, you see, I don't think that anyone else who comes to help Randy really understands. I'm probably the only one around who knows what it's like. After all, they said the same things about my future, too."

My parents looked at me in stunned silence.

"Well, in that case, by all means go," my father told me.

About 200 people volunteered to help Randy that fall. Five of us were needed for each therapy session. As the months rolled by with excruciatingly little progress, I began to lose my fervor. Shortly before Christmas, I quietly stopped going. Mom had been right: it was very hard to watch and realize just how little you could do.

"Well, Frank. Which college have you settled upon?"

I looked at Mr. Hidlay, the senior high guidance counselor, in confusion. "Uh, I haven't."

He smiled. "Better get started, Frank. I've just seen the results of the Preliminary Scholastic Aptitude Test battery you took last month. Your scores, combined with your grades here, are most encouraging. There's no question that you're college material."

I was on cloud nine when I arrived home.

My mother was somewhat bewildered as I sent off for catalogues from Trinity University in Texas, Arizona University, and a host of other Southwest colleges.

"Frankie, you wouldn't go two thousand miles away, would you?"

"But, Mom, you can play tennis down there twelve months a year."

She sighed. "Frankie, don't get your hopes up."

"Why not?"

She rubbed her forehead. "Honey, I'm just so afraid you won't meet the requirements to get into college."

"Doesn't sound like you, Mom. You're always a big booster, like Dad, in the Frank Bowe fan club."

She smiled. "One of my moods, I guess. You've been sick. Your father's been sick. It's not always easy living with someone so principled about everything he does, you know."

"O.K., Mom. Wherever I go, it'll be pretty nearby."

"Thank you, honey."

Two days later, when I dug out the addresses of Dickinson College, where Glenn Limbaugh was going, and Gettysburg College, Mom's mood was much brighter.

"What do you want in a college, Frankie?"

"Well, Mom. I've given this a lot of thought. First, I want a small college. No more than three or four thousand students. I'm a small-town boy. But more important, I want the chance to get to know people. I'm afraid a big school will leave me even lonelier than I've been here.

"Second, I want a strong academic program. A good school is important. It's four years of my life, after all.

"Third, to be honest, I want a school that's competitive but not like the Ivy League schools are. I know your brother Henry went to Princeton, but I know too that if I went there, every day would be like eighth-grade algebra was. I couldn't get through a day without wondering what I was doing there."

Mom smiled. "Sounds like you've got it all thought out."

I nodded.

"If I may say so, Bucknell meets all your requirements."

I shook my head. "No, Mom. I've got to break away some time, and this seems like a good time to do it."

"At least, apply. That way, if you change your mind, you still have a chance to go to Bucknell."

I agreed.

By Christmas time, I had narrowed my list down to three schools—Bucknell, Western Maryland College, and Gallaudet College.

Western Maryland attracted me because it was safely distant from Lewisburg, just the right size, featured a tough academic program that had a solid reputation for excellence, and had a student body whose qualifications matched my own.

I liked Gallaudet because it was especially for deaf students. I was excited about the idea of finally meeting other deaf people. Gallaudet's biggest attraction, I thought, was that I'd be allowed to develop into a well-rounded person. Since I wouldn't be different, I saw no reason I couldn't have some semblance of a social life. I hoped, too, that I'd be able to play varsity sports.

That's when I ran head-first into the fears my parents still carried, like leftover baggage, from their innumerable trips to doctor after doctor fifteen years ago.

Without telling me what she was doing, Mom wrote a letter to the admissions head at Gallaudet outlining all the reasons why Gallaudet would be wrong for me. Not surprisingly, Mr. Greenberg replied that I surely should be allowed to pursue higher education at a regular four-year college. My mother showed me the letter.

"See! Even Gallaudet says it's not the best place for you to go."

I tried in vain to get a copy of the letter she'd sent to the college. Mom claimed there was no copy. At length, I gave up, but not before I extracted a promise from both my parents.

"Look, you guys. I'm almost 17 years old. I'm a junior in high school.

Pretty soon, I'm going to be an adult. And I have some ideas of my own about what kind of a life I'm going to lead.

"I'll try Bucknell or Western Maryland, if they'll have me. But I want the right, if I fail there, or if I'm unhappy, to transfer to Gallaudet. After all, it's the only college in the world especially for people just like me."

Dad spoke for the two of them. "We'll give you that right."

"And, Frankie," Mom added. "If it's companionship with other deaf people that you want, Reverend Bowers conducts a sign language ministry at the Lutheran Church here in town. If you wish, you're free to go."

"When did you find out about this?" I demanded.

Mom looked at Dad. "It doesn't matter, honey. Go if you want."

The Rev. George K. Bowers, I discovered, had a slight hearing loss himself. He had developed a liturgy presented in sign language for the benefit of deaf adults from a nine-county area; people had come from as far as New York and West Virginia to attend his services. In addition, twice a month, he showed captioned movies, films with subtitles deaf people could read to keep up with the dialogue.

I attended a service two weeks after Mom told me about it.

As I walked into the community meeting room where the liturgy would be held, I felt strangely anxious. On the one hand, I was excited about meeting other deaf people; yet, on the other, my parents' worries concerned me.

As it happened, I could not understand the services any more than I could understand any meetings of hearing people.

Sign language wasn't a language people understood just because they were deaf, I discovered sadly. It was something I'd have to spend months, even years, learning.

I realized, with a start, that it would be useless to "interpret" my school classes as this sermon was being interpreted, because I would understand no more with the signs than I did without.

All the people who came to Mr. Bowers' service were my parents' age or older. I had little in common with them except the fact that we were all deaf. I sat in the back of the room as lonely and as bored as I ever was in our school auditorium. Even here, I sighed, I'm still an outsider.

As I returned home later that evening, I felt a keen and bitter disappointment. "I don't belong anywhere," I muttered to myself as I turned off Third Street onto Brown.

We went, as a family, for a campus visit to Western Maryland College in Westminster, Maryland.

C. Wray Mobray, a tall, lanky, easy-going man with a crew cut and a fondness for tweed jackets, was Western Maryland College's director of admissions. Equally important to me, he coached the tennis team.

"Well, Frank," he said when we sat down to complete the admissions process, "your record places you solidly in the middle of our students

144

here. I think your background is about average. You'll find it a challenge here. But I think you'll surmount that challenge. We're prepared to accept you on an early-admissions basis, subject to satisfactory grades in your senior year of high school."

Four years earlier, being called "average" would have filled me with a warm sense of contentment. But that was four years ago. Now it made me determined to prove him wrong.

"To be honest with you," Mr. Mobray continued, "you'll be competing with a number of high school valedictorians and many more students who maintained a straight-A average."

I sighed.

"Frank, I want you to make it. And not just because I'd like the college to win some of our tennis matches over the next four years. It's more important to me that you realize two things. First, that it won't be easy. And, second, that everything I know about you tells me you will do well here."

"As long as I don't have to take music."

He laughed. "We have electives in the art area. Instead of music, you can take fine art or dramatic art or both."

I relaxed.

"Now that we've finished that, how about a game of tennis to celebrate?"

Later, I joined my parents at Lee's Motel down the road from the Hill.

"How'd it go, Frank?" Dad asked.

"Well, I asked for it and I got it. I want a real education, something that will stretch me, make me draw upon everything I have. And there's no question that four years here will give me exactly that."

"Do you think the academic requirements are that rigorous?"

"Well, I suppose so. But I'm talking about tennis. Mr. Mobray blew me off the courts out there. There's no question about it: Western Maryland is going to be very educational."

With the next several years of my life decided, I turned my attention to what I really cared about: tennis.

All summer long, I arrived at the Bucknell courts by nine in the morning and didn't return home until nearly nine at night.

I learned two lasting lessons that summer.

The importance of being prompt was one of them. When someone was late showing up for a 10 a.m. match, my entire day's schedule was disrupted. Because matches were booked for every other hour, ten or eleven hours a day, seven days a week, this was a serious matter. Ever since, I've been almost Teutonic about being on time for my appointments.

It was, I must admit, an absolutely delightful problem. Never before had I had to worry about scheduling my social life, for the simple reason that almost no one wanted my time and attention. With tennis, though, I had people from a four-county area calling the house to set up matches. In addition to regulars like Glenn Limbaugh and Pete Walters, I had doctors, lawyers, university professors, stockbrokers, real estate executives, state politicians, and local merchants calling for appointments to play singles and doubles. And to think I had envied Robin her social life!

"It's remarkable," I told Mom after she had taken three calls in one half-hour period. "It's just amazing."

"What is, dear?"

"What people will overlook if you're really good at something. These people want a good tennis partner. They couldn't care less about the fact that all my ears do is hold up my glasses. You see? They don't care!

"Remember Dov Landau in *Exodus?* He avoided death at the hands of the Nazis because of his skill in forgery. The Germans were willing to overlook a lot because he had that skill.

"If I can just develop something in which I'm as good as I am in tennis, my handicap won't matter any more."

That revelation sustained me throughout my final year at Lewisburg High School.

Nothing that happened in my senior year made more of an impact on me than did reading William Golding's *Lord of the Flies.* On one level, this is the story of a small group of British boys stranded on an island. On a different level, however, it is an exploration of the role of the social contract in permitting men to live in peace with one another. Golding's theme is that without the structure that society gives to us, man's inherent tendency toward evil will emerge to dwarf his nobler qualities.

We see this as Ralph, chosen by the boys to be chief, struggles helplessly against the darker impulses personified by Jack and his band of hunters. For the boys to be rescued from the island, a visible signal must be made and maintained. But the boys neglect the fire, preferring to hunt and kill pigs. Under Jack's leadership, this hunting soon turns to murder, first of Simon, then of Piggy, the group's obese and asthmatic intellectual. Finally, Jack's gang hunts Ralph himself.

I could not stop myself from identifying with Piggy. With his glasses broken, he was handicapped; asthmatic, he was the object of universal scorn; bookish, he was somewhat socially naive.

Golding's book brought me face to face with the issue of evil in man. I always had found it possible to acknowledge, intellectually, the existence of such human characteristics. But to take the next step and to recognize evil in my own neighbors, and in myself, was something else altogether.

I had read with horror about the atrocities in Nazi Germany. But I could not imagine such barbarities happening in my own country, certainly not in my own town.

What *Lord of the Flies* did, and what nothing else I had experienced had been able to do, was to show me just how easily inhuman cruelty could emerge even in Lewisburg.

Like Piggy, I'd been subjected to the brutalities of which children are capable: mocked, scorned, beaten up. Unlike him, and this for me was the point, I had been able to escape because of the imposition of adult authority. The social structure around us had halted the beatings before they got out of hand. Remove that structure, I knew, and the cruelties would escalate, feeding one upon the other.

This must be, I thought, what had happened to Nazi Germany. When a culture encourages debasement of a people, and no restraining hand confines that debasement, it is not long before the people debased are visibly harmed. They become thin, bruised, nervous. This evidence, in turn, must stimulate their oppressors, much as the wounding of a pig excited Jack's gang. It is then but a short step to destroying altogether the debased people.

The following summer I saw something else that can happen to people who are oppressed. In Philadelphia, in the Bedford-Stuyvesant section of Brooklyn, in Jersey City, and in Rochester, New York, angry blacks ravaged a thousand stores. Hundreds were wounded. The riots of 1965 were the anguished cry of people desperate for attention. With their lives so devoid of meaning and their property so devoid of value, the wonder is that they had not rioted earlier.

The answer, I thought, must be that they had only recently begun to hope. That, if true, would constitute a devastating comment on America: fully 100 years after emancipation, millions of blacks were only beginning to feel they could aspire to social justice. *Brown v. Board of Education*, Martin Luther King and the Southern Christian Leadership Conference, the march from Selma to Montgomery, the march on Washington, and the passage of the Civil Rights Act of 1964: all of these filtered into the ghettos of America's cities, offering a glimmer of the possible to many thousands who had never dared hope.

It was not that something especially terrible had happened in the spring and early summer of 1965 to the blacks in the ghettos of Philadelphia, Brooklyn, and Rochester. In fact, almost the opposite.

"People think that revolutions begin with injustice," someone was reported to have remarked to King. "They don't. Revolutions begin with hope." Saul Alinsky made the same point differently. The world, he observed, was divided into the Haves, who know what they have and seek to protect it; the Have Nots, who have had all dreams beaten out of them; and the Have-A-Little, Want-Mores, who strive because they have hope.

The Civil Rights Act of 1964 prohibited discrimination on the basis of race and ethnic origin. It said nothing about ending discrimination on the basis of handicap. An employer still could say, with total impunity, "We won't hire deaf people—period," just as a school or college could deny a disabled person admission. And no federal law required public buildings to be accessible to individuals with physical disabilities. If revolutions begin with hope, a revolution of handicapped people was nowhere on the horizon.

I learned something else from that summer's riots. It is perhaps the saddest part of social justice. A people emerging from oppression have been deprived not just of hope but also of self-respect. In their anger and frustration, they will turn on themselves much more quickly than they will on the true sources of their misery. In Jersey City, Bedford-Stuyvesant, and Rochester that summer, most of the hundreds of people who were injured were not white but black; most of the thousands of buildings and businesses that burned were located in their own communities. People who hate themselves and their lives will tear down others like themselves.

Bob O'Dell's valedictory address at our commencement exercise was, the program informed me, about the Free Speech Movement that had begun the previous October at the University of California at Berkeley. What Bob had to say about Mario Savio and *in loco parentis* I had no idea as I sat rolling my program. And I didn't much care. Immediately following the program, the school sponsored a graduation party. I skipped it, as I had almost all high school social events. I didn't mind being alone that night. It was enough for me that I'd made it to this day, graduating 17th in a class of 188.

Two days later, I started my summer job at the local Ceco steel plant.

My father got me the job, after explaining as gently as he could that my chances of lining up some other job in the community were just about nonexistent. "Be honest with yourself, Frankie. You can't work in a store because you won't understand the customers' questions. In this area, there isn't much else in the way of summer jobs for high school graduates."

My assignment was easy enough: transfer order and shipment information from one set of records to another.

What I noticed very quickly, however, was how different my work was from that done by the employees all around me. They spent almost half of their time on the telephone; the other half, it seemed, was devoted to meetings. Since I could not use the telephone and since lipreading in meetings was almost impossible for me to do, the experience was a sobering one.

About a week before I left for college, I sat down in the living room with my father for a man-to-man talk about the business world.

"Dad," I began. "Thanks for getting me that job. I thought it would answer a lot of questions for me about working. It has. But it's raised a lot more questions that I desperately need answers to."

My father sat up, drumming his fingers on the coffee table, and nodded.

"First, there is such a thing as discrimination. You can't refuse to hire someone just because that person is black."

"Right, Frank. That change was long overdue, and I, for one, am glad it's on the books now."

"Me, too. Now for my question: Is there anything like this for people like me? I mean, is it illegal to reject me just because my ears don't work?"

Dad shook his head. "No."

"No, what?" I insisted.

"It's not illegal. There's no law anywhere that I'm aware of that says that you are protected against discrimination on the basis of your handicap. I'm a businessman, so I would know if there were any such law. And there isn't."

"None?"

"Frankie, why do you think I lined up that summer job for you? Did you think you could just get a job as a checkout clerk at Weis Supermarkets the way Chuck Vollmer did? Do you think you could become a host or waiter at the Pancake House like Robin did?"

"All these jobs require the ability to hear."

I slumped in my chair. "Dad, what am I going to do with my life?"

He smiled. "That's up to you, Frank."

"But how?"

"You'll find a way. It won't be easy. You will have to prove that you're twice as good as the next guy to get a job."

"But, Dad! If the jobs require hearing, nobody will hire me. I might be a great candidate, but if the job qualifications sheet says normal hearing is required, I won't even get a foot in the door. Nobody will even let me show them I can do the job, let alone that I'm better than somebody else!"

He shook his head. "Somebody will recognize your ability. You'll be hired. At any rate, you have a few years before you have to worry about it."

I was silent for a while.

"Dad, will it ever end?"

"What, son?"

"Having to work twice as hard, trying to be twice as good?"

He motioned me to the seat beside him.

"Yes, Frank. It will end. Remember what I told you about being a pro, when we were in Spring Lake, New Jersey? That it takes a hell of a lot of work to become good, but once you are, it's really rather easy. And look at yourself on the tennis court. As you told your mother and me, they don't care out there whether you can hear or not. Someday, it's going to be like that in your work, too."

I smiled as Mom came in to sit with us.

"Do you think," I asked them, "that they'll change the law so that handicapped people have an equal chance? So it won't be necessary to do a Superman imitation just to get a foot in the door? Like the law they changed giving blacks at least a ghost of a chance?"

Mom nodded. "I'm sure someone will."

My father shrugged. "Maybe they will, maybe they won't. But you can't wait for them. If it takes being twice as good, that's what you'll have to do."

I nodded. "O.K., Dad. I guess you're right. But someday, somebody's got to provide some rules. Because, you see, I'm very confused now about my future. I can think of a hundred jobs I can't do, or I'm not allowed to do, but it's awfully hard to think of even a handful I can do and will be allowed to do. That doesn't seem right.

"Why should my life be defined by what I don't have in my ears?"

My father looked into my eyes for what seemed a long time.

"Frank, you're more important than the rules are."

"But, Dad! You don't see. There have to be rules. It's just not right that most of life is closed off to me just because I was sick when I was small. It's not fair."

"Tell you what, Frank. You do this. First, you complete your college education and get yourself ready for a good job. And I mean ready: superbly prepared, so that you are without question the best candidate available, twice as good as anybody else.

"After you've done that and got the job, you can see what you can do to change the rules of the game.

"Until then, these are the rules by which you'll have to play."

Chapter
Eleven

From my first days at Western Maryland, I knew I'd made the right college choice.

It was absolutely wonderful to walk across the campus and see people say "Hi, Frank!"

They knew my name. They talked to me.

I was in Heaven.

People made the little efforts that made the big difference for me. Coming back from class one day to find Pat Fleeharty and Ron Clawson laughing in the hallway, I was startled when Pat turned to me: "Have you seen that movie, Frank?" He actually cared about my opinion.

For the first time in my life, I was included in bull sessions. One afternoon, I watched with fascination as Pat and Ed Coursey debated the existence of God; the group's conclusion was that Pat, an avowed agnostic, was the winner. Toward the end of the discussion, I tossed in a comment that Jeff Ludlow disagreed with. Treating me exactly as he treated everybody else when they said something he thought was stupid, he told me: "Fuck you!"

Perhaps nothing, aside from religion, captured quite as much of our attention as did the issue of race relations. We were very sensitive to the fact that ours reportedly was the first class in the College's history to include blacks. We boycotted a local barbershop when its proprietor claimed that cutting blacks' hair would damage his equipment. Probably we were naive. But we brought a passionate caring to our social activism, determined that in some small way we would improve the communities in which we lived.

And every Friday, we headed off campus for a "Gee, I'm Glad It's Friday" (GIGIF) party. In those pre-drug days, we were perfectly content with beer.

I quickly discovered who the good note-takers in my classes were and arranged to borrow their lecture notes. Sometimes, I almost wished I hadn't.

One of the best-attended courses in the freshman curriculum was Religion 101. The instructor, Dean Ira Zepp, was wonderfully popular because he was so relevant and down to earth. He didn't care, he told us, whether we looked at the Bible as literal truth or as literature, whether we preferred the Talmud or the New Testament. More important than the specifics of what we believed, he insisted, was the reality of what we did. If we lived

151

our lives according to a philosophy which reflected the values espoused by religion, we were being faithful to the highest virtues to which man can aspire. Dean Zepp spent more time discussing the moral emptiness of the secular Sixties than he did the teachings of the world's religions.

Now, a big problem with being deaf is that you miss out on a lot of what people really say, the kind of thing that doesn't get printed in newspapers and in books. I was picking up on a lot of that in our dorm bull sessions; that was where I learned, for example, that to say "fuck you" to someone could actually be a civilized comment. But I still had a long, long way to go. Just how far was illustrated the morning I trudged through the snow to the student center to find Larry Suder, whose notes I'd borrowed to get ready for the Religion 101 exam. I found Larry sitting with twenty other guys in the middle of a crowded room.

"Larry," I said as I arrived at his table. "I've found something in your notes that I don't understand. Sometimes you use initials, you know, and these appear so often throughout the notes that I really can't make sense of Zepp's lecture unless you explain them to me."

"Sure, Frank. What initials? And speak up. There's a lot of noise in this room."

I nodded. "V.D.," I shouted.

Twenty men bawled with laughter.

"Hey, Frank! You putting us on?" yelled Greg Getty.

"O.K., guys, calm down. I'm stepping out for a moment with Frank," Larry said. And taking me to a corner, he patiently explained that the initials stood for venereal disease.

I soon decided upon a triple major: English, philosophy, and religion. English because I still needed to master the coin of the realm, and because a bachelor's degree in English would help me in a broad range of fields from journalism to education to law. Philosophy because I wanted to develop a personal philosophy by which to guide my life; nothing, I thought, could be as important. And religion because it is through the world's religions that men have grappled with the great philosophical issues of the meaning of life and the value of man. Having worked so hard to be able to live a life at all, I wanted mine to have meaning and value.

One theme permeated almost all of my courses in English, philosophy, and religion. And that was Existentialism. It almost caused me to despair of ever working out a personal philosophy.

For Socrates, the Stoics, Spinoza, and others, philosophy was a way of life. For the existentialists, it sometimes seemed that philosophy was a way of death.

It probably began with Dostoevsky's *Notes from the Underground,* a shrill voice screaming that no good society can save man from depravity. I was reminded immediately of Golding's *Lord of the Flies.*

Nietzsche took Dostoevsky one step further. In *Antichrist,* a caustic

Glenn Limbaugh, left, and friend: Exuberance and a TR-3.

Fraternities are serious business: VP Bowe is below the coat of arms, President Pat Fleeharty is at right.

critique of Christianity, Nietzsche proclaimed, with a kind of awed horror, the death of God. In a fascinating passage, Nietzsche has the Madman bring the message that man himself has killed God, a terrible but glorious accomplishment.

The implications of the "death of God" philosophy were then explored by Sartre in *The Wall* and by Camus in a similar story called *The Stranger*. Both portray a man facing death. Sartre maintains that the highest value man possesses is that of integrity; his protagonist in *The Wall* remains true to his friend Gris even in the face of certain execution for something Gris has done. At *The Wall's* end, he is spared only to learn that Gris has been killed at a cemetery. Life, Sartre concludes, is absurd; it has no meaning. Nothing is finally important; there is no point to life. Yet, recognizing that and absorbing it in all its awful implications, the absurd man makes something of his life by remaining true to his own values.

In *The Stranger*, Camus insists that nothing, not even the death of another person, is important. Monsieur Meursault kills a man for no apparent reason; it is not an act he regrets, even when he is condemned to die for it. What he does regret is that his own life is to be shortened. I understood Camus to be saying that what matters is to live this life fully, to enjoy it for what it offers, and to regret nothing that it presents.

I thought the highest expression of existentialism was achieved in Camus' *The Myth of Sisyphus,* a volume of reflections on the Greek myth of the man who was condemned by the gods to an eternity of pushing a rock up a mountain only to have it fall back again. The gods, Camus points out, thought nothing could be worse than this futile exercise. Yet Camus insists that we must imagine Sisyphus happy: he knows his own fate, is conscious of it, and scorns it. For these reasons, his fate belongs to him and he transcends it. Sisyphus, then, is the absurd hero: he scorns the gods, he hates death, he has a passion for his own life.

The message that Nietzsche's Madman brings, that man has killed God, is a shattering message. Modern man, the existentialists maintain, has lived as though there were no God; the day-to-day reality of modern life is undeniably secular. What is devastating is to remove man from a world in which God is pervasive, if only in framing the beginning and ending of life and permeating it with meaning, to a world in which man is truly and finally alone.

Religion, existentialism insisted, belonged to the childhood of the human race. As adults, we must face up to the fact that we must define our own lives with no hope that they will have any "meaning."

While the poet Matthew Arnold would flee in horror, as in "Dover Beach," the existentialist would leap with joy: "I am Free!" And he would proceed to exist fully each day, dependent upon no one and caring about no one other than himself and his own independently arrived at values.

But existentialism, I found, ultimately was empty. All the "death of

God" theorists had demonstrated was the obvious: modern life is secular. And as the eminent Jewish theologian Martin Buber pointed out, to speak of "the death of God" is the height of arrogance. What has died, or at least declined, is man's own ability to have faith in a higher intelligence, not that intelligence itself. Buber reminded us that the God of the Talmud made an eternal covenant with the people of Israel, a covenant that stands regardless of any fluctuations in man's interpretation of its meaning.

And I could not accept the idea that having sacrificed so much to be able to live a life of any quality, the struggle finally was in vain, as for the existentialists it must be. There had to be something for which all of this effort had meaning.

One answer I found a bit later in Chaim Potok's *The Chosen*. For Rabbi Saunders, life assumes meaning in carrying on the mystical Hasidic traditions. For David Malter, it is in bringing rationality to interpretations of the Talmud. And for their sons, Danny Saunders and Reuven Malter, life's meaning arises from scholarship to help others, Danny in psychology and Reuven in the rabbinate. Only Danny bears even a faint resemblance to Ayn Rand's character Howard Roark. Yet in all five characters, one theme emerges: a life given in pursuit of a dream is the highest of callings. As David Malter puts it: "I am doing things I consider very important right now. If I could not do these things, my life would have no value. Merely to live, merely to exist—what sense is there to it? A fly also lives."

Existentialism, I concluded, taking its meaning literally, would lead me merely to exist, not to live. By contrast, pursuing a dream would allow me to live in the fullest sense of the word.

Social life at Western Maryland was dominated by the school's four fraternities and four sororities; to be an "independent," that is, not a fraternity or sorority member, was either to be very daring or to be a social outcast. Not wanting to be either, yet almost certain that none of the frats would select me, I played the rushing game with an anticipation masked by feigned indifference. And then one day as I walked off the tennis courts after a hard-fought match with Gettysburg College, the Black and White's vice president approached me on the Hill.

"Frank! Good to see you! We'd be delighted if you'd join up with us. That is, if you haven't already committed yourself to another house."

I was astonished. Somehow, I mumbled something to the effect that I'd be honored to be a Black and White.

"Great, Frank! We've got a great group this year. It may be our best pledge crowd in memory. I'm so glad you'll be part of us, Frank."

With that, he excused himself to pass the word at the frat. Watching him go, I was deeply pleased that he was so pleased.

It made my year.

Brooklyn blew again that summer. But it was startling to learn about race riots in Omaha, Nebraska; Des Moines, Iowa; Providence, Rhode Island; and Minneapolis, Minnesota. Even Pompano Beach, Florida, was razed. By the time the summer ended, some 40 cities had been hit.

When I returned to college for my sophomore year, all we in the frat house could talk about were the riots—and the avowed racist who had captured, somehow (no one knew quite how), the Democratic nomination for Governor of Maryland. His campaign motto, "A Man's Home is His Castle," said it all. It was a sickening reminder that Maryland is south of the Mason-Dixon line.

Like Pat Fleeharty, Jeff Ludlow, and most of my frat brothers, I vowed to act on behalf of the great cause of racial justice. Here, I thought, I could find the overriding purpose I sought in life, a *raison d'être* that would justify the sacrifices I'd made. Yet it was not to be so simple. Unlike Pat, I found myself thoroughly confused by the direction the movement was taking.

My world seemed to have turned on its head. It was not just that I found myself supporting Spiro Agnew for Governor; I could justify that as the lesser of two evils. But the criticism of King and his Southern Christian Leadership Conference for their tactics of non-resistance by the likes of Stokely Carmichael was something else altogether. Everywhere I turned in my search to find a place and a role in the equal-rights movement, I found more militant groups—primarily of younger blacks—doing their best to reject me and everything I knew. Stokely's Student Nonviolent Coordinating Committee seemed, despite the name, bent on inflaming, not dousing, the burning hatred between the races. The chant, "Black Power," seemed calculated to make me feel guilty, and unwanted, because my skin was white. Pat could overcome all of that by ignoring it, but I couldn't.

A few trips to Baltimore, a couple of weekends in the backwater flats of Westminster, and I knew I was unwanted in this movement. Just walking in the door produced sneers from the very people I'd come to work with. I felt compelled immediately to prove a negative: that the fact of my skin color did not mean I was one of "them."

If my life had taught me to recognize one thing, it was when I was not wanted. Yet, I could not understand how a civil-rights movement expected to be successful by alienating its own supporters and potential supporters.

I still needed a cause.

By April, I thought I'd found it. The Johnson Administration had singled out Appalachia as a region as much in need of help as any of the world's developing nations. And Western Maryland's students had responded by organizing a Student Opportunities Service, popularly known as SOS, to conduct summer projects in Mohawk, West Virginia, a tiny mountain town near the Kentucky border. I immediately signed up to accompany Walt Michaels and Ellen von Dehsen to Mohawk in late summer.

Partly to plan the project, and partly because carrying three majors was proving to be a burden, I stayed at the college in June for the first session of summer school. By the end of my first week, I'd almost forgotten about Appalachia.

Bonnie was beautiful, her long brown hair and large brown eyes sparkled with warmth, her bright white teeth flashed in an easy smile. In the Library one morning, I was captivated immediately by her smile as I opened the door for her—and drawn magnetically by the sadness behind her eyes.

"Why, thank you."

"You're welcome, uh, uh."

"Bonnie."

"My name's Frank. Why haven't I seen you around here before?"

She smiled. "Because I haven't been around here before."

I saw her that evening at supper.

"Mind if I sit down?"

"Sure, Frank. Please do."

"Bonnie, where have you been?"

She sipped some ice tea. "Well, to start at the beginning, Red Lion. That's in the southern coal regions of Pennsylvania."

"I know. I'm from Lewisburg."

"Oh, yes. Bucknell."

"So what brought you here?"

She sighed. "I need a few more credits to qualify for teacher's certification. So I'm here to take a Spanish course this summer."

"And then you'll teach?"

"Yes. Finally."

"Huh?"

"It took an awfully long time. This is the first job offer I've got, so I don't want to lose it."

"Did you plan to be a teacher?"

"No. That's why I need these extra credits. But it's the only thing open, I'm afraid."

I waited for her to explain. After a while, it became evident that she wasn't about to. So I changed the subject.

"May I walk you back? Unless of course you're living off campus?"

"No. I don't drive."

I was silent.

"It's a terrible burden, sometimes. I hate being so dependent on the cab companies."

As we walked across the side of the hill to McDaniel Hall, Bonnie talked about helping a girlfriend of hers in the Miss America pageant.

"Bonnie, you could have competed yourself."

"No. I couldn't do that."

The next morning I met her at McDaniel so I could walk with her to class.

"Have you seen 'The Sound of Music,' Frank?"

I admitted I hadn't. "I don't go to movies that much."

"Oh, you must see it! You really must. It's my favorite movie!"

"It's a musical, isn't it?"

"Oh, yes. The songs are beautiful. You'll love 'Climb Every Mountain.' And my favorite, 'I Have Confidence.' Promise me you'll see it, Frank? Please?"

That weekend I drove up to Gettysburg to see it. Twice.

She was right: I liked it. "Climb Every Mountain" struck me as a stirring song of hope, something like "The Impossible Dream." But I noticed that Maria sang "I Have Confidence" precisely because she did not have confidence.

I found Bonnie walking through the quad to lunch a few days later. With her was another Spanish student.

"Hi!" I said. "I saw it. I liked it."

"Oh, Frank. This is Betsy. I'm glad you liked it. Betsy and I were talking about, of all things, boxing."

"For what it's worth," I said, "you've not seen anything until you've seen Cassius Clay."

"Oh, yes!" Bonnie agreed. "You've just got to see him, Betsy. There's a beauty and a grace to Clay that no one has ever had."

Suddenly, I felt very close to Bonnie. And understood, all of a moment, how the simplest banalities in conversation can have another kind of meaning.

That evening as we strolled slowly around the track field, Bonnie grasped my hand firmly and swung my arm in rhythm with hers.

"You know, Bonnie, I think I'm starting to fall in love with you, mystery woman that you are."

She stopped. Looking deep into my eyes, she seemed lost in thought. Then we started walking again, more slowly this time.

"Frank, there's no mystery."

"I think there is. So many unanswered questions. You're beautiful, yet you don't think you can enter a beauty contest. You don't drive. Your favorite song is about hoping to believe in yourself but lacking all confidence. You had such a hard time landing a job, and it's not even what you planned to do with your life."

She was silent. The dusk was growing, and with it my worries that it would soon be too dark for me to lipread her.

"I'll tell you, someday. If you really want to know. But I doubt you do."

"Bonnie, give me a little credit. I care for you, as much if not more than

158

I have for anyone else in my life. I hope you'll accept that and perhaps respond in kind."

"All I can tell you, Frank, is this: You can't love someone else until you love yourself."

It was my turn to be silent.

"And I don't love myself. So you may be asking too much of me."

I left her at the door to McDaniel and returned to my dorm, overwhelmed with confusion.

And then the trip to Mohawk was upon me. With a goodbye kiss, her address in Richmond, Virginia, and a promise to write every week, I was off.

My father had arranged for me to use an ancient green pickup truck. I drove it ten hours through breathtaking valleys and heart-thumping mountain curves to reach the one-road town of Mohawk.

Staying in the homes of the people we worked with, Walt and I plunged into our work. We assembled a library of books and converted part of a schoolhouse building to house them; we took a dozen kids in the pickup truck to the state park for swimming every morning; we traversed to Charleston to argue for a new paved road for Mohawk. Each Friday evening, we joined the men for pickup games of softball. We helped the community scrape up the funds for a school bus. And we urged the townsfolk, in every way we could, to speak up about their own needs, to ask for what they wanted, to organize so they would get it.

Slowly, despite our feverish activity, I began to wonder just what we were doing there. The teenaged boys were waiting until they could enlist in the Army, which would take them out of the mountains. I knew they'd never return. The men worked hard, played hard, and christened their coal trucks "Widow Makers." The women appreciated our library but seemed hardly likely to use it. All our arguments about political strategy and community organizing seemed to fall flat before the smiling faces of the people of Mohawk.

They were a warm, wonderful, genuinely human group of people. But their sense of values differed so much from ours that I doubted the chasm could be bridged. I loved them, cared intensely for them, but knew, somehow, that what we were doing would mean very little to them in the long run.

And I couldn't forget Bonnie. Three or four times a week, her letters arrived. She was settled, looking forward to school; Richmond was hot; and would I come when I finished in Mohawk?

My six weeks in Mohawk ended almost before they had begun. I packed my clothes into the pickup and began the long, long drive to Richmond. All the way, I thought about how I'd tell Bonnie about the projects, about my life (we'd never gotten into it, strangely enough), and about the idea of bridging cultural values.

Walt and Ellen and the rest of us, I decided, probably had taken more from Mohawk than we'd given to the people there. We brought with us a set of values, a way of life, that those people probably could never know. We knew, after all, that we'd go back to college. Most of us knew what we'd do with the rest of our lives. We were able to plan them. For us to come into a mountain town like Mohawk and work on our "projects" made us feel good. But how did it make them feel? Five years later, what would they remember most? The library—or the remarkable optimism and carefree banter of the self-assured, politically active, college students?

It was a sobering thought, one I was eager to discuss with Bonnie.

I never got a chance. Five minutes after I entered her apartment, I found her crying.

"Oh, Frank! I just can't take this any more. I'm so dependent on the cabs all the time, and it gets me down so much I don't even know where up is any more."

"I think you'd better explain, Bonnie."

She nodded.

"It's my epilepsy. I have the grand-mal kind. But I haven't had a seizure in more than a year, Frank. The medicine controls it very well. I still have those petit-mal seizures, but they're not seizures at all, just little blinks of the eye.

"Anyway, that's why I'm not allowed to drive."

"And the beauty pageant?"

"Frank, can you imagine what that kind of pressure might do to me? The excitement? Those girls look like they're cool as cucumbers out there, but let me tell you, I've seen it from the inside, and it's as competitive as anything you can imagine. I'm afraid it would set off a seizure."

I nodded. "Does the school know about it?"

"Oh, yes. They have to. But they were the first who were willing to take a chance on me. After waiting so long, Frank, you can see why this is so important to me."

"Bonnie, of course I do. Now let's get on with your life. As long as I'm here, I'll take you anywhere you want to go. You can forget about cabs today at least."

"Oh, good. Then let's go to McDonalds. I love it there!"

The next morning I stopped by her school on my way out of Richmond.

"I have confidence. In you, Bonnie."

She smiled.

"I really do."

Just before I started my junior year, I was saddened to read that H. Rap Brown, Stokely Carmichael's successor at the Student Nonviolent Coordinating Committee, had attacked Zionism and American Jews. There go your biggest supporters, I thought, as I read story after story commenting on Brown's demand for "separatism."

A few days later, I read about the Chicago gathering of the National Conference for New Politics. Floyd McKissick was reported to have demanded that blacks be given the votes to control the convention—and they were. Shouting: "What right has a white man amending the black man's resolution?" he pushed through proposal after proposal, insisting that the white man had to demonstrate his trust in blacks by adopting the blacks' proposals without change.

It was in a somber mood that I returned to Western Maryland.

The rules were breaking down, I thought. Brown and McKissick reminded me uncomfortably of the hatred of Nazi Germany—and of Golding's *Lord of the Flies*.

The so-called "New Left" student movement against paternalism on campus and the war in Vietnam made little more sense. I could support their goals wholeheartedly, as I could those of black Americans, but their tactics seemed just as shortsighted as those of Carmichael and Brown.

And the music of the times left me helpless. I could not begin to understand what "acid rock" was all about. Reading about Jefferson Airplane and The Grateful Dead in *Time* and *Newsweek,* I found I could not even understand the words used to describe their music.

I was feeling very alone, very much of a stranger in my own country. But, back on campus I was quickly caught up in the routine of classes, homework, and studying for exams. First semester flew by.

One afternoon in February, I journeyed to Frederick to report a story for my journalism class. I did the interviews as best I could, took voluminous notes, and returned to the campus to type up the piece.

Two days later, Nancy Winkelman returned my paper.

"This is good stuff, Frank. But you've made a number of factual errors. I'm surprised at you."

"I must have misunderstood some of what they told me."

"I guess you did. But Frank, accuracy is the first requirement of good journalism. If you want a career in this field, you'll have to work out some way to interview people in person and on the phone so you get your facts straight."

I folded my paper and refolded it.

"I kind of hoped to do editing rather than reporting. That way, my ears wouldn't matter so much."

"I'm sorry to disappoint you, Frank. But in journalism everybody starts as a reporter. They send you out on hundreds of stories before you build up enough of a reputation even to be considered as an editor. One mistake in those stories they might forgive; two they won't.

"And you should know that editors spend more time, if anything, talking to people and on the phone than reporters do."

I could see the door closing.

Teaching was out. Business was out. And now it seemed writing, the one thing I did well, was also out.

I could not, for the life of me, think of what was in.

I felt like chucking it all when Pat Fleeharty barged into my room to announce that he was running for fraternity president, to serve in our senior year.

"How'd you like to be vice president, Frank?"

"Me?" I could not imagine a more farfetched notion. Me, a person the world finds useless, running for vice president of a fraternity I was lucky even to be a member of?

But Pat was persistent.

"Guys," I said in my campaign presentation in our meeting room one evening in March, "a fraternity is supposed to be a brotherhood. Yet a lot of you fellas are acting as though it means nothing to you.

"Well, let me tell you, it means a great deal to me. You guys were the very first group of people to select me as a member of a social organization. I can't even begin to tell you what that meant to me, at a time when I really needed it.

"If elected as your vice president, I'll work with our new president to do whatever I can to make this body as meaningful to all of you as it is to me."

I sat down. "Great speech!" Pat gestured.

Somehow, I won, polling almost as many votes as Pat did for president.

Well, I thought: here's reason at least to look forward to one more year of life.

On April 4, 1968, James Earl Ray shot Martin Luther King, Jr. at the Lorraine Motel in Memphis. It seemed the end of King's "dream." I remembered his remarkable speech in 1962 from the Lincoln Memorial, one of the best I'd ever read. It seemed so long ago now, almost another era, a time when things made sense.

The riots that followed dwarfed anything we had seen before. That spring alone, some 200 cities were hit by race riots.

And then on June 4, Robert Kennedy was killed in the Ambassador Hotel in Los Angeles. All I could think of was Bobby Kennedy quoting Jack Kennedy quoting George Bernard Shaw: "You see things, and you say 'Why?' But I dream things that never were and I say 'Why not?' "

Then there was Nixon and his "Silent Majority." The only answer was Hubert Humphrey. But the New Left, inept as always, killed his campaign before it could begin. When Chicago burned as the Yippies fought Mayor Daley's policemen, one could almost feel the last gasps of hope drain from Humphrey's campaign.

There was nothing left, I thought, as I watched the election returns the

162

following November. It was my senior year, but I could see no purpose to my life after college; no career into which I could move.

I thought of Randy, my high school classmate still paralyzed back in Lewisburg, and of my frustration at being unable to offer him anything of value. I knew from my parents' letters and visits to Lewisburg that his condition was unchanged. Despite several trips to Richmond, and many letters, I was unable to help Bonnie out of her despair. And, when I learned from Walt that the bus we had helped the folks in Mohawk purchase had overturned on the way to a football game, killing several students, I knew again the rage of helplessness.

Reading John Updike's *Rabbit Run* was perhaps the final straw. Rabbit Angstrom had once been good at something—basketball; but once he left school, everything went downhill. He failed—and he ran from his failure. I could visualize, with very little little effort at all, leading just such a life, if "life" is the word for it.

Staring bitterly at the snowstorm raging outside my window, I drafted "By The Time I Get Some Hearing," offered here with apologies to Jimmy Webb:

By the time I get some hearing
They'll be laughing, yes they will
They'll change the game on me, leave me
hanging there
And they'll keep on changing it again and again
'Cause they've planned that way
with such precious care.

By the time my ears start working
They'll be moving, yes they will
They'll move the frequencies past what
I can hear
And they'll keep on moving it up and up and up
to where only they can hear.

By the time I figure it out
They'll be playing, yes they will
A game of questions, twenty questions
And they'll win just like they always did
and always will.

It was then that I selected the topic for my honors thesis: the absurd in John Barth and Albert Camus, with consideration of the implications for suicide. The Existentialism I had so firmly rejected just two years ago now seemed, damnably, accurate. And I knew that suicide was something I was going to have to take seriously as an option. I didn't want a life like that led by Rabbit Angstrom.

The low point came during final exam week in December. Crushed by the burden of preparing for four finals in two days, exhausted from the effort of the two finals already completed, certain that there was no way I could master the mountain of material I needed to memorize for the remaining two, deprived of any hope that it would mean anything, I staggered from my study cubicle in Memorial Hall across the blizzard-swept quad.

I'll just have to give up, I thought.

Eighteen years of struggle, frustration, pain, and sacrifice. And finally, ultimately, it was pointless.

Then, half-way back to the frat house, I thought of my father.

His face shone through the endless curtain of snow: "If you're not going to do your best, don't do it at all."

And I saw again the note he wrote on the back of the picture of our championship Little League baseball team: "We just like to put all we have in everything we do."

I turned back, unpacked my books, and studied.

A week later, I learned I'd got A's in three of the four finals.

Still, I came back to Western Maryland after the holidays heavy with gloom. Without quite knowing how, I drove west from Gettysburg instead of south, and found myself in Frederick.

I might as well stop over at the school for the deaf, I thought.

A few minutes later, I found myself escorted to a classroom filled with eleven- and twelve-year-olds.

Dropping to one knee, I talked with each of them. They flicked their fingers and swept their hands in rapid gestures, none of which I understood. But they seemed fascinated by my hearing aid.

One boy, whose name tag said he was Danny, walked up to me, pointed to me, and then to himself. Then he made a simple gesture joining the two of us.

"He's saying 'same,' " my escort translated.

I turned back to Danny.

"Same," I signed.

His face lit up. A few moments later, the group crowded around me. It was all my escort could do to keep up with the questions. Where was I from? When had I become deaf? What did I do? Did I have any brothers or sisters?

I answered all the questions, then begged to depart.

I was overcome with emotion, just overwhelmed at a sudden and very powerful sense of kinship, of belonging, and, yes, of being needed.

I knew I had little to offer these kids, other than myself. But I knew where to learn what I had to know: Gallaudet.

Moving quickly, I applied to and was admitted to the Gallaudet Graduate School master's degree program in education of the deaf. From the federal government, I secured a fellowship covering tuition and expenses, plus a generous allowance for subsistence.

My final semester of college was a whirlwind of activity. There was fraternity business. As captain of the tennis team, I had to help Mr. Mobray get our young squad together. Induction into *Omicron Delta Kappa*, the national men's leadership society, moved me deeply as a manifestation of the fact that I'd done more than study in my four years on the Hill.

I finished my honors thesis in a week. Blasting Albert Camus for a bleak, rudderless view of life and dissecting the flaws of Todd Andrews' reasoning in John Barth's *The Floating Opera,* I concluded triumphantly that life was worth living because ideas and beliefs, particularly those that mold people's lives, are worth a person's life and more.

My father's ruddy face never had seemed so peaceful as it did the evening before commencement.

Almost everything he said to Mom and me over dinner reflected the pride he felt, yet could not quite believe. "I told you so!" was the unspoken message of almost all his reminiscences that night.

As coffee was served, he turned to me.

"Well, son. What will you do now?"

I smiled. "Rest."

"Seriously, Frank."

"Seriously, Dad, I want to get my M.A. at Gallaudet. It will do two things for me. First, it will teach me what deafness means to me and to others; I need to separate out deafness from the rest of me, just to find out who and what I am. I can't remember ever not being deaf, you know, and it will be good to understand what this thing is all about that I've been fighting so hard for almost two decades."

"Fighting hard—and winning!"

"Right, pop! Probably more important, it will help me do something I feel strongly about.

"When I was growing up, there was nothing there to help me. I notice there still isn't. I know there are little Frankies throughout the Susquehanna Valley area—and it looks as if no one will give them the help they need unless I do. So I will.

"I learned in West Virginia that good intentions aren't enough. I've got to equip myself with the ability to provide those kids with the education they need.

"Once I'm satisfied I've done that, and that what I've built will stand, I'll complete my education. Probably get a doctorate in psychology, since, after all, I'm interested in working with people.

"But there's only so much I can do in a classroom or with a Ph.D. if people still respond only to my deafness. The fact that I've won under these rules doesn't mean I like them. Someday, I want to change the rules of the game."

I smiled.

"That's about as far down the road as I want to look right now."

My father grasped my shoulder. "If that's all you do, you'll have lived a full and magnificent life."

"You know, Dad," I added as he paid the bill. "Commencement doesn't signal an ending. The word itself means beginning. I'm glad you're proud of what I've done so far. But I'm only starting, Dad. It's just beginning."

The following afternoon I sat through another mindlessly boring assembly, understanding nothing for three interminable hours.

But I didn't mind.

Sitting in the balcony, his body held high with pride and joy, was my father. His attention was not on the speakers. Rather, it was on a piece of paper he held in his hand.

The paper said: "Frank Bowe. *Summa cum laude*."

Chapter
Twelve

Gallaudet College sits on a quiet 99-acre campus in Northeast Washington, D.C., just off Florida Avenue and Eighth Street.

It is an amazing place.

From the classrooms to the dormitories to the dining hall and library, everything is designed to reflect the fact that the people using the college's facilities cannot hear. Everywhere, there are closed-circuit television monitors showing the same programs one sees elsewhere—except that these are captioned, so deaf people can read the dialogue others hear.

All of the instructors are skilled not only in fingerspelling but also in sign language. They talk in two languages at once, spoken English and the language of signs. Even in the smallest, most out of the way office, a deaf person finds someone who can sign.

So completely is the college devoted to meeting the needs of students who cannot hear that even the hearing staff and faculty often sign to each other.

Only at Gallaudet can a deaf person eavesdrop on the conversations of everyone else in the dining hall.

One of the first things I did after coming to Gallaudet was to have my hearing tested by its expert audiologists at the college's Mary Thornberry Speech and Hearing Clinic.

Based upon my memories, now becoming rather faint, of audiometrists in Danville and New York, I expected somehow that my lack of hearing would cause some comment or reaction by the testers. At Gallaudet I got no such response; then I realized: Of course. They test deaf people every day here.

To no one's surprise, my hearing registered at 110 decibels in the speech range; I made no response at all to most of the pure tones they offered me.

So now I saw it certified with my own eyes: You're profoundly deaf, Frank!

I had not been at Gallaudet two weeks before I learned that McCay Vernon, the eminent authority on the psychology of deafness, had accepted a professorship at, of all places, Western Maryland College. My *alma mater* was starting its own graduate program to prepare teachers of deaf children, complete with experts on the faculty, interpreters, and notetakers for the deaf students.

The irony of it all was not long sinking in. I could have used some of that kind of help while I was there, I thought angrily as I read the college's announcement. But the feeling passed as quickly as it had come.

The next weekend I drove up to Westminster to meet the great man.

Dr. Vernon met me at the door.

"Ah, Frank. I've heard of you. Come on in!"

I sat, expressing my thanks that he could spare a few moments for me.

"Not at all. Not at all. It's my pleasure to meet this young man about whom I've heard so much. And about whom I'm sure I'll be hearing much more!"

That was Mac Vernon.

I returned to visit with him several times throughout the year, more to soak up his inspiring confidence and joyful expectation than anything else. He believed I could do something, that I would make a contribution. And he convinced me he was right.

Mac introduced me to several federal officials responsible for research and demonstration projects funding in the areas of speech, hearing, and vision. They, in turn, arranged for me to work with them as a research assistant while I completed my studies at Gallaudet.

Exposure to the state-of-the-art in national research on deafness, blindness, and speech impairment; the chance to come to know Mary Switzer, the agency's head and a giant in rehabilitation; and the opportunity to understand the potential of scientific study in rehabilitation and special education—all these made my job at HEW (the Department of Health, Education, and Welfare) fascinating. L. Deno Reed, Sc.D., to whom I reported, urged me to consider going to a federally funded university program for my doctorate; he especially recommended New York University.

I was tempted.

But then on a holiday visit to Lewisburg, I committed myself again to doing something for the children I knew were there, needing help, and not getting it.

It took me nearly a year to master sign language.

I learned by watching the interpreters Gallaudet supplied for every graduate-level class.

These wonderful people move their lips, fingers, hands, and arms to provide a total visual interpretation of everything they hear.

They will tell you if they hear a jet go by, if someone in the room coughs. Through their facial expression, they will convey the moods of the person speaking: sarcasm, anger, humor, delight.

The hands were at first distracting for me. I moved my head to be able to see the lips.

Gradually, imperceptibly, I began understanding the signs.

Then one day in the spring, I had it.

It was a most remarkable day.

168

Our instructor, Miss Heidinger, had asked a question, the answer to which I knew. To my astonishment, three of my normally hearing class-mates offered obviously inaccurate answers.

I looked from the interpreter to the students, my eyes wide with amaze-ment.

They're not superhuman after all! I thought.

From that moment, something in me relaxed.

Equally important was the opportunity knowing sign language gave me to understand what people were saying to each other.

For the first time in my life, I didn't have to take someone's word for it. I didn't have to read about it in books or ask my parents to explain.

I could see it, right there in front of me.

I spent hour after hour sitting in group rooms, watching one conversation after another.

It was a wonderful, settling experience. At last, I knew. This huge mystery I had wondered about for years. On one level, I was disappointed: most of the conversations were incredibly dull. Yet on another level, I was fascinated. What people actually say is only part of what they mean. I could see two people who knew each other well, interrupting each other, finishing the other's sentences. I could see, too, a kind of verbal shorthand between two close friends, a great deal left unspoken.

At Gallaudet, I learned a great deal about deafness and about techniques for teaching and rehabilitating deaf children and adults. Perhaps most intriguing for me was the research, just then underway, that was beginning to demonstrate that sign language was in no way harmful to deaf children. Astonished, I read study after study comparing the speech, receptive language, expressive vocabulary, academic achievement, and other char-acteristics of children reared with signs and other children reared without them. By the end of 1970, I was satisfied that "total communication," a term referring to an approach which includes speech, lipreading, finger-spelling, and sign language, probably was the best communication strategy to adopt with children deafened early in life.

My conviction led to long talks with my parents each time I returned to Lewisburg on vacation.

It was not a question of convincing them they had been wrong twenty years ago; I did not think they had been wrong at all. The issue was academic, at any rate. Given the information available to them at the time, they made the only decision that made any sense to them. My father, of course, was determined that he had been right. I didn't argue.

Something else, though, was of great importance to me.

"Look, you guys," I argued. "I've learned signs. Because I have, I've seen people talk. I've talked to people using real, long, genuine conver-sations. I know now what I didn't know for two decades: how people talk

169

to each other. And now that I know it, I realize what I've missed all these years.

"All I'm asking is that you learn some fingerspelling and a few signs so that we can communicate more fully. I know what a difference it will make. It will bring us closer as parents and son.

"For a very long time, I didn't mind the restrictions in communication around here, simply because I didn't know what I was missing. Now I do know it, and I do mind. It hurts to sit here and realize how far apart we so often really are."

Perhaps ten years earlier, things would have been different. As it was, though, my pleas fell upon unlistening ears, almost as though they now were deaf. No, they wouldn't learn signs. No, they didn't want to. They didn't mind that I knew signs, but they were not about to try to acquire another language at this stage in their lives. Besides, there were all those emotions they still had mixed up in all of this sign language business.

"We're tired, Frankie," Dad said, speaking for both of them. "We're old; change is something we don't want any more. And we feel we've done our job as best we knew how. We put you through college. Now, our part is over. You're on your own now. Please don't ask again. We're not going to learn that hand language."

Mom nodded her head in agreement. "You can, Frank. That's fine; it's your choice. But don't force it on us."

The time had come, I knew, to stop asking them to change their lives for me. They had done enough.

Intellectually, I knew that. Emotionally, however, it was very hard. I knew there was much that my parents never said to me. And I knew I missed a great deal of what they said to each other and to visitors in my presence.

I couldn't change their minds, though. At Thanksgiving, Christmas, and other holidays or vacations, the strain remained.

I remember feeling keenly disappointed—and somewhat angry at my parents. Here at last was a chance to make the give-and-take of normal family conversation easy for us all. To some extent, I interpreted their refusal to learn sign language as a rejection of the intimacy and warmth that closer communication would bring. Yet I knew that was wrong; they were tired, they had a lot invested in the proposition that they had raised me correctly, and they were getting older.

Just as they once had accepted me as I was, I knew now I had to allow them to live as they wished. I had forced enough changes upon them already.

When I received my master's degree in May, I returned immediately to central Pennsylvania to search for the opportunity I wanted to help the many children I knew were there in need of special education services. It was not long before I found it.

Bloomsburg, Pennsylvania, is about twenty miles east of Lewisburg. On a tall hill north of the world-famous Magee Carpet factories sits Bloomsburg University, part of the state system of teachers colleges, this one specializing in special education, particularly speech, hearing, language, and mental retardation.

I was hired by Russell Gilbert, district supervisor for the Central Pennsylvania Intermediate Unit, to locate children needing special education, screen them, select the most promising candidates for the program, install the class in Navy Hall at the university, teach the class, and do whatever else was necessary to administer and manage the program.

Immersing myself totally in the task, I did just that.

I found Glenda in tiny Dewart, north of Milton; in five visits to her kindergarten class, I did not see her say or seem to understand a word. Chris and Craig were in classes for retarded children. Hope, although old enough, was not in school at all. Profoundly deaf, severely visually impaired, seriously emotionally disturbed, and physically uncoordinated, she badly needed help. Steve I found at home; he had been expelled from the Pennsylvania School for the Deaf. Pamela came to my class when her family moved to Selinsgrove from Florida. And Tina I found in a Lewisburg kindergarten.

The schedule was brutal—and intensely rewarding.

From seven in the morning until three in the afternoon, I handled the classroom and taught the children. At three, I taught a daily sign language class to a group of fifty college students. At four-thirty, I napped (teaching small children is absolutely exhausting!). At six, I taught interested adults sign language at a Berwick church. At seven, I visited one of my seven children's families. I tried to see each family once weekly, if possible, but at least twice monthly. These were perhaps the most rewarding sessions; the parents used the signs they learned, put into practice the suggestions I offered on child psychology, and gave me invaluable insights into the children I was teaching.

By mid-year, the benefits of having the class at the university became apparent. A steady stream of student teachers and student therapists worked, under my supervision, to help each child with priceless individual attention. And the students, in turn, benefited greatly from the day-to-day contact with the children. I took the students with me to attend area meetings of organizations of deaf adults and to activities deaf people themselves had planned.

On Saturdays and Sundays, I worked with a nonverbal, nonvocal 47-year-old man who lived with his mother in Berwick. He had almost no communication whatsoever: a mute testimony to the devastating effect of deafness when educational intervention is not timely and powerful.

There was little I could do to help him; it was just too late.

But the children thrived! Craig demonstrated a mischievous intelligence

171

and joy in life that made me want to strangle the people responsible for placing him in a class for retarded children. Glenda's growth was so rapid that I had no doubt at all that she would be able to enter a regular first grade the following year. Shy, nervous Chris blossomed into a real leader, primarily because his parents were the most enthusiastically involved of all parents in the program. Hope's furious tantrums disappeared after the first two months—and one day she actually started talking to Chris! I was so stunned that I drove to her family's home that evening to report the news to her parents.

Pamela somehow became trusting, open, and warm despite what I knew was a traumatic, nomadic family life that had left her with nowhere she could call home. And Steve, ah! Steve was the artist, a consummate master of the hand and the eye.

I closed up the classroom for the children's Christmas vacation, turning out all the lights. And then I noticed a flickering light across the hall, in one of the speech-therapy rooms.

I lifted the shade and peered into the one-way mirror which revealed the happiest woman I'd ever seen smiling mischievously as she continued to give her lesson, though aware that she was being watched.

Her *joi de vivre* made her, for me, irresistible.

It was an effervescence that almost never wavered. As we talked, got to know each other, talked some more, and dated, I found it a lift just to be with her. And when our affair started, the friendship we had formed deepened and enriched the entire experience we found in each other.

Was she beautiful? Not especially. Unless you say, as you must, that personality can infuse a face and a body with beauty.

Anne had grown up her father's girl, the youngest child in a family with three older brothers. She was accustomed to men doing things for her. So she was demanding without quite realizing it. She thought nothing, for example, of asking me to drive three hours just to pick her up at her parents' home and drive her to Bloomsburg. When she asked, usually at the last moment, it had the effect of a demand.

But a man hopelessly snowed under always will obey.

She said she loved me. And I believe she did. But our codes of conduct were just too different. She always asked me to wait until Thursday of any given week before asking to spend a weekend evening with her, so she would know her plans. I waited only until Monday and insisted on an answer.

Boyfriends visited her at the small home she rented with two other girls—and stayed overnight.

Seeing that, I refused to talk to her for a week.

She asked me to drive her and a girlfriend to Baltimore one Saturday—they spent the weekend in an apartment shared by two men.

I terminated my involvement with her for three weeks after I found out who was in that Baltimore apartment. But somehow she made it seem insignificant and secured my forgiveness.

The affair went on and on. It was stormy, violent, and ecstatic. It lifted me to unimagined heights and plunged me to unspeakable depths.

Finally, I found myself being torn apart just too much. On the one hand, I thought I loved her; yet, just as intensely, I hated her. I could not conceive of what seemed to me to be such flippant amorality, the flitting from man to man like a bee among flowers.

Love, I concluded, must contain within it the element of trust. And when all was said and done, I could not trust her.

I was delighted to find at Geisinger Medical Center, in nearby Danville, someone who understood hearing impairment as no one there had twenty years before. Frank Rousseau worked with us in Navy Hall to set up a screening and evaluation program for preschool-age children in the area. We also worked with staff of the Danville State Hospital to test the hearing of persons admitted for psychiatric treatment; Rousseau and I were particularly concerned that some of the patients had been placed in the institution because their lack of hearing had been interpreted to indicate, not deafness, but mental illness. Muteness and apparent lack of interest in what other people say characterizes undiagnosed deafness as well as some mental disorders.

By year-end, the sign language classes held in the afternoons at Navy Hall had grown to seventy-five students. Of these, eight were promising enough to be prepared as sign language interpreters. For Hope, Steven, Pam, and other children and adults in the area who needed interpreters to attend regular schools or to enjoy cultural and entertainment offerings in the area, these eight students would now be available.

The children's parents completed an extensive evaluation of the program, rating it very favorably, and urging its continuation. They were particularly pleased with their children's development in reading, writing, use of residual hearing, speech, lipreading, expressive and receptive language, and social skills.

Mr. Gilbert of the Central Susquehanna Intermediate Unit agreed that the program had demonstrated its effectiveness and committed the agency to continue the services. In fact, expansion to include preschool education and resource-teacher assistance for children placed in regular schools were among his priorities for the following years.

Satisfied that a foundation had been established, I turned out the lights in Navy Hall for the last time. It was time to move on.

New York University's Washington Square Park campus in the heart of Greenwich Village includes a School of Education, Health, Nursing,

173

and Arts Professions. On the fifth and sixth floors of 80 Washington Square East was a federally funded research and training center specializing in deafness. I worked full-time there as a research scientist while pursuing my doctorate in educational psychology. As if the research and graduate studies were not enough, I also enjoyed teaching in graduate and undergraduate courses on deafness education and rehabilitation.

My work took me across the country for national conventions, student psychological assessments, survey research projects, and studies of employment discrimination against deaf individuals. My experience in Pennsylvania had made me sensitive to the special needs of persons with visual impairments, emotional disturbance, mental retardation, and other disabilities, so it was with keen interest that I plunged into projects dealing with the problems of multiply handicapped individuals. And the skills I had learned at Western Maryland helped me prepare numerous voluminous reports of research and training projects and deliver scores of speeches from coast to coast.

The work was rewarding and fulfilling; I knew my life was making a difference. That is why the 1974 selection as one of America's outstanding young men was meaningful to me; it came as recognition that what I was doing was having an impact upon the lives of people around me.

My doctoral courses proved equally engrossing. I was fortunate to have the services of excellent sign language interpreters in all of my classes, one of the benefits provided by the federal funding the university received for its research and training center. These remarkable men and women were able, somehow, to translate into visual symbols the arcane and complex vocabularies of advanced statistics and psychological research design.

I especially enjoyed Sue Wolf's interpretation of Professor Elazur Pedhazur's rapid-fire lectures on statistical models in behavioral research. Sue would walk into the room, greet me, and take her chair at the side of the room. As soon as Dr. Pedhazur began speaking, she closed her eyes as if to sleep and flawlessly translated language far removed from that her own exposure to mathematics had ever taught her. How she handled three solid hours of uninterrupted monologue, almost none of which she understood, fascinated me nearly as much as Pedhazur's easy mastery of the material and great talent for teaching it. Here's a sample of what Sue had to cope with:

"The basic data matrix for multiple regression analysis is the rectangular matrix of raw scores or z scores. The matrix for canonical analysis has the first subscript of each X stand for rows and the second subscript for columns. Notice the broken vertical line I've drawn here—it partitions the matrix into the k independent and the n-k dependent variables. The variables are intercorrelated, and a correlation or R matrix is formed. This matrix, too, is partitioned similarly. In the multiple regression correlation matrix, the dependent variable is partitioned from the independent variables. In canonical analysis the correlation matrix is partitioned using broken lines, and the independent and dependent variables are labeled. R equals the whole correlation matrix of the $k + (n-k)$ variables; R sub 1,1 equals the correlations of the k independent variables; R sub 2,2 the correlations of the $n-k$ dependent variables; R sub 1,2 the correlations between the independent and dependent variables; and R sub 2,1 the transpose of R sub 1,2.''

If I had needed any demonstration of the fact that the language of signs can handle anything the English language can present, Sue provided that evidence.

I doubt very much that without her help, and that of the interpreters who worked with her, especially Kathy Diamond, I could have completed the university's rigorous program of studies, let alone maintained an A average doing so.

And I doubt that without something else I could have enjoyed my stay in New York quite so much. For the first time in my life, I was able to make telephone calls on my own—with no one assisting me.

The remarkable invention by a deaf man named Robert Weitbrecht of the modulator-demodulator coupler (''modem''), which allowed a telephone to be connected with a typewriter-like keyboard device, produced what was then called a TTY, since the keyboard used was often an old teletypewriter, and is now known as a TDD, the initials standing for telecommunications device for the deaf. Its use is simple. One places the telephone receiver on the coupler, turns the machine on, dials (or punches) the number desired, and, once the connection is made, types a message and reads the responding message.

I could use my TDD only to call others who had a device like mine. But that was quite enough for someone who never before had made a telephone call unassisted. I spent delightful hours calling friends I had made across the country, running up monthly phone bills in the hundreds of dollars, which I was more than pleased to pay.

And then I discovered the network of volunteer services known as ''Contact.'' By calling these people on my TDD, I was able to reach anyone who had a telephone. I just typed what I wanted to say. The Contact staff person would relay my call, read my message aloud to the person I was calling, and then type that person's reply for me to read. The process was almost instantaneous, requiring little longer than would the same call between two persons who can hear.

The TDD that Lee Brody brought to my Washington Square Village apartment did as much as anything else to end my feeling of isolation from the world around me.

It was Contact that enabled me to return the phone call I received one evening from the director of the New York City Mayor's Office for the Handicapped. Eunice Fiorito, blind from childhood, was founder and president of a volunteer coalition of organizations representing people with all kinds of disabilities.

I met with her again and again, at her apartment on 33rd street and at her lower Broadway office. I found Eunice to be remarkably easy to lipread, something I can say for extremely few blind individuals; somehow, making their faces and lips easy for deaf people to understand is very difficult for most people who are blind. But Eunice, in this way as in so many others, showed that blindness limits her not at all.

And what she had to say to me brought back all of my memories of the civil rights struggle of the Sixties, the mistakes its leaders and those of the New Left made, and the political genius that was Martin Luther King, Jr. She spoke for hours on end about her dream of creating a national civil rights movement to be run by disabled people themselves to capture, at long last, an equal opportunity in all aspects of American life.

Her organization, the American Coalition of Citizens with Disabilities, had no office and a budget of little more than one hundred dollars—but it had, she said, "a heartful of hope." As the group's chairman of the board, it was her job, she said, to find a way to take these dreams and translate them into reality.

Blind people, Eunice told me, had experienced much of the same kind of discrimination I had faced all my life. People with physical disabilities could not even get around the city independently, since none of the mass transportation systems were accessible. No American city, she explained, offered accessible transportation even approaching the bare minimum needed to get to and from work. Employment discrimination was rampant. More than half of all disabled adults were not even in the labor force— they had been forced to give up jobs. Discrimination in housing was so severe that thousands of disabled people were staying in institutions or hospitals simply because they could find nowhere else to live.

I listened, fascinated, as she talked. I vowed that if ever I got the chance, I'd work for the goals she had outlined with such vivid clarity. At last, I could picture for myself a possible future—a challenge that excited me, that would draw upon all I had learned, and that would drive me to learn, and do, much more. Now I knew how I could change the rules.

Everything was coming together, I thought, as I neared completion of my doctoral studies. My ancient nemesis, the English language, was now a treasured friend, although surprises always lurked just around the corner.

The difference, I knew, had been my reading; the thousands of hours alone with books had paid off. Without really noticing it, I had absorbed the language, the nuances of its denotations, and the subtleties of its connotations. A major help, too, had been Latin: more than sixty percent of all English words have a Latin root.

I had survived the social isolation I knew as a teenager. I smiled to recall the embarassing moments at Eagles Mere and my invitation to Beth to see "Son of Flubber." It had taken a while, years longer I knew than was true for most people, for me to become comfortable in social settings and to enjoy the small talk I had found so difficult to understand. But now, I knew, I was much more complete as a person for the agonies I had endured.

I had shown that I could do good work—in teaching, public speaking, writing, research, and other areas. I had a record to show the skeptics who were so sure that it was impossible for me to do these things. My disability now was more a hindrance to me than a handicap. I knew how to surmount its effects and how to function despite its restrictions. With an interpreter, in fact, I was not handicapped at all.

I understood, too, how similar other disabilities were to deafness—and how to help people overcome these impairments. For the Randys and Bonnies in my future, I would have more to offer than just my sympathy and interest. Most important, I now knew how to love and accept love. And just in time.

I returned from the week-long retreat at Poor's mansion in Tuxedo Park able to think of little else than the beauty, character, intelligence, humor, and love of the most wonderful woman I had ever met.

I spent the weekend planning ways to impress her with my sophistication, world-weariness, and wit. The sight of her was enough, however, to make me forget all of those elaborate plans.

"Hi."

"Hi."

"Uh. How 'bout some coffee?"

"I'd love it."

A week later, I took her to see the movie, "Don't Look Now." Afterwards, we sat huddled in a booth in a small Village restaurant, unhurriedly catching up on each other's lives.

She loved horror books and movies, I learned; the gift of a novel of demonic possession one afternoon earned me a much-coveted hug. The next day I gave her two dozen and pouted when she stopped at one kiss. She shared my dislike of *Rabbit Run* and *The Floating Opera*. The evening I gave them to her she sent me off to buy Baskin Robbins ice cream; when I got back, the books were gone, and she was curled up with a story of supernatural horror.

By the time I took her, a month later, to see Woody Allen's "Sleeper," I knew for sure that I was hopelessly in love. I spent about twenty minutes looking at the screen. For the balance of the movie, my eyes were locked with hers.

Our six-month courtship was light as often as it was heavy. Desperate to talk to her late one evening, long after Contact's offices had closed, I wrestled with myself about calling her at her parents' home. At last, the urge was just too strong to resist. I dialed the number, verified on my TDD that the ring had been answered, picked up the receiver and spoke: "Phyllis, please." After waiting what seemed a suitable length of time for her to come to the phone, I began talking about what it was that I so urgently needed to tell her. For half an hour, I poured out my heart to her and hinted, as obliquely as I could, that perhaps we could consider the next step in our relationship.

When I saw her after Pedhazur's class two days later, I asked her if my call had been all right.

"Oh, yes, Frank," she said with a sparkling smile.

"Did you, uh, did you like what I said?"

"That's a good question. But I can tell you, my father enjoyed it very much."

"Your father!"

"Well, look at it this way. At least now he knows you really care for me."

"But where were you?"

"Asleep, Frank."

She squeezed my hand happily as we watched "The Fantastiks," off-Broadway's longest running hit. She laughed about her diet as we sampled almost every restaurant and club in the Village and East Village area. She sighed with contentment as we spent hours walking slowly through the exhibits set up all over Greenwich Village for the semi-annual Washington Square outdoor art show. She shrieked with terror atop a ferris wheel during an Italian festival in the East Village. And she mocked me with feigned sorrow until I took her to all her favorite Broadway shows.

I called her every night, sometimes just to say "Hi!"

I'd learned my lesson; I went through Contact to be sure it was she to whom I was talking.

By March, we knew it was right.

"I'll have a little surprise for you when we get together for dinner tomorrow, Phyl," I told her as I kissed her good night on the Ides of March.

"Oh, no you won't! I want to pick out this little surprise by myself, thank you very much!"

And she did—a beautiful, sparkling white diamond that cost about three times as much as I'd planned to spend. Well, after all, I had always known she was a woman who had very good taste. We picked it up a few days later, a bright, brisk, surprisingly windless day.

"You'll take care of me?" she asked, with her little-girl face as she slipped the ring on her finger.

I nodded and bent to kiss her.

"You promise? Really promise?" Satisfied, she nodded to herself and repeated *sotto voce:* "Ah, he promises!"

I called her, through Contact, that evening to ask if her parents liked it as much as she did. Phyl assured me they loved it, she loved it, and most important, she loved me. Content, I hung up.

One minute later, the phone rang.

"This is Contact," I read. "We just wanted to say that we've all been hoping for both of you. We're all delighted here. And we wish you the very best of everything."

"Frank and Phyllis have come here to affirm publicly their love for each other," Mel read from the script the three of us had prepared together.

"Today, they will become man and wife. It is a special time which they ask you to share with them."

My parents sat on one bench behind us, Phyl's family on a bench nearby. Behind them were the few close friends we had invited to the ceremony.

I thought of Phyl's laughing plaintive "Promise me!" For the first time, I would be responsible for someone other than myself. Far from making me solemn, the idea brought a quiet smile to my face. I'm ready, I thought, and there's no one for whom I would rather be responsible. I'm ready, too, to face the world and to take whatever it may throw at me. It's wonderful knowing that you'll be at my side.

I noticed Mel was still speaking.

"Blessed be he who comes in the Name of the Lord. O God, supremely blessed, supreme in might and glory, guide and bless this groom and this bride."

I looked at Phyllis. Her eyes lowered demurely, she looked as calm and as peaceful as I had ever known her. Yet I knew that in a few moments she would once again be a frisky fawn gallivanting through the crowd.

Mel led me in the pledge: "Phyllis, I take you to be my wife. I promise to be true to you, in good times and in bad, in sickness and in health. I will love you and honor you all the days of my life."

I smiled. Phyl had insisted that the word "obey" be removed from the ceremony. I had not objected, pleased with her assertion of her rights as a woman.

Phyllis took my hand. I had never seen her so happy, so completely

179

content and peaceful. "Dear Frank, with this ring I thee wed, and by it be thou consecrated unto me, as my wedded husband according to the Laws of God and man."

She slipped the gold band on my ring finger and gazed wonderingly into my eyes.

Quickly, I took Phyl's hand in my own. "Dear Phyllis, with this ring I thee wed, in token and in pledge of our constant faith and abiding love. I pledge to you my love."

"We invoke upon you an ancient blessing taken from the Book of Numbers," concluded Mel. "May God be with you and help you develop together. May you enjoy peace of home, of mind, and of heart together.

"May the Lord bless you and keep watch over you.

"May the Lord cause his face to shine upon you and be gracious unto you.

"May the Lord lift His countenance upon you and grant you the blessings of peace and of health and happiness and harmony—with each other, with your loved ones, with your fellowmen, and with your God—now and forever more. Amen.

"Congratulations to you. Now, you may kiss the bride."

Phyllis and I settled into a new apartment at Washington Square Village. I continued my work at NYU. In the evenings and on weekends, we explored the city—she, delighted to introduce me to a metropolis she had known all her life. I, rather awed by Manhattan's sheer magnitude and seemingly endless neighborhoods. And every few weeks, I would visit Eunice Fiorito, increasingly convinced that the American Coalition of Citizens with Disabilities was the vehicle I needed to begin to change the rules.

The key to my growing excitement about ACCD was its potential to make real the promise of section 504 of the Rehabilitation Act of 1973, the so-called "bill of rights for handicapped persons," that never had been implemented. Eunice shared my conviction that section 504 could advance the lives of disabled people as nothing else could; literally, it could, potentially, revolutionize the entire experience of living with disability. She took me, again and again, through the history behind section 504, making sure that I understood what had happened, why the law was now meaningless, and how it could be made to emerge as the powerful instrument we both believed it someday would be.

On January 20, 1972, Senator Hubert H. Humphrey had introduced a bill to "amend the Civil Rights Act of 1964 in order to prohibit discrimination on the basis of physical or mental handicap in federally assisted programs." S. 3094 was needed, Humphrey had said, because:

180

The time has come when we can no longer tolerate the invisibility of the handicapped in America. . . . I am insisting that the civil rights of 40 million Americans now be affirmed and effectively guaranteed by Congress—our several million disabled war veterans, the 22 million people with a severe physically disabling condition, the one in every ten Americans who has a mental condition requiring psychiatric treatment, the six million persons who are mentally retarded, the hundreds of thousands crippled by accidents and the destructive forces of poverty, and the 100,000 babies born with defects each year.

These people have the right to live, to work to the best of their ability—to know the dignity to which every human being is entitled. But too often we keep children, who we regard as "different" or a "disturbing influence," out of our schools and community activities altogether, rather than help them develop their abilities in special classes and programs. Millions of young persons and adults who want to learn a trade, work like other people, and establish their self-worth through a paycheck are barred from our vocational training programs and from countless jobs they could perform well.

In the House, Representative Charles Vanik introduced a similar bill. No hearings were held on either bill. Neither was brought to a vote in committee, let alone on the floors of the House and Senate. Both bills died a quiet death.

Jack Duncan, staff director of the House Select Education Subcommittee, would not let the idea go away, however. Eventually, his persistence paid off. Late in August, 1972, seven staff members of the U.S. Senate Committee on Labor and Public Welfare met to discuss changes in the Rehabilitation Act, which was up for reauthorization. Recalling Senator Humphrey's ill-fated S. 3094, one of the committee staff members (no one remembers who) suggested adding language to the Rehabilitation Act to accomplish the purpose Senator Humphrey had sought to achieve in his bill: the prohibition of discrimination on the basis of disability in all programs receiving or benefiting from federal financial assistance. The staff inserted the change as the last sentence in the Rehabilitation Act. They called it section 504.

On October 27, 1972, President Nixon vetoed the bill. A year later, on September 26, 1973, Eunice told me, President Nixon signed the Rehabilitation Act of 1973 (PL 93-112). Its final sentence, unchanged from the staff version of August 1972, prohibited discrimination on the basis of disability in schools, colleges and universities, state governments, hospitals, libraries, and all other programs receiving or benefiting from federal grants. Unless the executive branch issued implementing regulations, however, section 504 would be little more than a statement of Congressional intent. "It's sort of like saying that all people are created equal; it's a motherhood-and-apple-pie kind of pronouncement," Eunice said. Now, in 1976, no one took it seriously. Certainly, no school, hospital, or library she knew of was complying with section 504.

On July 21, 1976, Doran Windsor Bowe, our first child, was born. Although Phyl and I had attended months of Lamaze classes, I was still unprepared for how nerve-racking the experience would be for me. Phyl's doctor didn't make things any easier: he decided as he walked in the door to prepare her for childbirth that no one, including me, would be permitted in the delivery room; I spent from three in the morning to early afternoon worrying downstairs while Phyl went through a very intensive labor. It was all worth it just to see the two of them, tired but well.

A few days later, taking Phyllis and Doran home from the hospital, I was able to give Phyllis some news of my own: the ACCD Board of Directors had selected me as the organization's first chief executive officer.

Chapter
Thirteen

I arrived in Washington to find that the national headquarters office of the American Coalition of Citizens with Disabilities, Inc., consisted of a 10' × 15' corner storage area at the end of a hallway in a Connecticut Avenue brick structure owned by the International Association of Machinists. Standing there, talking on the telephone, was the biggest blind person I'd ever seen. Roger Peterson, a gifted, sensitive man, had many talents, but making himself understood by me was not one of them. A volunteer who came to the office a few hours a week, he had a long beard and an almost immobile face.

Acting quickly, I arranged a personal loan from Riggs National Bank to cover the deposit for a larger office, lured a former NYU student of mine to become my interpreter, and started the long haul I knew would be needed to establish the organization as a presence in the nation's capital.

I learned very quickly that information was the currency with which Washington conducted its business, much as money was in New York. A Ph.D in research psychology destined me to certain failure as a lobbyist. I had to learn a great deal, and I had to do it fast. In nine months of meetings, midnight reading, and more meetings, I accumulated the information I would need: demographic statistics, judicial decisions, unpublished studies, sensitive memoranda, and hundreds of newspaper clippings detailing the concrete reality of discrimination against disabled people in twentieth-century America.

My research convinced me that the final section of that rehabilitation law enacted three years earlier held the key to equality of opportunity for handicapped people in our country. Section 504 of the 1973 Rehabilitation Act was sweeping in its scope and absolute in its terms: "No otherwise qualified handicapped individual in the United States . . . shall, solely by reason of his handicap, be excluded from participation in, be denied the benefits of, or be subjected to discrimination under any program or activity receiving federal financial assistance." The vast reach of United States Government funds, from schools to hospitals to mass transit facilities, meant that almost all of American life would be affected were section 504 to become effective.

But I knew, too, that there was an unwritten rule in Washington: any provision of law that has not been implemented within three years of its enactment is, for all practical purposes, dead.

I had just started. But already I was in a race against time.

The inauguration in January, 1977, of Jimmy Carter gave us the opening we sought.

Joseph Califano, Carter's new Secretary of Health, Education, and Welfare, was the one person whose signature could transform the lives of tens of millions of disabled Americans. We had to get Califano to issue formal regulations that would enforce section 504. I didn't know Califano, but my friend Clarence Mitchell did. Mitchell, the then-Washington-office head of the NAACP, was one of the greatest, and unfortunately least-celebrated, civil rights leaders of the time. He arranged for several of us to accompany him to a meeting with the new Secretary within a week of the inauguration.

Califano, I found, was unusually frank for a Cabinet official confronting frustrated activists. He readily admitted that he had never even heard of section 504 until just a few days before. Despite our urgent pleadings, however, he declined to issue regulations immediately.

Eunice, as ACCD President, told me after the meeting that we had no choice but to go to the White House to bring pressure to bear on Califano. Searching for an entry point, I instinctively canvassed my acquaintances in the Washington media. One name surfaced repeatedly: that of domestic aide Stuart Eizenstat. "Stu's the best appointment Carter made," I heard again and again. Eunice, who had met him once in Atlanta during the Presidential campaign, agreed.

I liked Eizenstat immediately. Warm, open, unpretentious, with a vast knowledge of the federal government (*he* had heard of section 504!), he was nevertheless cautious. "The President is committed to Cabinet government, Frank. He wants Califano to have the leeway to do what he thinks best. But don't worry; Joe Califano is a reasonable man."

No sooner had I returned from meeting with Eizenstat, than HEW General Counsel Peter Libassi was on the phone. In a soft, unhurried voice, he explained that he was following up on our meeting with the Secretary. Would we come over to HEW to talk about section 504? Yes, he told me, he knew about the statute: he had been director of the department's Office for Civil Rights under Johnson and had always believed that handicapped persons were long overdue their own bill of rights.

Libassi, it turned out after the first few minutes of our meeting, was yet another very nice man. I liked these people—but I couldn't get them to move!

Meanwhile, pressure was building across the country as ACCD's news-letters began to circulate among thousands of self-help organizations from coast to coast. Letters, phone calls, and telegrams poured into our new office. Tinged, as always, with a barely controlled despair from so many years of oppression, they now sounded a new note of hope. People sent money to support our efforts. Organizational membership doubled, then tripled, as people with deafness, blindness, cerebral palsy, paraplegia, quadriplegia, mental retardation, and epilepsy, together with their families, counselors, teachers, and friends, sensed in ACCD a vehicle for the long-awaited breakthrough that would transform their lives.

ACCD's Board of Directors caught the frenzy that was building and bombarded us with information, suggestions, and orders. A dozen lawyers affiliated with Washington organizations, notably the Children's Defense Fund and the Georgetown University Institute for Public Interest Representation (INSPIRE), offered closely reasoned advice. Syndicated columnist Jack Anderson's aide Les Whitten summarized the cascading messages in his usual succinct style: "This isn't a legal battle, Frank. It's a political one. What you need now is pressure. And more pressure."

There is only one way to build pressure: talk to people. Over the next several weeks, I flew around the country to generate grass-roots support in key Congressional districts from Houston to New Hampshire to Berkeley. I think the fact that the arcane workings of Washington: NPRM's (Notices of Proposed Rule Making); IFR's (Interim Final Regulations); and the like were as new to me as they were to my audiences helped me to communicate with people whose closest contact with the nation's capital up to that time had been their annual filing of income-tax returns.

Each time I returned to town, some Congressman or Senator would contact us, expressing bewilderment about "this sudden onslaught of mail about something about the disabled," offering me the opportunity to build yet another bridge to Califano. Libassi, meanwhile, reported progress: the regulations would be issued shortly; no major changes were foreseen that we wouldn't like.

It was Eunice who understood that the time had come to strike. "Frank," she told me as my interpreter's hands flew to keep up with her, "I want you to draft a plan the Board can consider in Denver. Something dramatic. This will drag on forever unless we, the ACCD, act and act now!"

I responded as I typically do when I'm confronted with something I don't know much about: I read everything in sight that might apply. In this case, what I wanted was some background on how other oppressed groups had created, *de novo*, an instant uproar. "You'll have to ask God," one of the Board members told me. In explanation, he handed me a copy of Saul Alinsky's *Rules for Radicals*. "Alinsky is the God of the oppressed," he went on. "I think you'll get some ideas from him."

I did. On the plane to Denver, I broached an emerging idea with several of the Board Members. "Here's my reasoning. Califano's the only one who can do what we want done. *Ergo*, we have to concentrate national attention on him. He's got to feel pressure he doesn't know how to deal with, something coming at him that's outside his experience. There's only one thing I can think of that meets those criteria: thousands of severely disabled people in his own offices."

Meeting the Washington press outside the White House: "Tell Jimmy Carter we will not be moved!"

With ACCD Board chairwoman Eunice Fiorito (center), interpreter Michael Hartman, and President's Committee on Employment of the Handicapped executive director Bernard Posner (right): Accepting a collection of memorabilia from the struggle for section 504.

Fred Fay, a quadriplegic Ph.D. psychologist from Boston, picked up on the idea immediately. "A take-over!"

"Right. HEW has a headquarters office in Washington and regional offices in ten other cities. Our people come in on the same day at the same time. And they don't leave until he signs the regulations."

Eunice liked the idea. She put it on the agenda for the final day of the weekend Board meeting. Just before I was to present it, I was called to the phone. Peter Libassi had tried all afternoon to reach me. It might be something important. When I reached him in his Connecticut home, though, I learned that nothing had changed. Libassi was anxious that we not embarrass the Secretary: "Frank, I know he'll sign the rules. And they'll be good ones."

I was noncommittal. By this time, after several meetings with the Secretary, I felt that I could trust him to do the right thing; this was a gut feeling that no rumors of impending collapse in the rulemaking process at HEW could quite shake. But Libassi and I were playing official roles now; we were actors on the stage of national issues, representatives of clashing organizations, not individuals. So I told the General Counsel none of my own feelings.

The Board immediately and unanimously adopted the plan. Flying back to Washington that night, I drafted a letter to the President, with a copy for Califano. The letter announced that unless regulations were issued by April 4, three weeks hence, ACCD would mount a massive sit-in demonstration in every HEW regional office coast to coast. The March 18, 1977 letter set out the three-year history of nonimplementation of the "bill of rights" 36 million disabled Americans deserved and needed.

The letter had two immediate consequences. One was a call from the White House, asking for a briefing. The other was a "freeze" at HEW: all employees of the department were forbidden to talk to me or to any of my representatives.

The pace quickly became so frantic that I left home at 4:30 every morning and often didn't get back until 2:00 the next morning. Yet I had never felt so alive in my life.

Les Whitten's sensitive ears picked up the growing tremors of a news story. "Frank, don't give out that letter until Jack and I get it on the wires. And, my friend, a word from Washington: your credibility is on the line now. If Califano doesn't sign, you have to produce that demonstration. You won't be able to back out no matter how much you want to." The story ran in a thousand newspapers that carried Anderson's column on March 26. Headlined "Handicapped Plan 10-City Sit-in," it summarized my letter to Carter and noted that the demonstration promised to be the greatest disabled people had mounted in the nation's history.

That story won us Ed Koch. Then the Representative from Manhattan's "Silk Stocking" district, Koch was still a liberal in 1977. His support gave me an idea: why not announce the sit-in from Capitol Hill, the site of the enactment of the law more than three years ago?

Representative John Brademas, Democrat of Indiana and the most powerful figure on Capitol Hill on behalf of handicapped Americans, promised his support. With his public backing, Congress got into the act in a big way. Democrats and Republicans alike went to the wells in their Houses to urge Califano to sign the regulations.

I knew that the pressure on Califano to sign the rules had to be intense. We learned from sources in the White House that the mail to the President on the issue was unprecedented; the continuing freeze on communications with me from HEW told us that the Secretary had to be feeling the heat. So why didn't he act?

As we entered the final days before April 4, our people became increasingly frantic. The phone in my Connecticut Avenue office never stopped ringing as people reported rumors, gossip, "inside information," and just plain fantasy. Within the course of a single day, I was told that the regulations had already been signed; that they had been discarded completely; that Califano was delaying to build pressure for the strong rules he wanted to issue; and that he was "gutting" (weakening) the rules every way he could. I was informed that the Central Intelligence Agency had "penetrated" some of our strategy meetings and that our phones were "bugged," just a few minutes before I was advised that the President has ordered Califano to produce great rules immediately so as not to embarrass Carter at the scheduled first-ever White House Conference on Handicapped Individuals, to be held in early May.

Joe Califano was wily as a fox. Waiting until the very last day, he summoned us to his office on April 4, and invited the national television and print media to observe. There he announced that he "endorsed" the demonstration that would occur the next day: "Handicapped Americans have waited for their lawful civil rights. I have asked all HEW personnel to cooperate fully with the protestors in their exercise of Constitutionally protected free speech."

Of all the steps he could have taken, this was the one I had least suspected. Was he calling our bluff? I knew his intelligence network was too good for that: he had to know we'd been planning for weeks and that we'd deliver on the threatened sit-in. If his "endorsement" was on the level, what was he up to?

I didn't have time to analyze the Secretary's motives. Immediately after the meeting, we rushed back to the office to put out the word: "Go!"

It was past three in the morning before I made it home to Phyllis and our baby daughter Doran. I walked in to find my sleepy wife rocking our little girl in her carriage.

"Frank, I've got to sleep. Rock her for a while. Sing to her."

"Sing? Me?"

188

"Please, Frank. I've been up all night."

"Sure, Doll. But if this works, it will be because going to sleep is the only way she can escape my singing!"

"This is no time for jokes. I'm exhausted."

"You think I'm joking! Phyl, you've never heard me sing."

"Just let me sleep for five minutes."

As I rocked Doran, I thought how Coretta Scott King probably had misled the nation into believing that civil-rights activists always had wives who took over their personal lives during a crisis. That may have been true in the early 1960's, but I could not imagine it being true any longer.

Had Phyllis and I not had so remarkably solid a marriage, I am sure the months of unremitting effort to get section 504 on the books would have destroyed the union. I thought, yet again, about how grateful I was to her for allowing me to give over twenty hours a day to the movement. Lesser women, with lesser commitments to their husbands, would not have permitted anything approaching what I did in the spring of 1977.

Eventually, Doran fell asleep. By then, however, it was five in the morning. With a soft kiss to Phyllis' forehead, I left to begin the demonstration.

The early reports were encouraging. New York was "going great. We'll be out in force!" Boston was already mobilizing at seven in the morning. Atlanta and Chicago promised to turn out every person they could find.

We scheduled the press conference for 10:00 a.m., traditionally the best time for evening network coverage. In a House of Representatives hearing room, I faced the cameras: "Today, disabled Americans are asking for the simple and just rights they've too long been denied. It's time that the rules were changed."

When we reached the bottom of the hill, we found that Joe Califano had been as good as his word: the doors were wide open for us, in a show of "welcome" for the protestors.

"Damn!" cursed one of the lawyers walking with me. "He's trying to co-opt us. This looks to the nation as if he's inviting us in! And to think it's against him that this sit-in is organized!"

Outside the Secretary's office, every foot of space was taken up by persons with every imaginable disability. Joe Califano stood under the floodlights, promising to issue the regulations "soon" and that they would be "fair."

"I thank the people here today for helping me draw the country's attention to the injustices this Administration is determined to end." And then he asked that, having made our point by coming, we leave. I found myself being pushed to the front. The Secretary looked at me briefly, then stepped aside.

"Mr. Secretary," I responded, "with all due respect, that statement is not what we came here for. We've heard 'soon' too many times for the word to have any more meaning. And if you are serious about ending the injustice we are protesting, we ask that you issue rules—and do it now."

The room erupted. At one end, I could see Eunice standing on a table, taunting the Secretary to come to her to debate the issues. But he turned and left the room without saying another word. The room was silent for a moment, as if all of us were contemplating what to do next. And then it began: a spontaneous chorus of "We Shall Overcome."

We were determined to stay for as long as it took to get the rules issued. But the Secretary's staff was determined to end the embarassment to the Administration.

Much later, after it was all over, Peter Libassi and I talked about the demonstration while sipping wine at the Palm restaurant in Northwest Washington. When I asked him about Califano's attitudes during our sit-in, Libassi responded: "You have to understand, Frank, that the last thing the Carter Administration needed during its first months in office was nationwide television news pictures of disabled persons being forcibly evicted from the HEW building. I just couldn't permit that to happen. The building managers insisted that all of you be removed. Fortunately, I was able to convince them that negotiations were preferable."

I could scarcely believe those negotiations.

"You're on federal property, Dr. Bowe," I was told repeatedly by the HEW lawyers. "We're asking that you leave. If you don't, we cannot assume responsibility for the consequences."

"And what consequences might those be?"

"Dr. Bowe, you know as well as we do that some of those people have severe medical conditions. No one is allowed to enter this floor. But anyone who wishes may leave. I think I make myself clear."

I knew that Fred Schreiber, the greatest leader the deaf community had ever known, was with us; Fred had a heart condition. There were others who would need medical supplies. ACCD First Vice President, T. J. O'Rourke, whom we'd chosen to speak for us, gathered the Board members who were with us for a discussion of the new developments. And then he helped the group as a whole come to a decision. It was nearly unanimous: we would stay the night.

The next day, however, wavering in the group's determination began to become apparent. Some were already planning to leave, citing medical emergencies. Rather than allow the group to dissipate, little by little, a vote was taken to repeat our demands one final time and march out together *en masse*.

But not before we had coffee and donuts.

The final negotiations were almost as unbelievable as were those of the previous evening. For three hours, we demanded food as a condition to any further discussion. And for three hours, we were told that this was impossible—unless we were willing to leave. Finally, it took a decision at the cabinet level to get each of us one cup of coffee and one donut: Joseph A. Califano, Jr., himself grudgingly made the concession.

As regrettable as the premature end of the Washington part of the sit-in was, it gave me the freedom to work the channels of power in Washington.

And at the ACCD office, reports came in every few minutes from sit-in cities coast to coast.

"Hello, Denver."

"Frank! Listen, Frank. We can't get arrested!"

"Huh? You can't?"

"They won't arrest us! They plumb refuse!"

"You better explain, Denver."

"Frank, we've blocked the main roads here with wheelchairs curb to curb. We've stopped rush hour traffic."

"Good thinking."

"But the idea was to get arrested, to attract national attention. But these guys won't cooperate."

"Any idea why?"

"Yeah. The jails are inaccessible!"

"Hello, Chicago."

"Frank. We're not sure how long we can hold out here. Some people have medical . . ."

"I understand. Stay as long as you can. But I don't want anyone's life or health threatened."

"That's our thinking, too. We've heard that's what happened in Washington."

"You heard right."

"Hello, San Francisco."

"Frank! We're really very disappointed in you. The nation is watching Washington. The people here all feel you've let us down."

"We did what the people here felt they had to do."

"But you couldn't do that to us."

"We could, and we did. Carry on as best you can."

"Don't worry. We will."

"Hello, Boston."

"Frank. If you think this is Boston, you've got to get a new interpreter."

I read my interpreter's frantic spelling: "It's your wife."

"Oh, hi doll. Boston's on the other line."

"Well, tell them to get off. I want you to get some medicine at the pharmacy. Doran is sick. Have a pen?"

"Yes, doll."

"Hello, Boston."

"What took you so long?"

"Pharmaceutical investments."

"Huh?"

"What's happening up there?"

"We did it, and we're really proud. We understand San Francisco and Chicago are still there."

"You mean you've left?"

"Had to."

"Yes, I know. Pharmaceuticals."

It went on this way all day. Finally, at seven, I was to tired to go on. I got the medicine for my daugther and caught up on my sleep. If I knew Califano at all, and I was beginning to understand him, it would be a long wait.

For the next three weeks, I divided my time between San Francisco (which got Safeway grocery stores to donate food, and Black Panther Party members to bring it into the HEW building) and Capitol Hill.

The California group (they were to stay 25 days and nights, a record for a sit-in in any federal building in history) sent a delegation to Washington to help with the lobbying. I went with them to see Eizenstat, who kept repeating "But the Secretary is a reasonable man!" and dozens of Senators and Congressmen. At one all-night meeting, I learned that California-style politics is in a world of its own. At two in the morning, the contingent from the coast almost voted to chain themselves to the gates of the Russian embassy; they would tell the press that conditions were better for disabled people in the USSR! At five, a group left for Califano's home, where they carried candles and sang songs, including one they'd composed while in the HEW regional office:

"Tell Jimmy Carter, we will not be moved;
Tell Califano, we will not be moved.
Like a tree that stands by the water,
We will not be moved!"

On Sunday morning, they followed President Carter to church.

Califano refused to budge. Finally, the Californians returned home. We were nearing the end of April.

I was plotting my next steps when, shortly after nine in the morning of April 28, 1977, I received the first call from HEW to our offices in more than a month.

"Frank?" It was Peter Libassi. My interpreter told me he sounded exhausted. "The Secretary's called a press conference for this afternoon."

"And?"

"I can't tell you anything beyond that. Trust me."

"Okay, Pete. I'll be there."

I arrived to see the Secretary announce the promulgation of the regulations he had signed at 7:30 that morning. As I looked over the rules, a tremendous sense of calm settled over me.

"The 504 regulations," the Secretary said, "attack the discrimination, the demeaning practices, and the injustices that have afflicted the nation's handicapped citizens. They reflect the recognition of Congress that most handicapped persons can lead proud and productive lives, despite their disabilities. They will usher in a new era of equality for handicapped individuals in which unfair barriers to self-sufficiency and decent treatment will begin to fall before the force of law."

The new rules, I learned, would banish "separate but equal" programs unless those programs were proven to be better for the individuals they served. Colleges would be required to provide interpreters and readers for deaf and blind students who met their criteria for admission. "No exceptions to these requirements are allowed," the document concluded.

As I stood easily in the back of the room while General Counsel Libassi fielded questions from the gathered press, an AP wire reporter pulled me out into the hall.

"What do you think?"

I explained that I hadn't yet had an opportunity to review the rules in any detail. "But from what I've seen, I think they're just, fair, and enforceable."

"You like them?"

"I think you could say that."

The demonstration brought into the "disability rights movement" thousands of individuals who had not previously been involved. It was exhilarating for me to watch as these people, previously so quiescent, spoke up with pride and dignity as they fought for rights so long denied them. We were able to bring these "footsoldiers" into the battle thanks largely to the efforts of the leaders behind the take-over: people like Judy Heumann, Kitty Cone, and Ed Roberts (in California), Tom Gilhool, Frank Laski and the Disabled in Action group (in Philadelphia), Fred Fay, Andrea Schein, and the Massachusetts Coalition of Citizens with Disabilities (in Boston), and Fred Schreiber, Terrence J. O'Rourke, and of course Eunice Fiorito (in Washington). Most of these people served, then or later, on the Board of Directors of ACCD; O'Rourke became its President shortly after the demonstration, succeeding Eunice. Each has his or her own story to tell. But one anonymous individual spoke for the legions of newly enfranchised people who benefited most from section 504 when he said: "Today, I stopped being a blind person who happens to be human. I am now, and forever will be, a human being who happens to be blind."

And there were people who were not disabled who made major contributions. At HEW, John Wodatch and Ann Beckman led the writing of the regulation. Wodatch's contribution was so great, in fact, that I've always thought of section 504 as John's rule. Both worked for Libassi. In Washington, a pivotal role was played by what was perhaps an unlikely organization. The American Association for the Advancement of Science (AAAS) worked with the American Council on Education to bring the nation's colleges and universities around from strong opposition through bare tolerance to active support. The woman behind that about-face was Martha Ross Redden, from Kentucky, who enlisted the legendary anthropologist Margaret Mead in the cause. Without them, I doubt we would have had so much to celebrate that April 28.

A few days later, the Secretary called. "I want to thank you for your role in this historic regulation, Frank. And I hope you will join me in implementing it."

I told him that now that I'd had a chance to read thorougly the lengthy regulation he had signed, I was more convinced than ever that we finally had changed the rules.

I think George F. Will, the syndicated columnist, expressed it most succinctly. In his May 5, 1977 column, Will said: "Nothing the Carter administration will do in the next three years will touch as many lives that are ready for a touch of justice."

A few days later, the President of the United States stood before some 10,000 handicapped persons at the Sheraton Washington Hotel to open the White House Conference on Handicapped Individuals. Referring to the new regulations, he asked: "Don't you think we're making progress now?"

That afternoon, I arrived home at the unheard-of hour of five in the afternoon. Phyllis was walking Doran.

"Hello. I'd like to introduce someone you might not know, but perhaps would like to meet."

"Who's that?"

"Me."

And I gave her a kiss.

Epilogue

The HEW section 504 regulation was published in the *Federal Register* on May 4, 1977. Immediately upon publication, it had the force of law.

The rule required that all new facilities built with federal funds or grants be made accessible to people with disabilities; all existing facilities had to be made accessible within two months, although in the case of structural changes, such as ramps or elevators, grant recipients had up to three years to make the renovations.

The new regulation also required that all public schools admit and educate, with accommodations such as sign language interpreters and notetakers as necessary, any disabled child residing in the district served by the school who was capable of learning at the school. In this respect, section 504 complemented PL 94-142, the Education for All Handicapped Children Act, for which implementing regulations were issued shortly after the appearance of the 504 rule. Under PL 94-142, states could, at least in theory, reject federal funds and thereby avoid having to comply with the requirements to provide a free, public education in the least restrictive environment. What section 504 did was to remove that loophole. Since every state and every school district receive and benefit from federal financial assistance, whether tied to PL 94-142 or not, they are obligated to adhere to section 504. Thus, a quarter century after Pat Halter reluctantly allowed me to enter the South Ward kindergarten program, federal law at last established the right of handicapped children to attend local public schools.

The 504 regulation also required colleges and universities to provide interpreters and other accommodations to disabled students who satisfied their admission criteria. Whereas I had been confronted with the "choice" of attending a college such as Western Maryland or Bucknell with no interpreting or notetaking services, or going to Gallaudet College with an exclusively deaf student population, any deaf college student now had the right, beginning in the 1977–1978 academic year, to attend virtually any of the thousands of colleges and universities nationwide and to receive there any necessary supportive services. Today, tens of thousands of disabled youth are benefiting from ramps, elevators, Brailled or taped textbooks, notetakers, specially equipped vans and dormitory rooms, and fair testing procedures in colleges and universities from coast to coast.

Finally, the new rule eliminated disability as a legal basis for employment decision-making. No longer could any employer whose programs or activities benefited from federal grants refuse to hire or to promote a disabled person merely because of disability.

While HEW Secretary Califano had changed the regulation somewhat, largely by streamlining its language, he had kept it a strong, enforceable rule. And he moved quickly to implement its requirements, drawing upon all of HEW's vast resources to reach into every area of American life touched by that huge department. Because I led a highly visible demonstration against HEW, there have been some who have thought I had my tongue firmly in cheek when I offered the opinion, which I still hold, that he was the best cabinet secretary with whom I have worked. The fact is that, despite the demonstration, I have a great deal of respect for him, for his judgment as a lawyer, and for his managerial ability in taming an unruly department. Califano told historian Edward Berkowitz that, for his part, he found me to be "someone I could work with. Frank Bowe made sense." The feeling was mutual. Even at the height of the demonstration, I knew that he was a man I could trust to make decisions that were in the best interest of disabled people and of the nation.

In 1978, the Congress extended the reach of section 504 to include the federal government itself. As of October 1 of that year, federal agencies themselves were required by law to make their programs and activities accessible to deaf, blind, physically disabled, and other handicapped individuals.

Also in 1978, in compliance with Executive Order 11914, section 504 rules began appearing from some thirty federal agencies other than HEW. Section 504 now regulated public transportation, public housing, public service programs such as the Legal Services for Corporation, and programs of the National Endowment for the Arts.

By 1979, it was clear that section 504 was changing the entire fabric of American society, from day care for preschoolers to public education, from vocational-technical trade schools to Harvard and Stanford Universities, from the subways in New York City to the airport in Seattle, from the libraries in Portland, Maine, to the senior centers in San Jose, California.

As section 504 took full effect, ACCD expanded to meet the growing needs of disabled Americans for information about their new rights. Probably the most demanding role I played as ACCD's chief executive officer was that of raising private monies to support our work. A coalition pressing for basic social change is not a "safe" charity for large corporations, yet we were able to get sizeable contributions from AT&T, Exxon USA, IBM, and other national and international companies as well as from several private foundations. To supplement these awards, I wrote six books during my five years as ACCD's CEO; the Coalition realized enough profits from sales of these books to pay my salary and that of my interpreter. To reinforce our commitment to private fundraising, we established a branch office in Manhattan. Soon I was spending so much time in New York that

Phyllis Bowe: The Sorbonne, the houses in Henry James, and "Tommy, Can You Hear Me"

Dr. Frank Bowe: "People come so close. They come within inches. Yet they are so very very far away. Sometimes I feel like I'm living in a glass box. I can see out but I can't reach out."

International Year of Disabled Persons, 1981

Delivering the commencement address after receiving an honorary doctor of laws (LLD), Gallaudet College

Phyllis and I relocated the family to Long Island, to be closer to our parents; I kept a small apartment in Washington.

Beginning in 1978, I no longer had to work up to twenty hours a day because we were able to attract top-flight staff members who took on much of the day-to-day activity of the organization. From a skeleton staff of three, we grew to twenty, including lawyers, researchers, trainers, and administrative personnel. Our budget quadrupled and then quadrupled again; by 1981, when I left the Coalition to form a private management consulting firm, ACCD was approaching two million dollars a year in program money. More than 100 disability groups had by then joined our coalition.

In keeping with our philosophy of hiring qualified handicapped individuals, we conducted nationwide searches to fill key staff positions. Indispensable was Marcia Miller, my interpreter, who was my ears on the world. Rita Varela, whom I recruited from Florida, headed our rehabilitation research and training program; her life-long experience with cerebral palsy added much to our effectiveness in working on behalf of people with physical disabilities. Jane Razeghi and Harriet Loeb, who was deaf, took over our education activities, bringing to their jobs a deep appreciation for the problems of local school districts and an expertise on vocational education. John Dystel, who had multiple sclerosis, and John Lancaster, a paralyzed veteran, were our two top lawyers. They helped immeasureably in tracking and interpreting legislative and judicial changes. They also helped us to translate section 504 into layman's terms, so we could communicate to disabled people how they could best take advantage of their historic new civil rights. And John Williams, who headed our public relations office, was instrumental in getting the national media to publicize these rights to millions of disabled Americans across the country; as a bonus, the quality of his work convinced many top media officials that stuttering was no bar to a successful career in journalism.

Meanwhile, my family was growing as well. Phyllis and I had "planned" on having two daughters. On Valentine's Day, 1979, when our first-born, Doran Windsor Bowe, was two and one-half years old, Phyllis gave birth to Whitney Paige Bowe. It was a joy coming home to my three girls. With them, I could relax. An interesting aspect of my family life, one that proved important to me in keeping the Washington work in perspective, is that unlike many other advocacy leaders, I could leave my work at the office because neither my wife nor my children were disabled. Someone like Martin Luther King, Jr. was helping his own family as well as millions of others by doing the civil-rights work he did; his family could justify to themselves the endless hours, days, and even weeks at a time he spent away from home as, in part, an investment in their own futures. My family did not benefit in the same ways from the equally time-consuming, if less historic, work I did. I hope my family will never need the fruits of my work on disability rights, but I owe them a great deal for accepting my commitment to the work I was doing, and for permitting me to do it.

Section 504 unleashed powerful social changes upon an America that did not quite comprehend what our civil rights meant. That a building should be accessible was sensible enough. But many people had difficulty understanding why people with disabilities asked to be educated in the same classrooms with other students, to do the same jobs others did, and to ride the same buses others took. Section 504 meant that the lives of millions of Americans would be forever altered. No such massive changes could take place without controversy, of course. The first tremors of a possible backlash were not long in appearing.

In North Carolina, a deaf nursing student, Frances B. Davis, brought suit under section 504 against Southeastern Community College. Ms. Davis claimed that section 504 required the college to provide her with special classes and to excuse her from attending some of the clinical courses. When the Supreme Court ruled, on June 11, 1979, that section 504 did not offer any such privileges, the news media were quick to sense a major story.

At CBS, Walker Cronkite, then managing editor and anchor of "CBS Evening News with Walter Cronkite," the nation's top-ranked network news program, placed the story at the top of the day's events. He assigned Carl Stern, a highly respected lawyer and Court reporter, to dig out the meaning of the decision. Stern lost no time in getting me before CBS studio cameras in Washington, just three hours after the decision had been announced. For almost an hour, we parried: Stern insisting that the Supreme Court pronouncement was a mortal blow to the rights of handicapped Americans, and I responding, just as heatedly, that it was nothing of the sort: "Frances Davis asked for things she had no right to under section 504. This Supreme Court decision therefore applies only to Frances Davis and to others who might make similarly groundless demands."

In the months that followed *Southeastern Community College v. Davis*, it became clear that the decision dealt with issues outside of the HEW 504 regulation. Not one word of the 1977 rule was changed. Joe Califano had done a good job in fashioning requirements that would be upheld in the courts.

We were not so fortunate in the area of transportation.

From my first days on the job as ACCD's executive director, I had been intensely frustrated at the abject failure of the nation's public transportation agencies to provide even the most minimally accessible services. People with physical disabilities, including tens of millions of older people, faced incredible barriers just to get to work or go shopping. Most people who use public transportation ride the bus; in fact, eighty percent of all trips on public transit are by bus. So ACCD rejoiced when US Department of Transportation Secretary Brock Adams announced a major new decision: all new large buses for urban transport henceforth would be the low-floor, wide-door, lift-equipped "Transbus," which Adams described as "the bus of the future."

The problem was: none of the country's bus manufacturers wanted to make Transbus. We met with Pete Estes, president of General Motors, and with his counterparts at Flxible. The only other bus company, AM General, dropped out of the business before we could contact them. Germany's Neoplan was interested in Transbus, but strong "buy American" regulations gave priority to General Motors and Flxible.

Through 1977, 1978, and 1979, ACCD devoted thousands of hours in what ultimately was a futile effort to get someone, anyone, to build Transbus. Then, one spring morning, my friend Bill Haddad called. Prize-winning New York journalist, co-founder and past associate director of the Peace Corps, and a power broker in national Democratic politics, Bill had read about our problems and thought he had a solution. Explaining that he had recently gone to work for John Z. DeLorean as vice president for planning at the DeLorean Motor Company, Bill told me he had a great idea: "We're thinking of setting up a plant, maybe in Miami, to build Transbus. Interested?"

We met in Washington, then in New York. DeLorean, Bill told me, had a "great concept": build a manufacturing facility in an economically depressed riot-torn area, employ "hard-core unemployable" workers, and produce solutions to social problems. He'd been talking to Mario Cuomo and Ed Koch about a plant in the South Bronx and with Miami officials about Liberty City. Using state and local money, DeLorean Motors would construct a plant and start manufacturing Transbuses. The more Bill talked about the idea, the more he—and I—became excited. It was do-able. At the very least, it would force General Motors and Flxible to stop stone-walling and start making the bus.

Working with Haddad on "the impossible bus" was an exhilarating experience—and a heady one. Bill brought in Otto Schultz, "the best bus engineer in the world," and his son Rainer, to help design an accessible, low-floor, wide-door bus. General Motors claimed that the bus couldn't be built—but Rainer showed how it not only could be made but actually would be less expensive for cities to operate than current buses. To introduce the bus to the American transit operators, Haddad brought to New York City one of Otto Schultz's West German buses, painted bright red, and called it the "DMC-80" (for 1980). Bill set the bus in the New York Hilton parking lot during the annual convention of the American Public Transit Association, surrounded by signs saying: "Welcome aboard the bus they said could not be built" and "This is the bus they didn't want you to see." I watched as Christina DeLorean, John's wife and an internationally famous model, greeted APTA delegates as they boarded the bus. The show was a smash.

Bill then took "the little red bus that could" to Washington. Senators, Congressmen, and US Department of Transportation officials rode the bus around the Capital, impressed; when they boarded the rival GM bus, it broke down at its second stop.

We were on a roll. All I needed, as ACCD director, was one manufacturer willing to comply with the Government's Transbus specifications. Increasingly, it looked as if Haddad would be able to be that manufacturer. First, though, he needed money. Moving with dazzling speed, Bill attracted the interest of the people behind the mega-hit "Star Wars." The plan, Bill told me, would be for producer George Lucas' lawyers to fund the bus plant start-up costs. Haddad was on cloud nine. "Imagine!" he exclaimed. "I can just see the headline: 'Star Wars to Build Bus That Couldn't Be Built!' "

And then the bubble burst.

One morning, at DeLorean's impressive headquarters offices on Park Avenue, Haddad told me he was no longer sure the plan was "do-able": "I asked John to make a commitment to the bus. He refused." Careful not to overstep the bounds of corporate confidentiality, Haddad explained that there were "problems" in the company that had nothing to do with him or with the bus. Over the next few months, as the press began reporting evidence of fiscal irregularities at DeLorean Motors, I began to understand why Bill had not been able to get the bus project moving. Eventually, bitter over what could have been a great adventure, Bill left the company and began a long process of discovering what had happened to the monies invested in the company. With him went the last hopes of disabled Americans for Transbus.

On May 31, 1979, the US Department of Transportation (DOT) published its section 504 regulation, which required that public transportation systems be made accessible to people with physical disabilities. The rule set forth a process in which all new buses purchased by local transit systems were to be lift-equipped, and all other transportation systems, including subways, were to be made accessible over a period of time. It was a good regulation, but it asked for more than most public transit agencies would be able to deliver. And, without Transbus, the guts of the regulation were gone. That didn't stop the transit agencies from protesting what they regarded as "utterly ridiculous" requirements. The uproar from the cities, including Ed Koch's New York, was such that the American Public Transit Association (APTA) brought suit on behalf of transit operators against DOT, charging that the agency had exceeded its Congressional mandate in publishing so broad and far-reaching a regulation.

In 1981, an appeals court agreed. DOT declined to appeal the decision to the Supreme Court and soon issued new, much less stringent rules. Although the revised requirements were less far-reaching in scope, they still called for "special efforts" by public transportation systems. The

DOT rule was by far the most controversial of all the section 504 regulations. However, it has still meant a great deal to disabled Americans. In 1985, for example, the courts recognized that the nation's airlines and airports were expected by section 504 to provide access to users of wheelchairs, special telephone services (TDDs) for deaf individuals, and informational signs low-vision and blind people can read.

Despite our difficulties with DOT, the essential meaning of section 504—that people with disabilities are also people with abilities, who can and should participate fully in society—continued to reverberate throughout America. Disability is, however, a worldwide phenomenon, and I was eager to do what little I could to awaken other nations to the potential of people with disabilities to become self-sufficient, contributing citizens. So when I received an invitation to a White House reception for Israeli Prime Minister Menachem Begin and his wife Aliza on the occasion of their first official trip to the United States, I accepted with alacrity. At the time, American press accounts portrayed Mr. Begin as an intransigent radical who held little promise of showing the flexibility needed in Middle East negotiations. I very quickly learned, however, that the Begins were both warm, unpretentious, and enormously appealing people. They invited me to visit Israel to help them expand that nation's efforts on behalf of thousands of disabled war veterans and civilians. In a half-dozen trips over the next several years, I came to appreciate the depth of the Israeli commitment to doing everything possible to help each individual reach his or her full potential. As Aliza Begin, talking in her Jerusalem home with my daughter Doran, put it just before she died: "Always give to life." It is a philosophy she followed every day of her life.

Then, in 1979, I was granted an exciting opportunity to spread the word further. Acting on HEW Secretary Califano's recommendation, Secretary of State Cyrus Vance named me head of the United States delegation to the United Nations for planning the 1981 International Year for Disabled Persons. I was the only head of a delegation among the 23-nation planning body who was disabled. After our first meeting in New York, however, Argentina, Sweden, and other member countries named as deputy delegation heads persons who were disabled. The delegates also agreed to my suggestion that the Year be renamed the International Year *of* Disabled Persons, to reflect recognition that people with disabilities themselves would participate actively in the Year.

Meeting in New York and Vienna over the next two years, we set an ambitious agenda of worldwide activities designed to highlight the fact that fully 500 million of the world's citizens, one-half billion people, were disabled—and that eighty percent of these people lived in the so-called Third World of developing nations. These countries are particularly concerned about resolving disability problems because, unless they can help their many disabled citizens to become productive, these millions of people

202

will be life-long wards of the state. Disability, then, is a shared interest of otherwise very different cultures; it can, and does, link Israel and Egypt, Switzerland and Sweden, the USSR and the United Kingdom, as does nothing else. Illustrative of this fact is that Libya was one of the prime sponsors of the Year. Even during that period of American-Libyan tensions, these two countries met across the conference table to discuss education and rehabilitation for people with disabilities.

In large part because of such cross-cultural ties, our efforts proved worthwhile. Of the several "Years" the UN has sponsored, the International Year of Disabled Persons certainly has been the most successful; more than 130 nations changed their policies to reflect a more mature understanding of the abilities of disabled individuals. I am especially impressed by the progress I have seen in Canada, West Germany, Japan, and Sweden.

Meanwhile, ACCD continued its pioneering work. It was a major factor in the successful drive to reauthorize the Rehabilitation Act in 1978 and in reforming Social Security legislation in 1980. We were able to make disability a topic that the media no longer restricted to the "medical columns." *Newsweek, Time,* and *US News & World Report* published feature articles on disability in their "life/style" sections. The *New York Times* offered full-page assessments of our progress on op-ed pages. And we helped disabled actors get jobs portraying characters in television and motion pictures, a major step for the entertainment industry, and one it had resisted for decades. Most important, ACCD guided implementation of section 504 in the critical early years of its life, ensuring that this law would survive to become an enduring feature of modern society.

I had told Eunice in 1976 that I was willing to make a five-year commitment to the Coalition, but that I was not sure I wanted to make a career of work that was so physically and emotionally draining. Fortunately, at the end of the five year period, the Coalition was in sound financial shape. It had a nationwide reputation for getting things done with uncompromising integrity. But I now felt that its board of directors wanted to move the organization in directions that I did not believe it should take; we had frequent clashes over organizational tactics and fund-raising strategies. In particular, I was disturbed by the tendency of some board members to place the interests of the local groups they represented above those of the Coalition, and by the board's seeming inability to decide how the organization's work should be financed. Probably, these tensions between us were inevitable. By that time, I had become closely identified with the Coalition, having been its first paid staff member and the only chief executive it had ever had. In November, 1980, things came to a head and I announced that I would be departing four months later. At its next quarterly meeting, the Board selected one of its own members to succeed me.

My new consulting company, headquartered near my Long Island home, quickly attracted contracts from such corporate giants as AT&T, Control Data, IBM, and Xerox. The work exposed me to state-of-the-art research on speech recognition and other aspects of emerging generations of computers, interests I found as consuming as I did the ACCD civil rights movement. The new work was, however, better compensated, and I was able to begin repaying my family for the privations it had endured during my years with the Coalition. Later, at the US Architectural and Transportation Barriers Compliance Board, an independent federal agency, I had an opportunity, at last, to use my doctoral training to direct basic and applied research projects on a wide variety of accessibility issues.

The changes ACCD made during my years with the organization have proven to be lasting ones, although the organization itself closed its doors early in 1986, primarily due to a lack of funds. The Reagan Administration, implementing a 1980 campaign promise to reduce the burden of federal regulations, reviewed the many agency section 504 rules as well as hundreds of other regulations. The 504 mandates' value, however, appealed as much to the Reagan conservatives as it had to the Carter moderates and liberals: Reagan made no changes in the section 504 requirements. And because section 504 mandates no "goals and timetables," the regulations were not affected by the Administration's debates about affirmative action policy.

In 1986, as this is written, several tens of millions of disabled Americans of all ages have benefited from section 504. They've been given an opportunity to get an education, thus equipping themselves to serve as citizens in our great nation. They've been offered a fair chance in employment, thus becoming able to support themselves and their families. Individuals with physical disabilities have been much more successful than ever before in locating the housing and transportation they need to live in and get about the community. Public buildings and polling places are more accessible than anyone would have predicted just fifteen years ago. All of this attests to section 504's status in 1986 as the single most all-encompassing civil rights statute ever enacted on behalf of America's 36 million disabled citizens.

A historic nationwide opinion poll by Louis Harris and Associates, released early in 1986, certified the progress we had made. In interviews with a randomly selected 1,000 disabled individuals from coast to coast, Harris found that "an overwhelming majority of disabled Americans believe that life has improved for disabled persons over the past decade" [1975–1985]. In addition, 67%, or two-thirds, told the Harris pollsters that the role played by the federal government, particularly in section 504, was instrumental in improving their lives. As Harris put it in their report: "The strength of this endorsement is unsurpassed since the Harris firm began measuring public support for federal programs and laws."

The rules have been changed.